THE REVOLUTION WILL NOT BE LITIGATED

THE REVOLUTION WILL NOT BE LITIGATED

PEOPLE POWER AND LEGAL POWER IN THE 21ST CENTURY

EDITED BY **KATIE REDFORD**
AND **MARK GEVISSER**

WITH A FOREWORD BY
JANE FONDA

OR Books
New York · London

© 2023 Katie Redford and Mark Gevisser
Individual chapters © their respective authors

Published by OR Books, New York and London

Visit our website at www.orbooks.com

All rights information: rights@orbooks.com

First printing 2023

Cataloging-in-Publication data is available from the Library of Congress.
A catalog record for this book is available from the British Library.

Typeset by Lapiz Digital Services.

paperback ISBN 978-1-68219-374-7 • ebook ISBN 978-1-68219-375-4

Contents

Acknowledgments

This book is part of the Power of Law, Power of People project, made possible through grants from the Bertha Foundation and the True Costs Initiative, and the Equation Campaign, a project of Rockefeller Philanthropy Advisors. We are deeply grateful to them, and to the Rockefeller Foundation's Bellagio Center, which granted Katie Redford the residency where she began working on "Rules for Radical Lawyers" and collaborating with fellow-residents Robin Gorna and Mark Gevisser on what would become this book. The Bellagio Center then hosted the conference that brought together most of the contributors, at which they presented the first drafts of their essays and discussed the issues addressed in this book. Thanks to Robin Gorna, for the role she played in planning the conference, and to Rhea Suh, for facilitating it.

"The Power of Law, The Power of People" is also the motto of EarthRights International, which was founded in 1995—with seed funding from Echoing Green—by Katie Redford, her friend and fellow novice-lawyer Tyler Giannini, and Ka Hsaw Wa, a movement leader from Burma. This book has grown from that seed. We are indebted to its founders, funders, and staffers, as well as to the Equation Campaign, which supports movements, leaders, and lawyers like those featured in this book.

Thank you to Jesse McElwain, who has been a vital member of the team and who, together with Kai Keane, is responsible for our website, https://www/therevolutionwillnotbelitigated.com. The following helped with networking and reading drafts: Patrick Boyle, Maggie Davey, Andy Hsiao, Bridget Impey, and Carol Steinberg. Thank you to Rebecca Nagel of the Wylie Agency for helping us find a publisher and readers, and to Colin Robinson from OR Books, the perfect home for this book.

The Power of Law, Power of People project is very much the collective effort of all the lawyers, activists, writers, and thinkers who have been part of it. We have learned so much from them, and are very grateful for the time they have so generously given, and the care they have taken. This includes all the contributors to this book, as well as Meena Jagarnath, Kate Thomson, and Hoi Trinh. Our thanks go to all the activists, lawyers, and movements who have inspired us and continue to do so.

Some Personal Reflections on People Power and Legal Power: A Foreword

JANE FONDA

My first run-in with the law was when Nixon's White House broke it, and *I* got arrested.

It was on November 3, 1970, at Cleveland Hopkins Airport. I had flown in from Canada, my first stop on a two-month-long speaking tour that would raise the funds to pay for the Winter Soldier Investigation. This was a project modeled on the Nuremburg trials that would bring active or formerly active soldiers from all branches of the US military to testify about the acts they had committed, or witnessed, in Vietnam.

The Watergate tapes would later reveal that President Nixon feared the GI movement more than any other part of the anti-war movement— he would do whatever he could to stop me, a famous actress, from providing a stage for GIs to tell the truth. As I went through customs in Cleveland, policemen were waiting to handcuff me and seize my luggage. When they found many small plastic envelopes of vitamins, I was booked on a trumped-up charge of drug smuggling. The arresting officer told me, bluntly, that he was acting on direct orders from the White House. Several months later, lab reports revealed the truth: the vitamins really were vitamins.

Later that year, as my antiwar activism gained momentum, the Nixon administration unleashed the CIA, the FBI, and its notorious COINTELPRO (Counter Intelligence Program) on me. This ranged from the planting of fake news articles about me to breaking into my home repeatedly to hacking my private bank account. I sued Nixon and seven of his henchmen. We settled, and got an apology from Nixon himself.

Was that justice? No! Justice would have been an end to the criminal murder of millions of Vietnamese soldiers and civilians and fifty-eight thousand American soldiers in Southeast Asia. But in the process of playing my role in the anti-war movement, I learned some powerful lessons about the themes of this urgent and necessary book, concerning the relationship between "the power of law" and "the power of people" in the struggle for justice. I have carried these lessons forward to my climate activism of today—and especially the Fire Drill Friday rallies and civil disobedience actions that have drawn so many into the fight for climate justice.

This book is filled with wisdom, with courage, and with a wealth of experience from some of the most effective activists and lawyers of the world. As I read it, one thing in particular has struck me, bearing out my own experience: the way "the power of law" and "the power of people" need to work together to bring about significant transformative change.

In my six decades as an activist, I have developed a keen sense of how important it is that we consider the law as a tool as we advance justice and social transformation. This book lays out many ways to do just that. It may be by seeking justice through litigation. It may be by using the law to defend ourselves against its abuse, even by its agents themselves. Or it may be by breaking the law, deliberately and purposefully, to draw attention to our causes.

This book works from the maxim that "it takes a lawyer, an activist, and a storyteller to change the world." If these essays hold valuable lessons for lawyers and activists and anyone interested in social justice, one of the most important is the very way they are written: they are gripping stories that will hold you even as they inform you. Their authors are all *doers*, people who have acted bravely to change the world. But they have come to understand, as I have, how public advocacy is nine tenths of any struggle—and that storytelling is what drives any public advocacy campaign, as it does any legal case.

Having spent a working life in Hollywood, I have witnessed the transformative power of an affecting and well-told story. I've spent a parallel life supporting causes ranging from the anti-war movement and the women's movement to the climate justice movement of today, and I have also come to understand the power of my own platform to draw attention to injustice and to seek protection for those being unfairly targeted. My intention has been to create a platform for others who have a story that urgently needs to be heard, be they the brave GIs or Indigenous activists. This has helped me appreciate the mobilizing power of the courtroom battle too: not just to change the law or get an innocent verdict, but to change hearts, minds, and attitudes through the power of storytelling. This book is full of such case studies, and as I read them, I thought about the Chicago Seven, and how Tom Hayden, Abbie Hoffman, and the other defendants used their trial to publicize what *really* mattered: not their own freedom, but the thousands of young American men being killed every day in an unjustified war on foreign soil.

Tom's lawyer in Chicago was his best friend, the legendary Leonard Weinglass—the man who represented me too, along with the American Civil Liberties Union, when I sued the Nixon administration. Sure, Lennie had all the attributes that we think make up a brilliant lawyer: He was sharply analytical, keenly strategic, he knew how to play to the jury, and he could be cutthroat when necessary. But he had other qualities too, essential for working with people who are fighting for their rights or even their lives: a certain quietness and empathy, an ability to listen with an open heart, and to find out through gentle questioning what was really at stake.

Now, half a century later, as I work to amplify the struggles of Indigenous people and those fighting for climate justice, I find myself working with someone who reminds me of Lennie: Mara Verheyden-Hilliard of the Partnership for Civil Justice Fund. The *Washington Post* has called Mara "the constitutional sheriff for a new protest generation," but she is so much more. She is someone who cares deeply about her clients, listening with that open heart to their pain, their trauma, and also their joy. She understands—as Lennie did—that this must be deeply embedded in legal strategy that aims to transform, rather than just tinker with, systemic injustice. As Lennie did with the ACLU and other groups, Mara works alongside movements as well as in a collective of lawyers and activists. Reading this book has helped me understand—as I hope it will for you—what it really means to be a "movement lawyer."

As I write these words in mid-2021, I am keenly observing a case Mara and EarthRights International are bringing against Canadian oil giant Enbridge and the Minnesota police. They maintain the corporation and the state police are acting illegally, in collusion, to expand Line 3. This is a pipeline carrying dirty tar sands oil through Indigenous lands and beneath more than two hundred bodies of water, and it is being constructed without adequate cultural or environmental impact assessments.

The police abuse in Minnesota—just two hours drive from where George Floyd was killed—is all too familiar to what I witnessed at Standing Rock in 2018. I will never forget the chilling image of a line of heavily militarized police on top of a hill, silhouetted against the sky—training their weapons down on the water-protectors whose arms were raised in prayer, exercizing their constitutional rights to prevent the Dakota Access Pipeline crossing their sacred lands and waters.

In Minnesota, at the governor's instigation, a fund with no apparent limit was set up by Enbridge to finance and reimburse all Minnesota's policing activities regarding Line 3, thereby incentivizing excessive harassment. Mara and the EarthRights lawyers believe they can stop this dangerous partnership, which is, among other things, a violation of the constitutional right to protest. It could set an important legal precedent.

Reading this book, I learned much about the power—but also the limitations—of such strategic litigation. I came to understand two things, most of all: The first is that a case is often only a means to an end, which is the advancement of your cause. Even if you lose the case you can "win" in a court of public opinion, or in the way you have brought people together to take action. The second is that, in this arena at least, there is no "power of law" without the "power of people": If you are seeking transformational change, a legal strategy must go hand-in-hand with a movement-building strategy. This is not only to get the evidence and the public support, but also to build resilience for the long battle ahead.

This book brilliantly sets out the three different paths for activists and lawyers to bring the radical changes we so urgently need. We activists can make the law through establishing precedent, such as in the suit against Minnesota and Enbridge. We can also use the law to defend ourselves, when it has been abused by the authorities to shut us down, as is also happening in Minnesota, and as happened to me in the early 1970s. And, of course, we can choose to *break* the law too.

Now in my eighties, I have found myself at the barricades once more. "Where are our elders?" the young people who went on strike for climate justice were asking in 2019. "We can't do this all by ourselves. We can't even vote." I was inspired by this, so I reached out to Greenpeace, an organization unafraid of taking bold action. I knew that, after forty years of marching and lobbying and petitioning and litigating and protesting, we needed to up the ante. Time is running out on the climate crisis. It was time for civil disobedience.

In 2021, twenty-five million Americans—over 10 percent of the adult population—were so alarmed about the climate crisis that they were ready to act. But they haven't done so because no one has asked. This is according to polling done by Yale University's Climate and Communications Project. I call these people "The Great Unasked," and the primary agenda of Fire Drill Fridays has been to use my platform to invite my compatriots to put their bodies on the line alongside me.

And so, in the fall of 2019, I moved to Washington, DC, and resolved to break the law every Friday until Congress passed the Green New Deal. Thousands joined me, and hundreds of thousands more supported us online—until COVID-19 compelled us to stop. Even though there was little risk for me physically in these weekly arrests, the spectacle of this eighty-three-year-old film star getting arrested—alongside so many powerful frontline activists and thousands of ordinary people—helped to create news, tell stories, and grow our movement. We have continued virtually through the pandemic, and nine million people have viewed our weekly program. Our volunteers called and texted over five million climate voters before the 2020 election, and we know we have influenced the progress made in climate policy by the Biden administration.

In March 2021 I travelled to northern Minnesota with Katie Redford (one of the editors of this book) and other lawyers and activists to witness seven water-protectors being arrested for civil disobedience. The water-protectors put their bodies between the bulldozers and their sacred lands in an effort to delay Line 3. All the time we were up there, as we drove across the vast, still-wintry expanses of that magnificent land of the Ojibwe nations, we were tailed by Minnesota police officers. They even pulled us over once on a supposed traffic violation (without issuing a citation). The outrage is that they were on Enbridge's dime, and we were law-abiding citizens exercising our most basic rights to freedom of movement. It's not that we were intimidated—of course we weren't! It was more the abuse of state personnel and intended chilling effect that this might have on local protest.

In Minnesota, I experienced a troubling flashback to 1970. Back then, as I travelled the country doing my anti-war mobilizing, I was constantly tailed. It was like having a shark constantly circling you. Those keeping tabs on me drove unmarked cars but wore trench coats as if from central casting; they wanted me to know they were there. Now, in 2021, being tailed by the Minnesota police, I felt the same tension in my body that I experienced back then. How disabling it can be when the abuse of "law and order" justifies crackdowns on those who speak truth to power.

Of course, my brushes with the law are nothing compared to what you will read about in this book; to what protestors are experiencing at the hands of the military regime in Burma right now, or what Alexei Navalny is enduring in a Russian prison as I write. Back in the United States, we might sigh in relief at the end of the Trump era, with its tyrannical bent. But we still live with "law and order" rhetoric from Trumpist strongmen, in Texas and Florida for example, and we have the very recent memory of the way Movement for Black Lives protestors were dealt with on the streets of our cities. We also continue to live with the way Black people are murdered, by racist police officers, on the street or even in their beds, just for being Black.

But if the law is being abused, *against* people, it is also being harnessed, *by* people and *with* people. This book shows how: from Standing Rock to Ferguson, from Moscow to Myanmar, from abortion rights in Poland to LGBTQ rights in Kenya, from land rights in Mexico to prisoners' rights in Lebanon, from the environmental movement in China to the climate movement in the United States. The anvil is white-hot at the moment, and we must use it quickly to ensure that the arc of history is, in the words of Rev. King, bent toward justice. Because when it comes to climate justice, or racial equality, or any of the other vital struggles you will read about in this book, time is of the essence.

This book shows how the law can be used, for better or worse. Reading it will show you how it's been used, across the world, to protect, unleash, and amplify people power. It has confirmed and deepened what I have known throughout my life, but have never put in words: The law is no magic bullet when it comes to bringing about change, but if you understand its power as a tool, *you* can harness it to bring about the change yourself—especially if you do it with others as a movement.

In this respect I have found *The Revolution Will Not Be Litigated* to be transformational.

I am sure you will too.

"It Takes A Lawyer, an Activist, and a Storyteller . . .":
An Introduction to This Book

MARK GEVISSER

The activist Ka Hsaw Wa remembers a conversation he and another young freedom-fighter from Burma (Myanmar) had nearly three decades ago with two American law students, deep in the jungle on the Thai side of the border of their country.

It was 1994 and the students, Katie Redford and Tyler Giannini, had come to the region as summer interns for a human rights organization, after their second year at law school. They had decided to study law—like so many—because they thought this would give them the skills needed to fight injustice and inequality; to make the world a better place. Instead, they were being taught the skills needed to win a case, and to earn them a place in the highly paid professional elite that they thought was part of the problem. Disillusioned, they now found themselves on the Burmese border seeking the kind of life experience that might connect their skills, knowledge, and ideals to actual work they could do as lawyers.

Ka Hsaw Wa was also seeking something different, in his life and in his activism. Having fled Burma after arrest and torture, he had witnessed unspeakable violence on his journey into exile. Somewhat ostracized within his own ethnic Karen community for refusing to take up arms—he did not want to perpetuate violence—he had devoted himself to documenting the human rights abuse of the Myanmar government, and giving these testimonies to human rights organizations and anyone else who cared to listen. This is why he was meeting these two American kids. The Burmese compatriot with him had information that villagers were being forced into slave labor and off their land by government soldiers, raped and murdered if they resisted, so that a gas pipeline could be laid down by American and French oil companies, Unocal and Total.

In his own way, Ka Hsaw Wa too was disillusioned: no amount of the documentation and exposure he had done seemed to have changed anything. And so—despite his credo of nonviolence—he did not disagree when his activist comrade burst out: "We've done everything else and they still ignore us, and our people keep suffering. Why would it be illegal if we just *blew up the pipeline?*"

But the way Katie Redford responded to this made Ka Hsaw Wa sit up and take notice: "We *can* blow the pipeline up, by using the law itself as our weapon."

The law, of course, was the enemy for Ka Hsaw Wa, given his experiences back home. But he listened intently as the two Americans described the way that, as he recalls it, "we would have the most success if we fought Unocal with their own weapons, on their own terrain: the American courts." That was a new way of thinking for him, "but I liked the idea of using their own tools against them—using law to lift people up, not to press them down. If I wasn't going to use a gun, what were my tools? The military had so many guns and so much power; all I had was a pen and, notepad." In this context, understanding *the law* as a weapon was a revelation, "particularly when it became clear to me that powerful people and abusive corporations were really scared of it!"

Out of this encounter, Ka Hsaw Wa formed an alliance with Katie Redford and Tyler Giannini, and then an organization, EarthRights International, that would take as its slogan the motto "The Power of Law, The Power of People"—side by side, as symbiotic and interdependent components of any change strategy involving the law. The starting point is that when movements and lawyers work together, the shift in power and transformational impact is greater than the sum of their parts, and this book's contributors recount their personal experiences of working with the law, working with movements, and bringing them together.

In the companion essays that begin this book, Ka Hsaw Wa and Katie Redford give their parallel accounts of the *Unocal* case germinated at that 1995 meeting. They worked on it for nearly a decade: Ka Hsaw Wa the activist channeling the movement, Redford as the lawyer working the case. If Redford's strategic objective was to use the case to establish a precedent that would mean US corporations could be held accountable for human rights abuse abroad, Ka Hsaw Wa's was to amplify and channel the struggle of his people. This, of course, was just a first step: toward the villagers getting their homes back or being paid just recompense, in a process of political empowerment that he hoped would eventually topple the military dictators.

Through the case, Redford developed the ethos that was to guide her legal career: "Win or lose in court, we wanted to make sure that we won the movement—that the communities had more power, more agency, more networks and confidence to engineer their own solutions after our case . . . than they did before." She also understood that by using litigation to build political power among those affected, they were strengthening the case itself: not just through the evidence (and testimony) that the movement was able to generate, but in the "court of public opinion."

In 1997, a US Federal Court made history by granting jurisdiction over *Doe v. Unocal.* Eight years later, Unocal finally settled with the eleven plaintiffs, all survivors of gross human rights abuses along the pipeline tracks. Ka Hsaw Wa and Redford are now a married couple, with children of their own; he describes the realization that dawned on them during their years of work on the case: "Not only were the people more powerful with legal tools in their hands, but *the law* was more powerful too, when the people on the ground—those with the most to gain and lose—were inhabiting and driving it with their own experiences."

*

"It takes a lawyer, an activist, and a storyteller to create positive social change."

In her essay on the experience of being Julian Assange's lawyer, Jennifer Robinson recalls that these words were first said to her by the legendary American movement lawyer Michael Ratner. At the time, in 2010, Robinson was a young Australian just setting out to practice law in the United Kingdom: "I really didn't think about my job as serving a movement," she writes. "I saw it as defending an individual and advising an organization, the traditional role I had been taught in law school. But then I saw how this person, with nothing more than a backpack and a small effective groups of volunteers, could shake the world's superpower to its core, with revelations about war crimes, human rights abuse, and corruption." Fighting Assange's extradition from the UK, she witnessed the way imperial, global power was being used to slur her client as such a threat to freedom when in fact "his work was designed to facilitate freedom: freedom of speech and the public's right to know."

Robinson came to understand that while her legal work was essential, defending Assange required public advocacy too. This meant working with activists and protesters, in the media and on the streets, to challenge the narrative and actions of the US government in order to protect his rights—rights, she had come to see, that were fundamental to democratic freedom.

From the activist's perspective, the veteran campaigner Kumi Naidoo—the former head of Greenpeace and Amnesty International—comes to a similar conclusion about using the law. He recalls that way South African anti-apartheid activists used court cases to talk "not just to the judge but to the people." On the one hand, they sent a message to the oppressed: "This is really bad, we must stand up and act against it." But they also sent a message to the oppressors: "This system is unjust, unfair, and untenable, and so it is not sustainable—the sooner you recognize the need to change, the better." Naidoo learned a lesson about "the communicative power" of litigation that he has tried to apply to his more recent work on climate justice.

"It takes a lawyer, an activist, and a storyteller . . .": this slogan aptly summarises the vision of this book. About half its contributors are, like Ka Hsaw Wa and Kumi Naidoo, activists who have used the law (or who critique its use) in their work as movement builders. The other half, like Katie Redford and Jennifer Robinson, come at the issue from a legal perspective. They describe themselves in many ways: "movement lawyer," "cause lawyer," "radical lawyer," "human rights lawyer," "community lawyer." What they have in common is that they practice law to effect social and political change; in so doing, they see themselves not only as lawyers, but as activists and storytellers too.

Narratives are "the lifeblood of the law, as well as the lifeblood of social movements," writes Justin Hansford of his involvement in the uprising in Ferguson, Missouri, following the police murder of the teenager Michael

Brown in August 2014. At the time, Hansford was a young law lecturer at St. Louis University; one of the few African American academics in the city of which Ferguson is a suburb. He took to the streets, in a groundswell that became the Movement for Black Lives, and his experience led him to think about the potential of movements. Hansford writes about how he has come to see that shifting the public narrative about Black Americans, and thus collapsing "the racial hierarchy of the United States, is far more important than any single legal victory or defeat."

In an essay that might be considered a prequel to Hansford's, Baher Azmy examines the way his organization, the Center for Constitutional Rights, used a high-profile trial to create a public narrative about racial profiling, by challenging the "stop and frisk" policies of the New York Police Department in 2013. One of the important functions of law resides in its power to translate lived experience into stories about individual and social fairness and justice, Azmy writes: "'I want my day in court' is a powerful phrase that operates as a shorthand for transcendent social values. The phrase also captures the basic human quest to tell one's story" and speak truth.

Hansford, Azmy, and many other contributors illuminate the way storytelling itself becomes a form of justice. As Redford writes: "Our clients found power, and victory, in taking charge of their narratives, and forcing a process where people had to listen." Seen this way, a court victory is not necessarily more important than the opportunity that a trial (or the mere threat of legal action) gives for being heard.

Writing from Kenya, the sex workers' rights activist Phelister Abdalla describes preparing for strategic litigation to decriminalize sex work, a case She expected her organization would lose, so as to present sex workers not as demonic sinners but as mothers looking after their families: "We want to use the case to give sex workers a human face." Her compatriot, Njeri Gateru, fresh from a bruising negative verdict in a suit to decriminalize homosexuality in Kenya, notes the value of the case anyway, in raising awareness, and attracting new supporters in parliament and the media: "Being yourself publicly also changes people's perceptions. People are unable to marry their hate or their ignorance with their understanding of your humanity."

Still, there is a healthy skepticism, in some of the contributions, about the role that lawyers should play in shifting public narrative. David Hunter, a law professor and veteran campaigner for the accountability of global financial institutions such as the World Bank, recalls a conversation with an activist who asked him what difference it would make spending the money on a policy brief from a lawyer or on creating street puppets for a protest, if it achieved the same result. It "hurts as a lawyer to be compared to a street puppet," writes Hunter wryly, "but the sentiment is worth remembering. In the long-term campaign for social justice reform, street puppets and lawyers are best thought of as tools in an overarching campaign. Certainly, we lawyers might be more helpful than street puppets in figuring out campaign strategy—but we also bring risks. Lawyers thrive in legalistic venues that simultaneously professionalize the discourse and risk devaluing the community's voice. The lawyer's role is to recognize that bias and support the community's right to choose whether to tell their story through puppets, through lawyers, or though their own voice."

*

If the contributors to this book understand the power of narrative as a tool, they also explore it as a personal methodology. They start from the premise that theories of change are not designed in laboratories or seminar rooms, but rather come out of a reflection on practice. And so all these essays and interviews are personal reflections, written as a counter to—or perhaps a companion to —the analysis of jurisprudence, or the polemics of manifestos.

There is a growing field of writing about the relationship between the law and movements, and even a new name for the concept: "demosprudence," a fusion of "democracy" and "jurisprudence," coined by the American law professors Lani Guinier and Gerald Torres to describe "the study of the dynamic equilibrium of power between law-making and social movements." Using examples from American civil rights history, they argue that social movements are critical not only to legal process, "but also to the cultural shifts that make durable legal change possible." Law is developed as much by social movement activism as by statutes and judicial decisions. In demosprudence, Guinier and Torres write, "neither the lawyer nor the client alone sets the terms or the goals of the relationship. Together they act out democracy." Written about the United States, their model presupposes democracy. But even in the more difficult places for law and democracy from which this book's contributors write—China, Russia, Poland, Burma, Lebanon, Mexico, Kenya—this sense of walking together drives their narratives.

This means that they are tellers of their own stories too, as well as those of their "clients" or movements. They take you into their worlds: Jennifer Robinson frantically helping orchestrate a protest outside the Ecuadorian embassy in London, providing the activists with the legal ammunition they needed to prevent the British authorities from storming it; Ghida Frangieh at the barricades of Lebanon's 2019 revolution, in the detention centers trying to access arrested protestors; Eimear Sparks in the vibrant, triumphant reproductive rights movement that saw a referendum in favor of legalizing abortion in Ireland; Nana Ama Nketia-Quaidoo working with Ghanaian villagers to reverse a land-grab of their chief. Ayisha Siddiqa, a shy Pakistani immigrant, finds community in her new home for the first time while leading the 2019 youth climate strike through Manhattan; Marissa Vahlsing and Ben Hoffman putter along an Amazon tributary in a *peke-peke*, to and from clients trying to resist an American oil company; Kumi Naidoo finds himself on a rubber dinghy in stormy Arctic seas as he races toward a Cairn Energy oil rig Greenpeace seeks to occupy.

All these accounts are not just engagingly descriptive of fascinating lives and work, but revelatory: of generational transitions; of epochal change and apocalyptic anxiety, particularly around the climate crisis; of the ethical dilemmas that define our age and how to plot a way through them; of what it means to do good when the odds are stacked against us; of how one can make a positive impact, at all, in an epoch of the Anthropocene and in the age of globalization. In their different ways, each contributor explores the complex, and often-awkward dance between legal or judicial reform and social change.

In her essay on female genital cutting, Julia Lalla-Maharajh describes this dance. Lalla-Maharajh, who has been one of the world's most effective campaigners against the practice, notes that in twenty-six of the twenty-eight African countries where it happens, there are laws forbidding it—and yet it continues. "Do you want me to lock up everyone involved in cutting a girl?" an African justice minister asks her. "How am I going to lock up 98 percent of the population?" More than that: the perps are often mothers themselves, fulfilling an age-old social obligation. Following the way community-based organizations have worked to shift these social norms, Lalla-Maharajh has learned that "if a legal norm does not mirror a social norm, then there is an inherent tension that can remain unresolved. The law should not be avoided, but nor is it a panacea; we need to work with people and social norms." It is from Lalla-Maharaj's own experience in the field that she can say that for the law to have effect, it must be "a living, breathing tool that has relevance and accessibility for communities." She brings this notion to life through vivid descriptions of newly forged passage-to-womanhood rituals in Senegal and Kenya, developed to replace genital cutting.

While some contributors, like the Polish abortion rights leader Klementyna Suchanow, think about the relationship between legal advocacy and movement building from the heat of an ongoing battle, others look back with hindsight at legendary struggles that have come to define this relationship. Joe Athialy reflects on his experiences as an activist in the "Save The Narmada Valley" movement in India, trying to stop a dam project that would displace a million people. JingJing Zhang describes her landmark litigation on behalf of pollution victims in China. Krystal Two Bulls recounts her activism against the Dakota Access Pipeline at Standing Rock, and the legal backlash against her. Robin Gorna recalls the campaign to boycott the 1990 AIDS Conference in San Francisco, because the US still prohibited the entry of HIV-positive aliens into the country, a campaign that introduced a human rights dimension into AIDS discourse.

And Mark Heywood describes the South African AIDS movement's courtroom victory in 2001, reversing a government decision to withhold antiretroviral medication from pregnant women with HIV. Fighting this case enabled Heywood and his comrades to strengthen a movement: his Treatment Action Campaign (TAC) used the case "to educate members on the constitution and the law"; this gave the new organization "purpose and internal coherence," while the court hearings themselves inspired demonstrations, and the organizing and alliance-building that went into them.

The flip side was the impact that "TAC's mass mobilization had on the legal process by influencing public opinion outside the court."

Fighting police torture in Russia, Pavel Chikov reflects on the power of this "court of public opinion": not just the cases his organization, Agora, has fought against police violence, but the publicity they have sought for these cases, and even the publicity they have generated by seeking out litigants through public appeals. Agora has evidence that the level of police torture is significantly lower in those regions where its lawyers have achieved high-profile convictions.

In Lebanon, the lawyer Ghida Frangieh has played a similar role, with her organization, Legal Agenda, and the Lawyers' Committee for the Defence of Protestors she has managed since that country's October 2019 uprising. "Law is too important to be left in the hands of lawyers alone," she writes of the very public campaign to popularize Article 47, the Lebanese Miranda Rule guaranteeing the rights of detainees. As with the Treatment Action Campaign in South Africa, litigation was a key—but certainly not the only—part of this campaign. The result was palpable: not just that detained protestors and their supporters insisted on these rights, but that parliament had no choice but to pass an amendment strengthening it even further, due to public pressure.

Frangieh's interest in the rights of detainees stems from her early legal experience representing refugees in custody; this sense of a journey— of reflecting on past experience and working hard to apply the lessons learned—characterizes so many of the essays in this collection. After winning a settlement in a landmark class action suit against a state chemicals company for polluting a community's water supply, JingJing Zhang writes about how she is now determined to hold China accountable for environmental and human rights abuse abroad. Joe Athialy describes the way he mobilized fisherfolk from Gujarat based on his experience at Narmada, bringing them all the way to the US Supreme Court. Farhana Yamin looks back, critically, at the years she spent drafting international climate treaties—from the perspective of an Extinction Rebellion activist gluing herself to Shell's headquarters in an act of civil disobedience.

Other contributors grapple with the implications of what it means when their clients reject the law as a tool. In the case described by Ben

Hoffman and Marissa Vahlsing, their clients decided not to sue the oil corporation polluting their Peruvian Amazon river, but rather tried to negotiate favorable labor contracts with them, using the illegal brinksmanship of occupying and shutting down the company's oil wells as a strategy. Hoffman worries that by adhering to the movement lawyer's credo of respecting community agency, he and Vahlsing—the legal experts, after all—might not have made a strong enough case to go to court. But when the community actually did shut down the wells, it forced a negotiation—with the government involved too—and this seemed like it might yield results.

Some contributors are, like Hoffman and Vahlsing—American lawyers—deeply aware of their outsider status in relation to their clients; both the power and responsibility it brings. Others, like Njeri Gateru, are very much members of the community they represent legally: in Gateru's case, queer Kenyans. At the meeting that kick-started this book, convened at the Rockefeller Foundation's Bellagio Center in 2019 and attended by most of its contributors, Gateru made the point that she did not see the "the law" and "the people" as two distinct columns, or two pieces of rope that needed to be twined together for maximum strength. She was one rope, both a lawyer and an activist, in both cases advocating for the rights of her very own people. Her life and her practice, her politics and her profession, were inextricable. In her interview in this book she describes the complexity of this: not just preparing the legal arguments for the decriminalization of homosexuality, but "preparing yourself as a person who participates in the movement" and "preparing the emotions of the community for whatever the outcome is of such huge litigation."

Finding the balance between feeling oneself to be part of a movement and maintaining the distance necessary to play one's professional role is a central theme of this book. Justin Hansford writes of the middleman role he played, as a Black law professor in Ferguson, and how if you are going to be a movement lawyer you need to accept this discomfort, never really at home either among the suits in the boardrooms or on the ground with the people, but—ideally—valued and trusted in both arenas.

*

"Meaningful and durable social change comes not from legal rulings, which are inherently vulnerable over time and contingent on political forces in the longer term," writes Baher Azmy. "They come from social and political movements that center communities most impacted by an injustice, as the agents of the change they demand." This point, made by several contributors to this books, seems particularly apt in the shadow of the United States Supreme Court's 2022 *Dobbs v. Jackson Women's Health Organization* decision, which withdrew from American women their fifty-year-old constitutional right to abortion.

Abortion rights litigation began in the women's movement: movement lawyers such as Florynce Kennedy and Nancy Stearns argued on the basis of equality—an argument arising, in turn, out of the civil rights movement. It was this argument that convinced New York state to pass the country's first abortion rights legslation in 1970. But when the Supreme Court finally ruled on abortion rights in *Roe v. Wade* in 1973, it relied rather on a case out of Texas that argued a right to privacy: an argument that Ruth Bader Ginsburg later said stopped the momentum of change, because it was more about "the physician's right to practice" than "the woman's choice." The implication of Ginsburg's critique, made in 2013, is that jurisprudence grounded in a mass movement for equality might be more robust over time. As Florynce Kennedy has put it about their strategy: "when you want to get to the suites, start in the streets."

This book is not an investigation into movements themselves, and what makes them effective or sustainable. Rather, it is about movements' relationship with the law, and with legal advocacy as a strategy among many, to achieve meaningful objectives. Still, both the lawyers and non-lawyers think deeply about what movements are, in an effort to understand their relationship to legal strategy, and it is clear, from their experiences, that while there is no blueprint for how to use the law to help shift power, there is a common pattern of experience. Here is how the Power of Law, Power of People project has distilled this common pattern of experience: "Movements are born of pain and anger. They sustain momentum by creativity and community, by empathy and joy. They navigate uncertainty and chaos using the imperfect tools of the law to seek justice and relief."

The "pain and anger" is clear: from Justin Hansford and Baher Azmy's American city streets where young people of color are targeted and dehumanized; from the horrific stories of police abuse in Lebanon and Russia recounted by Pavel Chikov and Ghida Frangieh; from the fear and the sense of urgency in youth climate activists Ayisha Siddiqa and David Wicker; from the experiences of Irish women forced to have backstreet abortions as recounted by Eimear Sparks and the anger of Polish women being stripped of their rights to abortion as recounted by Klementyna Suchanow; from the suffering of villagers and peasants from Oaxaca through North Dakota to India and Burma; from communities in the United Kingdom and South Africa devastated by AIDS.

It is out of the crucible of such emotion—rather than from the seminar rooms of strategists or legal advisors—that movements emerge, with their expressions not only of pain and anger, but joy and creativity too: so many of this book's contributors note the exhilaration and regenerative energy of being on the streets, at Black Lives Matter protests, pro-abortion rallies, the popular uprising in Beirut, climate justice protests the world over.

In her striking account of a three-decade-old debate with her friend the human rights lawyer Jonathan Cooper, the AIDS and feminist activist Robin Gorna writes that the power of movements is in the way they create connections between people—often very different—bonded together in common cause: "The best social movements connect the head—evidence, research, legal arguments—with the heart: identity, emotions, true connections." Gorna understands movements as "an art, not a science"—but she writes too of the importance of strategy in assessing whether to fight a legal battle: "Of course we've got to change the rules that matter most, but obsessing about legal change might mean missing opportunities," she says to her friend Jonny. "Who cares about perfect legislation if no one at the hospital will touch you because they hate gays and are terrified of infection? We have to start with what matters most in people's lives: the immediate struggles, changing hearts, minds, social understanding, getting more money in place."

Cooper shoots back that that the 1998 Human Rights Act he helped get passed in the UK now provides the basis for more effective activism: "Now when people with HIV face discrimination we go to court. We don't just make a noise!" The two friends eventually agree that the best recipe for social change is law *and* movements, rather than either/or.

For Krystal Two Bulls, an Indigenous warrior at the forefront of many campaigns, using the law to build and protect a movement is merely a form of "harm reduction," albeit one that is "very valid and very necessary given it can save life." Two Bulls was part of the movement that gathered at Standing Rock, in North Dakota, in 2016, to prevent pipeline construction through sacred Indigenous lands. Given that the Western form of law was "imposed on us" and used, in effect, to commit genocide on Indigenous people, "I'm conscious of how we are founded on this cracked foundation. No matter how many houses we build, paint jobs, renovations, it's not going to matter. If we are going to move toward the change we hunger for, needed for the survival of planet, we have to redo our foundation." Still, even from this perspective, activists such as Two Bulls understand the power of the law: "We have to infiltrate these systems and bring them into these spaces to prevent further harm done."

Njeri Gateru articulates a fundamental dilemma for "cause lawyers" such as herself: "When I think about what's at the root of the pain of queer Kenyans, and in other words for me too, it's the *law* itself. It's the law that permits all the violence and discrimination against us. And now I must go into battle to make things better by using the tools of that very same law that causes the pain in the first place!"

Gateru's comment illuminates the way so many of the contributors to this book grapple with the law (or its enforcers) as the enemy, as Ka Hsaw Wa did, given his experiences in Burma—or as Phelister Abdalla, the leader of the Kenyan sex workers' movement, first did, given her own experiences of the law: raped by the policemen she went to for help. Other contributors write about how the law is purposefully used against them and their clients, to curtail their activism. Krystal Two Bulls describes the experience of being the victim of a SLAPP (Strategic Litigation Against Public Participation) suit after participating in the Standing Rock camp. Klementyna Suchanow writes of how she and other abortion rights leaders are continually harassed with charges, as a way of attempting to disable them. If legal harassment is one strategy to cow activists, then unpunished extrajudicial violations of their rights is another.

A movement can have your back when you are victimized by the law, as Krystal Two Bulls describes, in the way a Protect the Protest coalition coalesced around her defense. It can give you the strength to challenge the illegal practice of the authorities collectively, as Ghida Frangieh describes, in the way the Beirut Bar, during the 2019 uprising, took a stand against authorities denying detainees their basic rights. And, as well as providing the evidence and the narratives required to win a case, a powerful social movement can enforce a verdict: Mark Heywood notes that, in South Africa, a key court victory on the right to shelter was never properly enforced because, unlike as with the HIV case, there was no movement to back it up.

Understanding legal activism as part of a broader political struggle also means having to make tough decisions about litigation, writes Joe Athialy, reflecting on a bruising loss for the Save the Narmada Movement in the Indian Supreme Court: "What if you lose your bid at the courts? Does it close all other avenues of negotiations? Will the state be more aggressive? Would that turn away the public support you might have garnered over the years? These questions weigh heavily on a movement deciding on whether or not to litigate. The buffer, of course, is to root litigation within a larger strategy of political struggle": if you have made the calculation that the propagation of a particular public narrative is worth the risk of losing a case, then you might proceed anyway.

Still, Mark Heywood cautions movements against seeking a "magic bullet" from the law "when what they actually need to do is organize."

*

The law, writes Mark Heywood, "can be catalytic and even cathartic. Yet on its own, it cares nothing for democracy or rights. On the other hand, people's movements, like people themselves, are hot-blooded, noisy, and messy. They are diverse. They don't often take easily to rules. They can be intemperate. Movements rise and fall. They breathe. They can die."

The fluidity of social movements is just one of many conditions that make the "Power of Law, Power of People" equation difficult to activate. The political context around them is another: in countries like Russia, China, and Burma there can be neither power of law nor adequate space for people power, given the way the state controls the judiciary and restricts freedoms. In the shadow of Russia's 2022 invasion of Ukraine, Pavel Chikov notes that the human rights situation has deteriorated to such an extent that "I don't see me and my team working on the ground in Russia even by the end of the year. We are one step away from massive repression." Culture and faith is a third condition to be negotiated, as Julia Lalla-Maharaj demonstrates with regard to genital cutting; Nana Ama Nketia-Quaidoo explores this further, as she tries to set the law of the land against the alleged supernatural powers of a tyrannical chief in Ghana.

And then of course there is the problem of time. When, in 2019, the US Supreme Court rejected the World Bank's claims of absolute immunity for harms to the fishermen of the Gulf of Kutch, meaning that they could proceed to sue the World Bank for damages on the power plant it had financed, Joe Athialy went back to the state of Gujarat with Budha Ismail Jam, the first plaintiff, to hold a victory celebration: "I could only salute his perseverance, and that of his fellow petitioners. But nothing, yet, had materially altered in his own life, and his own ability to earn his living on the Gulf of Kutch. I had been working with him for eight years already, but we had only just won the right to *begin* fighting the World Bank on its own turf! It would be a long time, still, before Mr. Jam felt any kind of tangible relief."

This is one of the most enduring critiques—leveled by most contributors to this book—of what is known as "impact litigation," or "strategic litigation": the treacle-like pace with which cases move through a justice system, set against the urgent need for change, on the ground, and in the lives of the people who have suffered the damages in the first place. By the time Alejandra Ancheita won a case for an Indigenous community against a mining company in Mexico, "the scars were already deep in the community and on the environment": the extraction that had already taken place. Still, she said at Bellagio, she learned a vital lesson from the experience: "I thought I was there to help them find solutions, but as I spent time with them, I understood and appreciated how *they* were using *me*: to buy them time, so they could figure out what to do next." The long spooling-out of litigation actually suited them, and helped her redefine her role as a lawyer.

Time is the major preoccupation of the climate-lawyer-turned-activist Farhana Yamin. Describing why "lawmakers" such as herself must become "law-breakers," she writes that no legal results will "deliver the transformational changes we need in the next few years unless and until they are accompanied by people also *breaking the law*—as part of a mass 'movement of movements' based on peaceful civil disobedience." In her conclusion to this book, Katie Redford describes why, in her own work, she has shifted from being a movement lawyer to running a campaign to keep fossil fuels in the ground: If the "long arc of the moral universe bends" toward justice, how do we grapple with the scientific truth that "we just don't have time for that arc to bend?"

This frustration reflects a constant tension in the book, and sometimes in the practice of each individual contributor, between the incrementalism they were taught in law school (and in which many of them believe), and the instincts for radical and swift political, social, and economic change. When Ghida Frangieh is approached by people asking whether they should post something on social media or organize a protest, she jokes: "It's a revolution, don't consult the lawyers!" No revolution "will be 'authorized' by law," she concludes. "But the law, if used appropriately, can create revolutions."

At the end of her essay, Ayisha Siddiqa, still an undergraduate when writing, contemplates her personal future. Like Katie Redford, who wanted to change the world three decades previously, Siddiqa thinks about law school. She wants to acquire all the skills she needs to take on the fossil fuel industry, "including the law." She has also "realized the limitations of mass mobilization": "You can have thousands of people on the streets chanting 'climate justice' at top of their lungs only for the people with money and power to ignore you." She imagines that a law degree will enable her to be "part of the decision-making process"; she wants "to learn the language of those making the policy."

Both Kumi Naidoo and Farhana Yamin encourage young activists to go into law, with some important caveats. "One of the biggest mistakes I've made in my own life has been to mistake access for influence," says Naidoo. Yamin, who spent decades as a high-level climate negotiator in the United Nations process, cautions that "law alone isn't going to work to tackle systemic injustices, so don't forget to be an activist in your community even as you dream big."

In her "Rules for Radical Lawyers," Katie Redford complains that rather than learning about how to fight "for truth and social justice" in law school, she encountered "lofty legal theory, judicial opinions, and one hypothetical fact pattern after another presented by brilliant law professors. But where was my practical primer about how to make real change for real people? Certainly not in the legal textbooks filled with Supreme Court decisions. I yearned for something based on lived experience, and reflective not only of laws and precedents, but of their contexts and impacts. This was why I set out to make this book: to add to the library of any law student or lawyer—in fact, any person at all interested in how to use the law as part of their activism—something that was so painfully missing, from mine, when I set out."

We hope that this book helps make the path clearer, richer and more rewarding for people who want to understand more about the relationship between "the power of law" and "the power of people."

*

"It takes a lawyer, an activist, and a storyteller . . ."

The process that led to this book began in March 2018, when a lawyer, an activist, and a storyteller found themselves in neighboring rooms as residents at the Rockefeller Center at Bellagio, on Lake Como in Italy. Each was there for a four-week period, working on their own book project.

The lawyer was Katie Redford, who had come to Bellagio to start work on a book she planned to call *Rules for Radical Lawyers*, a play on *Rules for Radicals*, Saul Alinsky's 1971 book, something of a bible for the American left. The activist was Robin Gorna, who was beginning a memoir of her life's work in the AIDS movement. And the storyteller was me, a journalist and nonfiction author, finishing up a book that would be published in 2020, about the new global human rights frontier of LGBTQ rights and the people who lived along it.

At Bellagio, Redford and Gorna began a conversation about the relationship between legal advocacy and movement building. They decided to convene a meeting of lawyers and activists involved in landmark struggles across the globe, and ask them to share their experiences of the "Power of Law, Power of People" equation. They approached me, as a storyteller, to be part of the process, and once they selected the participants, I began working with each one to craft an essay, the draft of which would be presented at a subsequent Bellagio meeting in 2019, and the final version of which appears in this book. Not all the participants at that Bellagio meeting were able to contribute to this book; others joined the project later on, and were not at Bellagio. Some, too, opted to be interviewed, rather than to write an essay.

There are, of course, far more stories about "The Power of Law, the Power of People" than can be contained within the finite covers of a single book, and this book is far from comprehensive. Rather, it offers insight into twenty-odd struggles, as recounted by twenty-eight people who were part of them—as lawyers, as activists, or as both.

Neither can this book claim to represent every kind of struggle, for justice and human rights, being waged in the twenty-first century. Still, in its range—from the Movement for Black Lives in the United States through the Lebanese revolution in the Middle East to the global climate justice movement—this book provides an unparalleled range of experiences, about the relationship between legal advocacy and movement building.

Often, in working with the contributors, I joked that they suffered from what I diagnosed as EBAS—Erin Brokovich Aversion Syndrome— because of their diffidence about putting themselves center stage, something that went against the grain of their commitment to the collective. But their EBAS symptoms are, of course, their strength, for out of the critical reflection on their roles has come the powerful collection of theories of social change, each rooted in actual experience, that you hold in your hands. Personally, I agree with many of them that the shifting or reframing of public narrative—sometimes through legal battles, but always through the practice of politics—can shift power relations more effectively than individual legal victories. And in this respect, I salute all of them for their willingness to embrace becoming storytellers themselves—and their manifest talent at the job.

In the end, my coeditor Katie Redford was so struck by the way this book's contributors had put the vision for a "Rules for Radical Lawyers" manifesto into practice that she decided to write it as this book's conclusion, rather than to embark on a whole new, separate project. Before she offers some very practical "rules," she notes some famous words that have rung through our ears while bringing this project to fruition and listening to its contributors. You might have heard them yourself, reading this introduction, in the words of Ka Hsaw Wa, Krystal Two Bulls, Ghida Frangieh, Njeri Gateru, Ayisha Siddiqa and others. They are the words of Audre Lorde, and they have inspired the Movement for Black Lives that was taking place all around us as we were putting this book together: "The master's tools will never dismantle the master's house. They may allow us temporarily to beat him at his own game, but they will never enable us to bring about genuine change."

Law, Redford writes, "is of course 'the master's tool' par excellence." What she has learned in her own work as a movement lawyer and as the coordinator of the Power of Law, Power of People project is "two things. First that we *can* use the law, very effectively, to beat the Master at his own game. And second, that if we use the law effectively, in conjunction with movements and their other actions—such as mass mobilization, protest, and public advocacy—we *can* bring about genuine change."

*

Given that I am South African, some other words have rung through my ears as I have worked on this book. They are Nelson Mandela's, from the Rivonia Trial of 1964, when he chose to make a speech from the dock rather than testify in his own defense. It was in this mesmerizing four-hour speech that he said the following: "I have fought against white domination, and I have fought against black domination. I have cherished the ideal of a democratic and free society in which all persons live together in harmony and with equal opportunities. It is an ideal which I hope to live for and to achieve. But if needs be, it is an ideal for which I am prepared to die."

His lawyers pleaded with him not to make this speech. They knew that by doing it, he would be heading for a certain guilty verdict on the charges of high treason, an almost-certain execution. But, as his lawyer Joel Joffe would later write, Mandela understood that "the heart and kernel of this case was not in this courtroom, but in the world outside." If the state was mounting a "show trial" to demonstrate that it would not tolerate dissent, Mandela would commandeer it to give his compatriots a message in resilience and moral courage—and to build global support too. A movement lawyer as well as a movement builder, he was a brilliant strategist: he wagered that by playing to "the world outside," he would attract such opprobrium toward the South African authorities that he would be spared the noose. This is what happened.

Mandela had steered the African National Congress (ANC) toward the Defiance Campaign of civil disobedience and then into taking up arms only because all legal avenues had been exhausted. But he kept his faith in the law, and once he saw from within his prison cell that the situation had shifted to such a point that a political settlement might be possible, he began the secret negotiations that led to my country's democracy and its exemplary constitution. In 1990, upon his release from prison and the unbanning of the ANC, a Xhosa praise poet from Mandela's home region, the Transkei, composed the following lines, which seem particularly apt as inspiration for this book:

Wayigqibezel' imfundo yakhe bayokudibana ngobugqwetha benyaniso,
Khumbula kaloku amagqwetha ukutheth' ityala lawo engagqwethanga
    kweliny'igqwetha.
Asuk' ema amagqweth' azigqwethela,
Kuba yayingagqweth' inyaniso.

Once he [Mandela] had finished his education they [the Boers]
    met the law of truth.
Imagine, lawyers representing themselves.
They just stood and defended themselves,
Because they were lawyers of the truth.

What does it mean to be a lawyer of the truth? What I hear, in these words, is an appreciation for the collapse of the traditional space between lawyers and the people they represent. Also, a celebration of the way Mandela embodied a rare unity, the unity for which this book's contributors strive: between the calculated actions of a legal strategy, and the heartfelt aspirations of the people such a strategy sets out to reach; the experienced realities of their lives it sets out to transform.

Further Reading: On "demosprudence": Lani Guinier and Gerald Torres, "Changing the Wind: Notes Toward a Demosprudence of Law and Social Movements," *The Yale Law Journal*, vol. 123, no. 8, June 2014. On abortion rights: Emily Bazelon, "America Almost Took a Different Path toward Abortion Rights," *New York Times*, May 20, 2022; Meredith Heagney, "Justice Ruth Bader Ginsburg Offers Critique of Roe v. Wade During Law School Visit," The University of Chicago Law School, May 15, 2013. On Nelson Mandela: Nelson Mandela, *Long Walk To Freedom* (Little Brown, 1994), Joel Joffe, *The State v Nelson Mandela* (One World, 2007). The praise poem is cited in Adam Sitze, "Mandela and the Law," in *The Cambridge Companion to Nelson Mandela,* ed. Rita Barnard (Cambridge University Press, 2014).

CASE STUDY

Human Rights: *Doe v. Unocal*

From Burma to the Bench: The Activist's Perspective on *Doe v. Unocal*

KA HSAW WA

Growing up in Burma during the military dictatorship of the 1980s, we used to say that when you hear the word "law," you run in the other direction.

Later, during the 1988 uprising, I would be arrested and tortured: I had just finished high school, and was waiting to go to university. But even before that I was often in trouble. My poor mother was once forced to pay a bribe, through a lawyer, after I got into a fight with military authorities who were bullying another kid. When I complained afterward about how corrupt and greedy all lawyers and judges were in our country, she retorted, "You better watch it; you complain about the law so much, you're going to end up marrying a lawyer one day."

Fast forward to 1993. I have been living in the jungle for five years, doing my bit for the freedom struggle by documenting abuses by the military dictatorship. Into my world stumbles a bright-eyed, long-haired American first-year law student, working as an intern for a human rights organization. I thought she might be useful in getting the word out about our predicament, so I didn't run the other way for a change. But given my experience of "the law," I didn't believe in its power to make any kind of change in a country like my own. Our debates about this characterized our relationship from the start.

"Change can only happen when people rise up together," I insisted, in one of our late-night arguments.

"The law can be a tool for justice—and change," she argued back.

The funny thing is, the only person in this story who was totally right was my mother. I eventually married Katie Redford, after she became a lawyer. Our meeting was life-changing for both of us, not just because we founded EarthRights International, started a family, and eventually moved to the US. For me, it also meant thinking about the law in a whole new way—its possibilities, but also its limitations.

*

One night, shortly after I met Katie and her compatriot Tyler Giannini, we were in hot discussion with another Burmese student. The student spoke about the abuses that were happening along a pipeline being built by the American oil company Unocal, together with Total of France, to carry oil from the Andaman Sea across Burma and into Thailand. Unocal contracted the Burmese military to provide "security," which meant that it turned a blind eye while people were being thrown out of their homes, press-ganged into forced labor, and punished with rape, torture, and murder if they resisted—and sometimes even when they did not. All this so that the corporations could get their gas from the offshore fields in the Andaman Sea and across our country into Thailand to the Thai border.

I had been taking Katie around and interpreting for her, helping her meet survivors of human rights violations associated with logging. In the process, I told her about my own efforts to defend human rights by documenting violations and trying to get these records out to the world. For me it was important that we were *seen*: in a country that had effectively implemented a media blackout, I wanted to protect people by making their struggles *visible*. But in our conversations, Katie and Tyler saw the human rights abuses in a different way: as violations of international law.

This difference between we activists from Burma and those law students from the US became clear in the conversation, that night, about Unocal. The student talking to Katie and Tyler became very animated. He itemized the way our people had worked with journalists to expose the abuses; how villagers together with NGOs had written letters to the company, and even to the US government asking them to intervene; how they had done everything within the realm of possibility to stop this project that was hurting our people so badly. Nothing had worked. "If we've done everything else that we can, and they ignore us, and our people keep suffering—why would it be illegal if we blew up the pipeline?" the student asked.

Katie and Tyler countered with a stunning proposition: We could "blow up the pipeline" by using *the law itself* as our weapon. We would have the most success if we fought Unocal with their own weapons, on their own terrain: the American courts. That was a new way of thinking to me, but I liked the idea of using their own tools against them—using law to lift people up not to press them down.

I sat up. Suddenly I was really listening. I was receptive to this idea because I had already chosen nonviolence, given my personal history. I'd come to the perspective that violence creates more violence, and it had become important to me not to go down that path.

My own history of violence began when I was seventeen. A friend who opposed authority had disappeared and the police wanted information about him. So they detained and tortured me. They beat me for three days until I passed out. Once I was released and had recovered in hospital, I joined the student movement. There wasn't a direct connection between being tortured and joining the movement: I was just pissed off. I started speaking onstage about what had happened to me, and how we needed to end the military dictatorship. I rose in prominence, speaking to and recruiting more people to join the movement.

In response to our words, the military took out their guns, and started killing us. A friend died in my arms. In September 1988, after the biggest crackdown, thousands fled into the jungle. I was among them. Along the way, I saw some really terrible things. I saw the body of a woman who had been raped and killed, her nipples cut off, with a tree branch forced into her vagina. I was so shocked to see that people could treat one another like that. Then I met an older woman whose son had been forced to have sex with her by the Burmese military. The son was so ashamed afterward that he committed suicide.

I wanted to kill the people who had killed my friends and killed these people. But I also noticed how senseless violence had terrified the people: villagers were afraid of anybody who came with guns, even so-called revolutionaries and students. Seeing those abuses made me think maybe I wanted to do things differently. I realized that revenge might make me feel better, and maybe confront my own anger, but it wouldn't help anyone else.

I became focused on trying to get international pressure on the Burmese government, to ease human rights violations. I would listen to a story, memorize the information, and write it down with my broken English whenever I got a chance. Then every time I saw a Westerner I'd give them the letter to mail to the *New York Times*, or Amnesty International, or Human Rights Watch. At first I got no support from my own community, the Karen people, one of the most abused ethnic minorities in Burma, who were in control of the border areas. The most they would grant me would be to allow me to live in the territory they controlled without having to join the resistance army. There was a lot of pressure to be a soldier, and when I refused to take up arms, people told me I didn't deserve to wear a man's sarong because I didn't have "manblood" in my veins. But my own history had taught me the dangers of violence. Violence was the problem in my country, so it couldn't be my solution. Instead of giving arms to the people I wanted to give them a voice.

But if I wasn't going to use a gun, what were my tools? The military had so many guns and so much power; all I had was a pen and notepad. It was in this context that understanding *the law* as a weapon was a revelation. Particularly when it became clear to me that powerful people and abusive corporations were really scared of it!

Katie, Tyler, and I founded EarthRights International to sue Unocal. We worked on the case for over a decade, from 1995 to 2005. The suit was filed in the US because law doesn't work properly in Burma. Katie and the American lawyers were sure they could hold the corporation accountable in the US and I thought, "My god, you can hold them *accountable*?" Such a foreign concept to a guy from Burma! Oh, good! That appealed to me because I felt sick and desperate about my other work, where I hadn't seen much effect. We were running out of possibilities, and if this was one way for us to be seen and heard, I was all for it.

*

It was a good match.

I'd been collecting documentation anyway, which was exactly what the lawyers needed to use in the court system, so it was a good thing for both of us. But now that I was a legal researcher, doing my fact-finding for a specific purpose—a *lawsuit*—I had to learn to ask questions differently. I started asking open-ended questions rather than leading ones, so we got information that was much more detailed and event-oriented, rather than storytelling-oriented. I had to understand which facts and information were most important, because not all of the bad things that were happening were relevant to the law. Villagers would want to tell me everything they had lost—they knew every egg, chicken, and buffalo that the military had taken from them, in addition to the abuses like rape and killing and torture. But I learned that the law was most concerned about the most violent abuses — so what mattered to the villagers didn't always matter to the law. I had to train a whole team to work clandestinely as human rights investigators, across the border, too, because the pipeline ran across the Tenasserim region, turning it into one of the most dangerous and militarized parts of the country. For four years, we interviewed victims and witnesses, using pencils, small notebooks, tape recorders, and disposable cameras we could hide in our sarongs and destroy quickly if we needed to. We were intelligence agents too: we would hide in forests and fields and use binoculars to observe the military presence, noting details such as battalion numbers on uniforms. We got hundreds of firsthand testimonies, and in the end we found powerful plaintiffs, all with horrifying stories.

To protect them, all our clients and witnesses were called "John Doe" and "Jane Doe." When the man we called John Doe 1 attempted to escape a forced labor program, he was shot at by soldiers. When the soldiers came to his village searching for him, they retaliated by beating and kicking his wife, Jane Doe 1, and their baby, into a fire: the child died of her burns a few days later, and the woman was severely injured. There were other terrible abuses like this, and we eventually found nine others to lodge claims against Unocal in an American court.

The villagers all had the same questions: When could they go home? And how long would the case take? I kept going back, walking into the villages in Burma and talking to people. I kept on explaining the procedures and difficulties to them. There was a time when Unocal got a summary judgment, which dismissed the case. The villagers were very frustrated, and I had to keep them motivated, which was hard. When we started the case, Katie had said she thought it would take a couple of years for this case to be finished. Maybe it was her idealism or maybe it was her inexperience at the time, or maybe it was because this was the first time a case like this had ever happened. But she was wrong; the case took ten years, which just proves my point: lawyers don't know everything!

What did happen in the first two years was a big victory not just for us but for the rest of the world. In 1997, we got jurisdiction. This meant that a US court was willing to hear our case, and that was the first time this had ever happened against a corporation. We now knew we could go forward and sue a company in the US for what they did overseas.

Finally, Unocal settled with us, in 2005. For the first time, a US corporation had to pay a substantial sum to survivors of human rights abuses in another country. This was a huge deal. But to be honest, I was not happy. I have the type of personality that wants everything or nothing, and I didn't want to feel like I was giving up after ten years of fighting this case. I wanted to keep fighting. I wanted victory more than settlement. It took me a while to realize that after we settled, there was a lot of winning too. Because the corporation lost, the practice on the ground changed. Our clients made their own decision and ended the case on their terms and demands.

The people in the area affected by the pipeline are also much better off now. This has partly to do with the country beginning its short-lived transition to democracy in 2013, and partly with the kind of pressure put on Unocal and Total by the case. The human rights situation there has improved significantly even though the junta reasserted its iron grip on the country in February 2021. I think this is because the corporations know people are watching now, and if the corporations care, so do the generals that profit from their operations. After our case, there were fewer violations; this gave the villagers hope. When you flee from the village, everything is losing, losing, losing. When you fight back and get a victory, that's the emotional part. The news made them happier and stronger. Our clients felt really proud of themselves because people elsewhere had less suffering because of them.

But I feel more complicated about the money part of the settlement. It felt like something that a corporation would do: kill and rape and torture and enslave, and then chuck money at the consequences to make the problem go away. Honestly, this felt like it *was* a kind of losing. Sure, the individual plaintiffs got a lot of money, and this helped many of them get on with their lives after so many years in hiding and fear. They could send their children to school, and pay for medicine when they needed it. They could build new homes and relocate and start over. Many of them used the money for their community, like building irrigation systems or churches or schools in their villages.

But for others, the windfall was ultimately negative. You cannot make the pain—the rape, the torture, the dislocation, the loss of loved ones— go away with money, and some drank their new wealth, and thus their health, away. Perhaps it would have happened anyway, but it seemed to me that some were destroyed by money, spending like crazy, marrying over and over, dying before their time. I feel this frustration—even anger—to this day: money wins, people lose. Even in the nonprofit sector, money makes people and organizations go in weird directions they don't want to go. Sometimes it seems that whatever you do doesn't really matter, because it all comes down to money.

So I've come to a different definition of what it means to win. My definition of winning is those smiles on the faces of the villagers, and the skills and power and energy you leave behind. When you make one suffering person smile with hope, you feel you are winning at the same time. Training, going back, working with the community to give hope so they keep fighting—that's winning for me! For lawyers maybe it will be different, but for me as a community activist, that's what it's all about.

*

Working on *Doe*, local villagers became legal workers—skilled in hearsay law and evidence law, learning about which kinds of abuses would stand up and survive summary judgment in a US court. A realization dawned on both Katie and me, proving that the activist and the lawyer were closer than they had initially thought in those early jungle conversations. Not only were the people more powerful with legal tools in their hands, but *the law* was more powerful too when the people on the ground—those with the most to gain and lose—were inhabiting it with their own experiences. This realization led to our decision to set up an EarthRights school in Thailand: to train more community leaders in how to use all the tools available—legal, campaigning, communications, financial—to take on corporate power. We used our experience fighting Unocal to build an entire curriculum, a yearlong training, to enable communities to fight corporations on their own terms wherever they showed up: not just in Burma, but all over Southeast Asia, and later in South America too.

I have run this school in Ecuador, and when I was last there, I met with a bunch of Indigenous Achuar people from the Amazon. I explained how we held Unocal accountable and changed the law. But not just about the law: I also spoke about Indigenous people in other places, and explained how Indigenous people can protect themselves. They listened to me in a way they were not prepared to listen to a "gringo." This is another kind of winning for me: when our almost-win in Burma helps people in other countries to get their own wins. If we talk to each other about how we dealt with the Unocal abuses, maybe other people can be helped, and then help others; it radiates out from there. The more communities are educated about how to negotiate with corporations, the stronger the resistance will be when corporations try to abuse people's human rights.

Meeting Katie and setting up EarthRights International put a powerful new weapon in my arsenal. When you sue a company they can't ignore you. They have to show up in court; they have to respond, at least for a while. This gives you the power to make them see you, and it also gives you the time to build your power and get yourself organized. When we demand that they listen to us, they can ignore us. But when the judge demands they listen, they have to at least show up and play the game. Still, I have never seen the law as something working in isolation. To me, law is a tool for campaigning, and campaigning is a tool to change the situation. Litigation is a last resort for holding people accountable, but I know from experience that threats and fear can also be powerful motivators.

At EarthRights International, litigation and legal advocacy are only pieces of what we do. Law is a useful tool but mobilization, training, and campaigning are more important in our ecosystem of strategies. Law is very limited, especially in countries like Burma. I feel this more than ever, writing these words in 2022, after last year's military coup, breaking the 2008 constitution. Now I'm stricken by how the military keeps unleashing murder, violence, and oppression on peaceful protesters, villagers, and civilians just trying to survive. The military's brutal wars continue in ethnic areas, displacing thousands of people. Meanwhile, this abuse directly serves the interests of high-ranking military officials and powerful oil and gas companies and will further undermine the human and environmental rights in Burma that EarthRights and so many defenders are already fighting to preserve, unleashing even more destruction and suffering.

Against this, I'm in awe of the youth and the women leading the civil disobedience movement. Hundreds of thousands of protestors have taken to the streets to stand up for their democratic freedoms and defy the coup. They have resisted the military's brutality with courage, ingenuity, and unwavering commitment—knowing full well that in doing so, they are putting their lives on the line. I am inspired by the unity and determination shown by diverse groups of people coming together from across the country.

What these people are fighting for is a return to the rule of law. But the law is not, at the moment, a tool they can use. Nor is it something that inspires the masses to put their bodies on the line. The people in my country are doing that because they love their country, their people, their land. When you come from a country such as Burma, and you understand this, you know that law cannot be the leader. It's a means but not an end to the work for transformation and justice.

Further Reading: On the *Unocal* case: "*Doe v. Unocal*," earthrights.org/case/doe-v-unocal/. On Burma: Zoya Phan, *Undaunted: A Memoir of Survival in Burma and the West* (Simon & Schuster, 2010); Charmaine Craig, *Miss Burma: A Novel* (First Grove Atlantic, Inc., 2017); *Myanmar's Enemy Within: Buddhist Violence and the Making of a Muslim "Other"* (Asian Arguments, 2017); Thant Myint-U, *The Hidden History of Burma: Race, Capitalism, and Democracy in the 21ˢᵗ Century* (W.W. Norton & Company, 2020).

The Revolution Will Not Be Litigated: The Lawyer's Perspective on *Doe v. Unocal*

KATIE REDFORD

Here's how I remember my first deposition. It's also my first memory of what it really means to be a movement lawyer.

It was the rainy season of 1997. I sat in the unnaturally cold, sterile hotel room in Bangkok.

We were suing the American energy company Unocal, which had built a pipeline through Burma with the brutal aid of the Burmese military government, and our first plaintiff was up. Jane Doe 1 walked in, wearing flip-flops and her sarong, and sat down at the long conference table with me, her other two lawyers, and Ka Hsaw Wa, the activist from Burma who had led the clandestine efforts to gather evidence and witnesses for our case. Directly across from us were the lawyers from Unocal, the multinational oil company. All of them were stern Americans in dark suits. Jane Doe 1 was 4'10" and one hundred pounds at most, and they towered over her. They were the big guys in the room (literally) and they knew it.

At the head of the table sat the court reporter, flown to Bangkok from Los Angeles to transcribe the sworn testimony of all of our clients. The deposition began. After the initial formalities—name, age, where do you come from?—a Unocal lawyer asked Jane Doe 1 a series of questions, including whether she knew why she was there that day.

Seems like a straightforward question, but at that early stage in our litigation, it confirmed what we already suspected about Unocal's theory of the case, and how they planned to defeat us. In *Doe v. Unocal*, the corporation talked about the case in ways that dismissed our clients and their lived experience—arguing that activists and political dissidents, like Ka Hsaw Wa, were using people like Jane Doe in a growing global movement that aimed to isolate and then overthrow the Burmese regime. They similarly suggested that anti-globalization and anti-capitalist activists were using our clients to paint negative pictures of corporations and what they did overseas. Or that our clients were pawns of environmentalists, who hated the pipeline because of its path through rain forests. They described our clients as victims of activists and movements who sought to use them in their own political battles. And they portrayed us, their lawyers, as militants using the legal system inappropriately for media and advocacy gains.

So when Unocal's lawyers asked Jane Doe 1 if she knew why she was there, they were probably hoping and expecting that she would say something to validate such claims. Something like: "I'm here because EarthRights told me to be part of this lawsuit." Or: "I'm here because Ka Hsaw Wa asked me to come." Instead, what they got were words to this effect: "I'm here because your company and the soldiers killed my baby and I want justice."

Silence.

After what seemed like a long moment, one of the lawyers blustered, "Move to strike, unresponsive"—an attempt to get the answer removed from the record. Judith Chomsky, one of our cocounsel, leaned over toward me and chuckled under her breath: "It *was* responsive, it just wasn't the response you were expecting."

In that moment, an early moment in a case that would take ten years, I felt like we had already won. In that moment, Jane Doe 1 was the most powerful person in the room, and everyone knew it. Most importantly, *she* knew it. It was at that point that I realized that one of my most critical roles, as her lawyer, was to open the door for her; to provide a forum for her to tell her story, to face those responsible, and to demand justice.

In the end, although we never went to trial, we "won" a successful settlement. Unocal paid a whole lot of money to our clients and the communities it had harmed. Jane Doe 1 was delighted to get the payout, but she told me that, for her, the money was not the win. The remedy for which our justice system allows—money—could not give her back her dead baby. It could not buy back the freedom and dignity lost by our clients forced to work as slaves on Unocal's pipeline project. The win was the process itself: the agency that Jane Doe 1 and her fellow litigants exercised in seeking justice for themselves, and then being part of a precedent-setting case that would open similar doors for others from around the world. That's what gave them power—and that power was there whether we won or lost the case.

*

Jane Doe 1 was one of our "best" clients.

By this I mean she was smart, articulate, had a great memory, knew exactly what had happened to her and why . . . and was able to describe, consistently over time, how the harms she had suffered were legally relevant, and how the defendant in the case was responsible for those harms.

But I also mean she had one of the worst stories you could ever possibly imagine. She had been a young mother with the bad luck of living in a village that ended up on the route of the Yadana natural gas pipeline—a multimillion-dollar project that became the largest source of foreign income propping up one of the world's most brutal regimes. The Unocal lawyers were not entirely wrong: movements targeted this pipeline as a way of weakening a financial lifeline for the dictatorship. Jane Doe 1's husband, John Doe 1, had been taken as slave labor on the pipeline and escaped after ten days. When soldiers came looking for him, they found her nursing her two-month-old baby outside the house, early in the morning, keeping warm by the cooking fire. When she refused to answer questions about her husband, they beat her, kicking her and her baby into the fire. When she regained consciousness, badly burned herself, she saw her baby, barely breathing, burned all over her body. A few days later, the baby died.

For the next ten years, Jane Doe 1's story, and the equally horrific stories of our other clients, would be held up in the media, in activist meetings, in testimony to national and international legislative bodies. Jane Doe 1 did indeed become a kind of poster child for a number of movements, from the Free Burma movement trying to topple the dictatorship to the anti-globalization movement aiming to expose the dark side of unregulated corporate power to the international labor movement fighting forced labor in Burma and globally. As radical lawyers, we appreciated this not only because it highlighted the unjust systems driving the abuses, but also because we saw how it helped our clients' case, by making it more visible.

Our first victory was in 1997, when the federal court in California granted jurisdiction over the case. This would be the first time a US corporation would have to defend itself in its home courts for human rights abuses abroad. From that moment on, corporations subject to jurisdiction in US courts were on notice that they were no longer above the law for violations of fundamental human rights. What happened in Burma no longer stayed in Burma. This decision strengthened the arguments of human rights and anti-globalization movements against the free-for-all of deregulation and laissez-faire economics. Open markets, they advocated, did not necessarily lead to open societies. They believed that economic globalization must be accompanied by a globalization of law and justice, and the federal court in California handed down a historic decision that bolstered that position.

When we gathered our clients together to share our thrill at the California judgment, establishing jurisdiction, they looked at us with wonder and excitement. "We are happy," one of them said. "So now it is safe for us to go home?"

My heart sank. Of course they could not go home. There was a highly militarized pipeline running through their ancestral villages, and no legal decision could change that. For them, nothing had changed. We were just at first base. They were still living in hiding, at this point still penniless and bereft. They couldn't send their kids to school or even buy medicine if somebody got sick. The law, to our clients, really didn't matter. We responded with as much encouragement as we could muster: "But because of you, Ken Saro-Wiwa's family in Nigeria can seek justice against Shell. Companies everywhere now know that they can't do this kind of thing with impunity. Because of the legal precedent you set, others from around the world can have a chance to face off against their abusers and demand justice."

We hoped this would provide a measure of consolation, but we underestimated what that meant, because a profound shift did occur: our clients felt their power. One of them said, "Who would have ever thought that a poor, small villager like me, from Burma, could ever do anything to help someone from Africa?" They had changed the system, adding new levels of legal and financial risk to corporate human rights abuses, altering decision-making in corporate boardrooms around the world. And they had shifted their ideas of themselves, from little and nobody to somebody with power to make change, and to help others.

I saw this dynamic play out again and again in this case, and others.

In *Bowoto v. Chevron*, EarthRights represented communities from Nigeria that had faced appalling violence at the hands of military and police forces hired by the American energy company Chevron to provide "security" for their oil operations in the Niger Delta. In 2008, after a decade of case development and litigation, we went to trial in California, where the company was headquartered. This itself was a major victory, marking the first time that a multinational corporation had to stand trial in the US on charges of serious human rights abuses—including extrajudicial killing, torture, and other crimes against humanity. But the jury ruled against us. Although it was a devastating moment for everyone, some perspective was offered by our lead client himself. When an EarthRights lawyer expressed his sadness and regret to Larry Bowoto, Mr. Bowoto was incredulous: "Did you really think we were going to win a court case in Chevron's own hometown?" He laughed. "*We* didn't think so—we've been fighting them for so many years! But we fought them *here*, and we told the court and everyone in America what they did to us. They had to sit in court and listen, and defend themselves. Because of this, we are not nobody and we can't be ignored. Our struggle will continue even though the legal case is over."

In *Bowoto v. Chevron* and in *Doe v. Unocal*, our clients found power, and victory, in taking charge of their narratives and forcing a process where people had to listen. Later, for the John and Jane Does in the Unocal case, this power would become more tangible, with help from the damages they received, and the way they could use it for themselves, for their families, and for the bettering of their community. But still, they would not be able to go home, to the villages from which they were so violently uprooted.

*

Even as I write about the "power" that litigants such our clients from Nigeria and Burma experienced, I realize I am doing so from a particular perspective. As a movement lawyer who looks at a case more holistically than most lawyers are trained to do, I might have broader ideas about what it means to "win" or "lose" in court. But even the power analysis that underlies my expanded definition of "justice," beyond the courtroom definition, arises from my own view of the world, and this definition might not be shared by the people I seek to assist.

So, too, are other seemingly straightforward legal terms complicated when they are read in the context of a social justice movement, or a human rights struggle, rather than narrowly in a court of law. I received a brutal lesson in this, very early in my career, on my first trip to Burma in 1993, around the term "evidence." I was working as a legal intern for an international human rights organization, tasked with collecting testimony from villagers about how they had been forced into labor after their homes had been burned down by Burmese army units charged with clearing the way for industrial logging operations. One of these villagers, a survivor himself, confronted me:

> He: You want to talk about extractive industries? That's you.
>
> Me: Um, I think you misunderstood me. I'm working for a human rights organization, and I'd like to interview you about what happened when logging concessions were granted near your village.
>
> He: Yes, I know. You're an extractive industry. Just like the loggers. Just like the journalists. You're all the same.
>
> Me: I don't understand . . .
>
> He: You people come here to our country from far away. You stay for a few days. You ask us to tell you our stories. You take our evidence back to your countries, and we never hear from you again. You put them in your reports or your newspapers, and you sell them. You get the benefit, and we don't. Why should I talk to you and give you what I have?

He was right, of course. What was evidence to me was his lived experience of horrific suffering and harm. And so many NGOs are based in the same global headquarters as the banks and corporations that we criticize, and operate in this same extractive way—parachuting in with promises to investigate, document, and expose the truth. We might well do so. But from the perspective of the communities we aim to help, we show up, we extract, we usually get paid for our time doing this, and we leave. In a way, we do "sell" their stories, and they often never know about or feel the impacts of that exposure. Sometimes it even puts them in greater danger.

And so when we established EarthRights and launched our first case against Unocal, we knew we had to do it differently. We knew we were challenging one of the most powerful extractive industries in the world and we couldn't be one ourselves. And just as we needed to approach our evidence with the sensitivity and understanding of what that was for our clients, so too did we need to be attuned to the notion of damages. What for the lawsuit were "great" legal claims for damages were for our clients horrific lived experience of suffering and abuse. And the process of seeing a case through from beginning to end—from client intake to gathering evidence to filing the complaint; from discovery through trial to assessing damages—requires that our clients and witnesses retell their stories, and relive their trauma, over and over again.

The process—such an important word for lawyers—was therefore as important as the outcome. Our legal strategy was a long shot, and for that reason, we needed to make sure that the lawsuit was both a means to justice and accountability, and an end itself. And when the case was over for us, we knew it would not be over for our clients and their villages. The oil companies we were suing, and others that might come behind them, would always want those resources, that gas, that land passage for the pipeline. Win or lose in court, we knew those companies were not going away. The real victory would be if the communities had more power, more agency, more networks and confidence to engineer their own solutions, and be more prepared for the next fight, after our case, than they had been before.

In that sense, we took our role as lawyers extremely seriously. We based our three-person, one-computer, one-fax-machine "headquarters" in a small town close to the border where the pipeline crossed into Thailand. We also made sure that leading members of our legal team, like Ka Hsaw Wa, were from the communities we represented, and could travel there at a moment's notice, whether they needed us or we needed them.

We also recognized the ways in which a lawsuit could be a focal point, and provide extra ammunition and momentum, for aligned movements and advocacy campaigns. We noticed the way ears pricked up when we were introduced to government officials, shareholders, corporate board members—people with *power*—as the lawyers and legal advocates in the lawsuit of *Doe v. Unocal*. Maybe there's a level of gravitas attached to testimony given under penalty of perjury; maybe it's the intrigue and drama associated with courtroom battles; perhaps images of lawyers and judges in wigs and black robes lend an aura of credibility. Whatever the reason, when we said "lawsuit" people listened just a little bit harder.

One example: The Free Burma movement used the *Doe v. Unocal* case as a kind of "Exhibit A" in global campaigns against the regime, calling for the sort of sanctions against Burma that had been imposed, previously, on apartheid South Africa. At Congressional sanctions hearings in the US, Naw Dorcus Mu, the coordinator of EarthRights's Women's Rights Project, spoke powerfully about the widespread violence against women in the pipeline region. Her testimony included devastating stories of rape endured by our clients Jane Doe 2 and 3 and other women at the hands of soldiers guarding Unocal's pipeline. There could not have been a more powerful reason for the American government to decide that US corporations should not be investing in that country, and risking complicity in those abuses. Robust economic sanctions were put in place, a key demand of the movement.

A lawsuit ups the ante. When Ka Hsaw Wa and others from Burma attended shareholder meetings of Premier Oil, Total, or Unocal, we were by no means the only activists advocating for shareholder resolutions on Burma. But we were the only activists with a lawsuit to back us up. It's one thing to tell investors that their company is engaged in bad, immoral, or even unlawful activities. It's another thing entirely to tell them that they are being sued for it. Suddenly, the corporation can no longer brush it off as "noise" of "whiny, complaining activists." In a lawsuit, the complaint may well be filled with examples of what the activists are also "whining" about. But those complaints are magically elevated by the formal, legal document that transforms the "noise" into the real threat of legal liability, in addition to related harms to their brand, their reputation, and their bottom line.

And, of course, the media loves a good lawsuit, and Jane Doe 1 became the story that everyone would know about Unocal's operations in Burma. In such instances, there can be rich reciprocity between the lawyers and the media. When Unocal's president John Imle was interviewed by *Nightline*, for example, he made numerous statements on camera that we were later able to use against the company in our case. Likewise, we were able to share with activists and the media some of the most damning evidence against the company, and their knowledge of abuses, that we gained during the discovery process. In his deposition, for example, Imle admitted under oath that Unocal knew about the forced labor on its pipeline.

In all of EarthRights's cases over the twenty-five years of litigation, opposing counsel has said in one way or another something along the lines of what Unocal's lawyers wanted to prove with Jane Doe 1: that we were abusing the legal system, and even our clients, for our own political purposes. Our response to such criticisms has been to prepare the strongest legal claims, based on the most solid evidence and analysis, and to do our jobs as lawyers for our clients first—knowing, of course, that the movements and activists will do *their* jobs, mobilizing people by putting the abuses revealed by the case into the world.

But this too is a particular risk for movement lawyers that must be navigated and handled appropriately lest it backfire, as it seemed to have done when we went to trial in *Bowoto v. Chevron*. With many of our Nigerian clients in California for the duration of the trial, we were looking forward to their once-in-a-lifetime opportunity to tell their stories not just to the jury, but to the world. Our clients too understood this opportunity to speak truth to power and to anyone else who would listen while they were in Chevron's own backyard. As in most trials, the defense objected, claiming that we were turning the case into a media circus. But in apparent recognition of the intensifying scrutiny from the media and the public on her court, the judge issued a sweeping gag order on the lawyers and litigants on both sides, right as the trial began. From this point on we were not even allowed to speak to our public relations firm or our movement partners.

Here was another moment where we had to make a decision that balanced the interests of the case with those of the movement: While it was our strong belief that such an order was an unconstitutional violation of our own and our clients' freedom of speech, we made the tactical decision not to appeal it. Given that trial was about to begin, and our case was in this judge's hands, we felt as lawyers that it would be a mistake to potentially annoy or anger her by going over her head and challenging her ruling with an appeal. "Yes, your honor," we thus said, and we proceeded with our case.

We lost that case. But even when we win, or settle—as in *Unocal*—victories can be complicated as a part of broader movement strategies. When we settled with Unocal on behalf of our clients before trial in 2004—because that's what *they* wanted—so many of our comrades in these movements sensed betrayal, were angry that we had "sold out" or that we had not consulted with them first. They felt we did not understand the strategic importance of having a public, months-long trial, with all the attendant media, organizing, and advocacy opportunities.

But what they didn't fully understand was that *Doe v. Unocal* was not their case. It was not our case either; it was our clients' case. And the eleven John and Jane Does we represented were not part of the labor, environmental, or anti-globalization movements. They were plaintiffs because they had been, in legal terms, "damaged" by this pipeline project, and those damages—horrific human rights abuses—gave them legal standing to sue. Even if they had gone forward with trial and won in court, the other side would have appealed (and vice versa). The uncertainty in their lives would have dragged on for years while they continued to live in hiding and in fear. We spent a long time with them, discussing the pros and cons of a trial versus a settlement: legal, practical, technical, and personal. In the end they made the difficult choice; it was theirs to make.

*

The backlash to corporate human rights litigation like *Doe v. Unocal* was swift and fierce. Industries and their lawyers, sometimes with the support of governments, spent the ensuing years opposing not only the specific cases, but the fundamental notion of corporate liability for human rights abuse. Subsequent federal court decisions both advanced and chipped away at the *Unocal* precedent until 2013, when, in *Kiobel v. Royal Dutch Petroleum Co*, the US Supreme Court held that most claims for harms occurring outside of the US would not be allowed to proceed in US Courts. Ensuing Supreme Court decisions continued to roll back the human rights advances of the preceding decades, holding in 2018 (*Jesner v. Arab Bank*) that foreign corporations could not be sued, and then, in 2021 (*Nestle v. Doe*) that US corporations could not be sued for their conduct outside of the country.

A few years after we won the *Unocal* settlement, the entire team reunited on the Thai-Burma border for a long-awaited victory celebration. The lawyers travelled from the US and our clients travelled from their various homes, bringing gifts that they had made, cooked, or hunted. We celebrated together with food, drink, and karaoke. But the best gift was accompanying some of our clients to their new homes and villages, seeing the ways in which many of them were rebuilding their lives, and using their money to help their people and establish themselves as leaders in their communities. Jane Doe 2 was supporting her church, and helping sponsor students to attend Bible study classes; John Doe 9 was using his money to put in wells and build irrigation systems in his village. Jane Doe 1 built a new home, and was sending her children to school. We travelled with John Doe 5 to his village, where he proudly showed us the beautiful community center and school that he built and continued to sponsor. This gave them all a renewed sense of social power within their communities.

The lesson I learned from *Unocal* is that it's all about power. We want our clients and their communities to feel more powerful, to *be* more powerful, because of our legal work and the process we help them access. And we want those who abuse power because they have too much of it to understand that they have less power than before they were hauled into court. Impunity breeds future abuse; and the threat of legal accountability deters it. Win or lose, if we haven't left our clients and their communities more powerful than they were before we started, we haven't done our job. Every time we set out on the road to legal action we need ask ourselves two questions: not only whether this will advance our case and help us win, but whether it will unleash the power of our clients and our communities for the long term.

That power can be personal, economic, or cultural as well as political. Jane Doe 1 regained a measure of control by taking action. When we were interviewing her and her husband during our client intake process, she lashed out at her husband in anger: "What kind of man are you? If I were a man, I would get a gun and go find those soldiers and kill them all." By giving her a forum to tell her story in a way that mattered—in a way that would "hurt" the company and make them change—she was doing something, and that transformed her from helpless victim to active, powerful survivor. And, of course, when we won the settlement, she had newfound economic power: she was able to educate her children, buy them clothes, build a new home, and move on with her life.

The settlement did not give Jane Doe 1 her baby back, or restore John Doe 9's freedom from his days lost to forced labor. But it did allow them—and all of our clients—to move forward with their lives with a sense of dignity and power that comes with being in the drivers' seat of one's own destiny.

Further Reading: For general information on *Doe v. Unocal*, see earthrights.org/case/doe-v-unocal; also: Katie Redford and Beth Stephens, "The story of *Doe v. Unocal*: justice delayed but not denied," in Deena Hurwitz and Margaret L. Satterthwaite, with Doug Ford, *Human Rights Advocacy Stories* (Foundation Press, 1997); Maria Armoudian, *Lawyers Beyo nd Borders* (University of Michigan Press, 2021); Oona Hathaway, "Has the Alien Tort Statute Made a Difference? A Historical, Empirical, and Normative Assessment," *Cornell Law Review*, vol. 107, 2022; *Total Denial*, film by Milena Kaneva, 2006.

LAWYERS ON PEOPLE POWER

Leadership and Learning Lessons in the Black Lives Matter Movement

JUSTIN HANSFORD

On August 9, 2014, on the twelve-hour drive back to St. Louis from Washington, DC, my phone started beeping more urgently than usual. In the weeks and months and years to come, almost all of us who became involved in the Black Lives Matter Movement would share a clear memory of first experiencing Mike Brown's death through an image that showed up on our social media timelines. For me, it was Facebook on my phone. First, there was the body covered in a white sheet, left lying for hours on the road. Next, a photograph of a man in jeans on the sidewalk holding up a piece of torn cardboard on which he has written in black marker: "FERGUSON POLICE JUST EXECUTED MY UNARMED SON!!!"

Sitting with me in the car was an old friend, an activist-colleague from my days as an organizer. I had been writing, already, about the death of a Black teenager named Trayvon Martin at the hands of an armed neighborhood watch volunteer in Florida in 2012; now we watched social media catch fire as we raced toward the gathering outrage over the police murder of an eighteen-year-old in Ferguson, Missouri. It seemed as if a tipping point had been reached. My friend knew the family of Emmett Till, the fourteen-year-old lynched in Mississippi in 1955 after being accused of insulting a white woman in her family's grocery store, and he called Emmett's cousin to talk about Mike Brown's murder. It felt like we were suspended in space, somewhere along the I-70 between DC and St. Louis; suspended in time too, between the histories of murderous violence against young Black men in the United States—and the possibility of radical change, if a movement could be sparked by the murders of Trayvon and Mike Brown.

Ferguson is a largely Black suburb in the greater St. Louis region; Mike Brown had been murdered about ten minutes' drive from where I lived in the city. Those first few nights back were a blur. I am someone who could've been in that same situation, accosted by police for being a young Black man seen to be threatening. I had my own troubled history of alienation. As a kid, I had been angry at the world, dealing with the absence of a father I had never met; I had been in and out of trouble as a teenager, and it had not been clear, at all, that I would make it through high school. But I was inspired by reading *The Autobiography of Malcolm X* to take my life more seriously and try to make a difference, and I had gotten into Howard University, and then Georgetown—and here I was, thirty-two years old, still a young Black man but now a law professor too, at St. Louis University, just home from a meeting in Washington, DC, with President Obama's Young Africa Fellows. I threw myself into the turmoil of those days of rage and exhilaration: rage at the injustice and a shared feeling of pain, but enjoying being out there too, in solidarity with so many others, from Ferguson and all over the country. It would take me some time to figure out my lane in all of this: how I could best use my legal skills to support the protests and then the movement that arose out of them. But in the beginning, only one thing mattered: being there, and being helpful, in any way I could.

This meant becoming the milkman for the protesters. Some local organizers were trying to create a safe space for people who were going to stay out past curfew, and I got involved in helping them buy medical supplies. We learned from Palestinians, who contacted us on social media after seeing footage of us being teargassed, to put milk in our eyes to dull the pain of the chemicals. I was a professor; I had a car and some money. And so I had a trunkful of milk that I was driving around with, late at night, after curfew, to help those with tear gas in their eyes.

I was a lawyer with a lot of fancy titles, but in that moment, what was needed was a guy who could buy milk and distribute it. There's a lesson in that for movement lawyers: not thinking that you have to be the fancy person making the Supreme Court arguments all the time to make a difference, but doing whatever it takes to support the community. There is an old saying that teachers use, one I think we lawyers could take on too: "People don't care what you know, until they know that you care." There were people in Ferguson who had to know that I really cared about the community and was willing to do things to help them before they trusted me as someone who they would go to with bigger problems. It was easy to care about the people who were out there protesting. In my eyes, they had shown that they were willing to be tear-gassed and face danger and great physical risks for my rights and well-being against the system that wanted to crush me. It was an honor to support them.

There were not many Black law professors in St. Louis, and by the second week, legal organizations from out of town interested in support-ing the protesters began reaching out to me. I would take them on a walk through Ferguson when they came to see the protests. And one of the rea-sons I was able to build some sort of a real trust with these organizations was because I had spent time on the streets: I could give directions not only on how to get around, but how to get plugged in.

Eventually, as the weeks turned to months, my contributions as the milkman became less valuable than the contributions I could make as a lawyer. After so many weeks of protest, establishment civil rights leaders, churches, and politicians had begun to take up space in the debate, and the original protesters were becoming agitated and confused about what could be done to create the meaningful change that had inspired them to risk their safety, to face tanks and tear gas, in the first place. They just didn't know what to do next. I came to appreciate that while there were so many ways that I might able to help logistically, this wasn't my expertise. The legal and political side was my lane. That was where my unique contribu-tion would come from.

Over the years, the legal profession has suffered from a poor reputa-tion in some quarters. But when there's a health crisis in your community, like the COVID-19 pandemic, you turn to doctors; when there's an injus-tice crisis in the your community, like racist police violence, you turn to the lawyers. The crisis in Ferguson escalated as more people took to the streets to protest Mike Brown's murder, and the police responded with violent force rather than compassion, arresting dozens of people. This, in turn, stoked rage, and because of all this, there were people in power who were being forced to pay attention and respond. Once that happened, people on the ground realized that they needed expertise in order to make fully informed recommendations. So organizers started to reach out to folks who could help them craft those responses. And again, they wanted to go to someone that they could trust.

I had to be multilingual. In the city, young Black professionals wanted to talk about establishment politics: how to leverage blue voters in a red state, what bill to support, et cetera. On the street, people who had never protested a day in their lives before this moment—my barber, the apartment building janitor, the local grocery store clerk—suddenly, all they wanted was justice: most of all, to get the killer police officer tried and convicted. And then there were organizers: people like me, who had crafted their political identity from involvement in grassroots organizations such as the Malcolm X Grassroots Movement, becoming skilled at demanding systemic change in order to overcome white supremacy. From this experience, I learned that when it comes down to discussing policy and demanding systemic change, you need to know what the law is—and have ideas about how to change it. People were asking me what to do. It's amazing how much the discourse has moved forward, thanks to the movement, in the few years since Ferguson: back then defunding the police was a fringe demand. I am embarrassed now to admit that in 2014 we were still promoting body cameras as a way of holding police accountable—today I disavow that method of reform. Overall, though, we were then and still are now demanding an end to policies of racial profiling.

At that time, I was also being tapped by the power establishment of St. Louis as someone who could speak on behalf of the movement. Elected officials were inviting me to meetings where people were discussing political responses to the crisis. It was a difficult position because one of the things that they would insinuate was, "Well, can you serve as a middleman? Can you get them to calm down? The natives are restless." But as a movement lawyer I knew even then that my obligation was to try to stick as closely as possible to the grassroots—while keeping a sharp eye on the law, and while navigating how to use my status and expertise to help the people who had risked their lives for my rights. I tried my best to bring in people who were out on the streets to negotiate at the tables of power. But even that process was fraught, because now you're put in the position of having to select a handful of spokespeople from the hundreds of protestors and organizers.

It was a constant balancing act, being in two worlds. I have a suit and tie on and I'm a lawyer, so in the eyes of many, I am not fully part of the protest community. But then I'm not fully part of the power establishment either, because I am hanging out with protesters and spending time in the streets. This feeling of always being the odd man out is something that movement lawyers need to be able to embrace: you will always tend to be a bit more conservative than the most radical protestors—while in the corridors of power, the courts or congress or the parliament or whatever, you're always going to be seen as the "radical." What I came to learn is that I needed, in both worlds, just to show up as myself, if I was going to be trusted. If this means wearing a tie while on the streets in Ferguson, so be it.

At one of those high-level meetings, attended by senators and congresspeople, I had met Ron Johnson, the State Highway Patrol captain—a Black man—who had taken over much of the response to the protests. When I was out at a protest one rainy night, I saw him among the ranks as a group of big, burly police officers began charging a line of young Black women who had locked arms and were blocking the street. There were going to be arrests, certainly, and—it seemed—violence against the young women too. So I put myself between the police and the protestors, walked directly toward Ron Johnson and called out, "Leave these people alone. They are not committing a crime."

Capt. Johnson recognized me: "Okay," he said, "leave them alone. Don't harm them."

This is part of the delicate trade-off. There's power that comes from being in those rooms—from participating at a high level in policy discussions, on behalf of the movements we represent. It's a power we can leverage in the street, to make things a little easier for people sometimes.

Then there is the power of litigation itself. I saw it being used most effectively in the challenge made to the way Black people were being incarcerated for being unable to pay minor fines, such as traffic violations. The organizations that led the litigation—ArchCity Defenders, the law clinic at my university, and others—borrowed the term "debtors' prison" to describe this plundering and mass incarceration of Black and poor people. The litigation had begun just before Mike Brown's killing, and the anger on the streets about the exploitative practices of the police department had much to do, I believe, with the way the people of Ferguson were willing to show up en masse to protest Mike Brown's murder.

I have written about the St. Louis debtors' prison litigation as a model for ethical movement lawyering. By adhering to some core principles, the lawyers in that case gained the trust of the movement and did real service to it. First, the lawyers stayed true to the movement's core values in all of their work. This meant, for example, a rejection of what is called "respectability politics" and taking on the movement principle that our lives matter even if we are petty offenders, and whether or not we conform to middle-class behavior patterns or societal gender norms. Secondly, the lawyers retained a high level of accountability to the movement, making sure that the debtors' prison work stayed in line with the goals and vision of the grassroots organizers to greatest extent possible. In the nonprofit world, where pressure exists to please funders, it's a challenge to put the vision of the activists at the forefront (especially if it's the funders that are paying the bills), but it can be done. Finally, the lawyers created change not just through litigation, but by demonstrating how you can use the law to shift public narratives about what constitutes injustice. Not only did the debtors' prison advocates provoke moral outrage by putting the heart-wrenching narratives of the victims into the public domain, but they deepened society's understanding about the mass incarceration of Black people, and how it is a function not just of racism or the "War on Drugs" but of the familiar kind of greed and the predatory desire to exploit the resources of the weak that has plagued society throughout human history.

Competence in public narrative is a vitally important but rarely recognized skill for movement lawyers. Consider the way the work of law itself is driven by storytelling. Clients construct narratives to share their problems with who might help them. Lawyers tell their clients stories about the law in order to inform them of their rights. Litigators then tell stories to the judge through pretrial submissions and again in opening statements and testimony to juries. Judges and jurors retell stories to themselves and each other through jury instructions and deliberations and certify one or another narrative through the issuance of a verdict or a judicial opinion. Journalists tell the story of what happened to the public. A trial is a competition of stories, and in many situations we may never know what the actual truth was, so the best story wins.

But if narratives are the lifeblood of the law, so too are they lifeblood of social movements.

The social movement scholar Marshall Ganz writes that movements gain the kind of momentum needed to bring about change through "the transformation of thousands of individual stories into a shared story." You can see this process at work, so powerfully, in the way people took to the streets as part of the Movement for Black Lives after the murder of George Floyd in 2020. There is a critical lesson here for those of us who consider ourselves to be advocates for this movement: the stories we tell through the legal process have a larger function. We need to be able to identify, cultivate, and disseminate public narratives: not only to support movement mobilization, but, more broadly, to shift the public narrative about who Black Americans are, and thus to collapse the racial hierarchy of the United States. This is far more important than any single legal victory or defeat.

*

Three months after Mike Brown's killing, I found myself in Geneva, Switzerland, in a nondescript conference room of the United Nations, looking on as my client—Mike Brown's mother, Lezley McSpadden—testified to the UN Committee against Torture about the murder of her son. Working with the US Human Rights Network and others, our immediate intention was to get the actions of the Ferguson Police Department censured by the UN itself as a human rights violation. But we also saw this process as a tool to help us shift the public narrative around police violence against Black people in the United States. From the slave narratives to the blues, from the song "Strange Fruit" by Billie Holiday to the miniseries *Roots*, sharing our stories has both bound us together as a people and opened a window to the rest of the world to experience our reality in Black America. Lezley's testimony was part of that tradition.

Lezley would have stood out anyway, a petite woman with vibrant magenta hair amidst the dark business suits; but what she said took the proceedings to an unexpectedly emotional pitch. She was able to articulate, from the depths of her heart, how she felt. She was doing more than simply explaining the facts of her situation so that a UN body could condemn it as a human rights violation. She was explaining her pain. It was extraordinary to witness the effect of this. As she recounted how she was forced to stand outside in the sun and watch her child's body lie on the ground for over four hours, I watched the way those powerful diplomats and human rights officials from all over the world were shaken to the core: they had those earpieces in their ears, they were each hearing Lezley's story interpreted in real time into their own language, and they were all in tears. There was this human being before them, describing the tragedy that would define her entire life. My colleague Meena Jagannath and I delivered a detailed report later on in the session. But I am convinced that Lezley's testimony moved the committee, more than any legal arguments, to state in its findings that racialized police violence in the United States deserved to be noted as a possible violation of UN Convention against Torture.

I had already been thinking about the way mainstream narratives—such as those in the news media—chose to tell the story of police murders of young Black men, and how we needed to counter them. Trayvon Martin had obviously been killed because he was young, Black, and wearing a hoodie; his murderer had escaped accountability because he claimed that he had believed himself to be under threat, and the powers that be believed his story. Similarly with Mike Brown, there was a concerted effort, from the pro-police side, to foreground thug-like images of Mike: the baseball cap turned backward or pictures of him throwing up a gang sign were meant to provide visual proof of their claim that he was a scary bad guy, sort of like illustrations in a storybook. There was a story all over the media that he had stolen some cigarillos and Swisher sweets right before getting killed, as if this justified the police officer Darren Wilson's violent response. We needed to counter this narrative. One way was to begin to circulate different representations of Mike Brown: there were also pictures of him as a young man in a graduation cap, on his way to college. Another counternarrative was to try to get the public to understand his murder not as the consequence of some kind of legitimate "stand your ground" defense by a fearful police officer, but as a human rights violation representative of a larger pattern of systemic injustice.

This is why we came to Geneva. And watching Lezley testifying before the UN Committee on Torture, I understood how, in the context of human rights advocacy and movement lawyering, testimony can engender both empathy in the listener and dignity in the teller. Remember the context: the way that Ferguson authorities, and even the media, had gone to such great lengths to suggest that Lezley did not have the right to feel such deep pain because her son's death was his own fault; that he was a thug and therefore that she must be a bad mother.

Going to Geneva had been a somewhat controversial decision. There were some senior organizers who explicitly forbade their members from joining us because they felt it was not a productive use of time, a waste of valuable resources. Perhaps because of the way I grounded my work in the teachings of Malcolm X, I disagreed. In 1965, just before he was assassinated, Malcolm had said that the problem of Black Americans was "not a violation of civil rights but a violation of human rights. Not only are we denied the right to be a citizen in the United States, we are denied the right to be a human being." At the time, Malcolm was working on taking the case of Black Americans to the global community at the United Nations. He wanted to get our situation to be understood alongside the other global anti-colonial struggles being fought at that time; to build more allies; and to avoid being limited to stating our plea before the same system that had been complicit in committing the crimes against us in the first place.

As advocates in this case, those of us who would go to Geneva felt that if we were to get a positive result at the United Nations, we could bring that back to the mayor and city council and governor, and make them fear how they would look in the eyes of the world unless they changed course in Ferguson. More broadly, I also hoped to use the decision of the UN Committee against Torture as a way to shift the narrative about Mike Brown's murder, and what it represented for Black Americans: by making it an international human rights problem, as opposed to just a problem of local policy. We weren't just some concerned citizens disagreeing as to when and whether police should use force. We were members of the global community making an assertion about morality, based on universal principles of right and wrong, making claims that were being heard and taken seriously by people all over the world. Through my study of critical race theory, I had come to understand that law is political, and the ultimate decision to charge the racist police officer would have as much to do with political winds and currents as with a reading of the language of a statute. The gamble was that pressure from the UN could shift those currents even more than the arguments made by the local prosecutor in his effort to protect this murderous cop from accountability.

It didn't quite work out that way. A grand jury decided not to indict Wilson in late November 2014. This was just days after the UN Committee against Torture explicitly noted in its findings "the alleged difficulties to hold police officers and their employers accountable for abuses," and specifically called on US officials "to investigate such force properly and prosecute accordingly." The city immediately erupted into chaos, angrier and more outraged than ever. But despite the mass destruction of property, the authorities responded, generally, with more restraint, and no one was killed. Records would later show that this was in part to avoid international criticism: given that our recent Geneva trip and the committee's assessment had received high-profile media coverage, it was on the minds of police and state officials as they planned their response. We didn't get justice in the form of charges being brought against Darren Wilson, but we gained power. We were there to be contended with on the world stage, from a human rights perspective. This affected the way the establishment saw us: we were undoubtedly taken more seriously. Perhaps more importantly, it had a profound effect on the way we saw ourselves.

It took a while for me to understand this point. Those weeks of anger and chaos following the failure to charge Wilson were a deeply dispiriting time for those of us who had gone to Geneva, coming so close on the heels of our victory there. In fact, on the night of the non-indictment, with the city in flames, I took a break from trying to locate friends and allies and coordinating safety measures and found a quiet place in a meeting room and just sat and wept. I was starting to understand the limits of what I was doing, trying to play on a playing field that was rigged by local policy and politics. We were hitting dead ends with politicians, with law enforcement, with prosecutors, and even internally within ourselves.

In the midst of all of this, one thing that provided me hope was the memory of a town hall meeting in a high school during those early days. One after one, people took the mic to talk, passionately, about their experiences with the police. I remember, most vividly, a young woman named

Cheeraz Gormon, a spoken word artist: In terms much more poetic than I can capture, she essentially said, "I want you to understand that what happened to you wasn't just a bad apple police officer, wasn't just one racist guy. *This is a human rights crisis. This is a human rights violation.*"

Suddenly the community members in the audience were standing up and applauding, some of them in tears. I saw with my own eyes the transformation that happened within them when the narrative around what was happening to them shifted; how it added both dignity and purpose to their struggle. The power of this redefinition and self-determination—of shifting someone's status and the way that they saw themselves—was that it could change the way they would interact with the world, and the way that the world interacted with them. That's the highest level of advocacy a movement lawyer can practice: the possibility of changing the way that people understand themselves, and of changing the way that people are understood by the rest of the world. It's that possibility of helping people achieve a higher level of human dignity that I constantly strive to achieve.

*

A month prior to our trip to Geneva, I was one of nine people arrested for illegally trespassing inside a Walmart near Ferguson. Here is the background: On August 5, just four days before Mike Brown's murder, a young Black man named John Crawford had been killed by the police inside a Walmart in Ohio. He was holding up a BB gun on sale and was perceived as a threat, so when the police were called, they killed him at first sight. Walmart had suppressed the surveillance footage, which revealed the horrific and unjustified nature of the murder. And so the in-store protest was called to highlight the corporation's murderous complicity with the police.

I was in Walmart that day as a legal observer. I was the only Black person among the five legal observers, and it was astonishing to watch the police officers walk past the other lawyers—one Asian and three white—and cuff me, leading me off with the others who had been arrested. We were held in the cells for a few hours and released on bail, after being charged with trespassing on private property. A lawyer from the National Lawyers Guild was appointed to represent us, and when he met us he advised that standing trial could result in some minor jail time, since we were in fact guilty of the crime. As the lawyer among the accused, I thought that jail time was highly unlikely, given that it was just a simple trespass in a protest environment. But in the WhatsApp group we set up, there was a strong feeling among the accused that we should follow our counsel's advice because of the way a trial and a sentence might disrupt our lives, and, in particular, make things difficult for the students among us. I went along with the majority.

I regret this, and I am sorry that I didn't see, or advocate for, the possibilities of a political trial; one in which we might have talked about First Amendment issues and the right to protest, and also revealed corporate complicity in the racial hierarchy. In my case in particular, there was clear evidence of racial discrimination. We could have highlighted all of this, but our lawyer didn't see, or perhaps didn't sufficiently articulate, those possibilities—and neither did I. This raises a complex question. Was it our lawyer's place to prevail on us to risk our freedom in order to forward the political objective? Or was it his prerogative, at least, to give us a detailed outline of the pros and cons of the possibility of a political trial, even if unsolicited, in light of who we were? In any event, given what I have come to understand about how a political trial can cause a seismic change in shifting public narrative, I primarily blame myself for what I see today as a missed opportunity.

That following summer I was headed to South Africa on a Fulbright scholarship to study the life and work of Nelson Mandela—a movement lawyer if ever there was one—and perhaps my excitement and eagerness to flee the country played a role in my stepping back from advocating for a political trial. Looking back, I see the irony in this, given what I have come to understand as a primary lesson from Mandela's own experience of the law: how it was so central to his life and work to engage in political trials, especially in the Rivonia case of 1964, a "show trial" that he would use to suit his own ends, stating the rationale for the armed struggle and the objectives of his African National Congress movement in the public domain at a time when it was illegal to do so. A key element of his political impact was his decision to give a statement from the dock rather than testify: a decision that made the death penalty more probable by forgoing the opportunity to make a sound legal defense, but which gave him the platform to give a political speech that echoed around the world for decades.

I don't want to suggest for a minute that our choices in Ferguson and Mandela's in the Rivonia Trial, exactly fifty years previously, were comparable: Mandela knew he could lose his life, whereas my worst-case scenario was a few weeks in jail. And Mandela's legal environment was much less sympathetic. We had a jury, so there was at least a chance for us to get jury nullification, whereas the South African freedom fighter and his codefendants were stuck with a hostile judge representing the very apartheid system they were seeking to overturn. But where I draw a parallel between his situation and mine is that we both had the opportunity to shift public narrative through political trials, and while Mandela grasped this, I did not.

I see it as a question of courage, of faith. Spiritually, I was not prepared to lead—to challenge our lawyer, to risk loss of career and experience a brief stint as a political prisoner; to walk down a different life path—and I have been reflecting on why this was. There most certainly are personal reasons, but there is also the fact of my training. There was nothing in my education to prepare me for how to make such decisions; how to straddle the streets and the courthouse; how to turn protest into policy; how to intentionally set out to shape public narrative; how to think both as a lawyer and an activist when facing charges and wondering whether it's possible to politicize one's case. If my education had provided me with some resources to serve as reminders of what types of questions I should have asked myself, what elements I should have factored in as I made these life-changing decisions, I strongly believe that I would have been better prepared for the moment.

In my own writing and teaching I often emphasize the importance of following the lead of the movement when you are a movement lawyer, and of deferring to the community, particularly if you are an outsider and not part of that community yourself. But Mandela's career teaches me that this humility should not never cross the line and become an abdication of duty. Sometimes it is the role of the lawyer to *be* the leader, even in movement spaces. We, as lawyers, have been granted access to certain resources: the benefit of a legal education; the training in how to parse a law-related document or situation; the experience of trials and mediations and negotiations. Is it right, then, to step aside and ask others, who have not had the benefit of those same resources, to bear the burden of leadership when legal issues are at stake?

It is helpful here to distinguish between leadership and management. If leadership means giving orders heavy-handedly, you certainly don't want lawyers doing that, because of the power dynamic between lawyers and clients. I see leadership more as helping to create a vision and then coming up with the strategies for realizing it, and also providing inspirational moments to energize your comrades in the pursuit of your common goal. To step down from leading in that capacity because, as many of us might say, "It's not my place, I'm just a legal technician," is an abdication of responsibility, in my view, if you define yourself as a movement lawyer. In the Walmart case, I believe I failed that test of leadership.

This does not mean elevating the law itself to some kind of sacred status, access to which gives you the right to call the shots. Doctors use medicine. That's their tool. Lawyers use the law. That's our tool. But it's just a tool. It's not really about the medicine—it's about the health of the person. It's not really about the law—it's about fighting for people to have a fair chance at life. If you are a movement lawyer, it's not just one person, but a whole movement that could use your help. Too often, students lose sight of that in school, and then in their careers. They forget that they are there because people are being treated horribly and they don't deserve it; and they are uniquely trained to find ways of fixing that.

Further Reading: By Justin Hansford: "On Trayvon Martin and the Cost of Suspicion," *Critical Legal Thinking,* April 11, 2012; "Demosprudence on Trial: Ethics for Movement Lawyers, in Ferguson and Beyond," *Fordham Law Review,* vol, 85, no. 5, 2017. By Justin Hansford and Meena Jagannath: "Ferguson to Geneva: Using the Human Rights Framework to Push Forward a Vision for Racial Justice in the United States after Ferguson," *Hastings Race & Poverty Law Journal,* vol. 12, Summer 2015. On social movements and storytelling: Marshall Ganz, "The Power of Story in Social Movements," August 2001, dash.harvard.edu/handle/1/27306251.

Who Owns The Streets?: Ending Discriminatory Policing in New York City

BAHER AZMY

It was April 2013, nearly three weeks into the landmark trial of *Floyd v. City of New York*, when these secretly recorded words were revealed in the courtroom:

> All right, I went out there to [Howard and Chauncey Avenues] yesterday and . . . we've got the old man out there with the grey hairs. A loud mouth. He thinks since he's 55 years old he's not going to get locked up. Well, guess what? I don't tolerate shit out there. He went in [to jail] and two of his pals went in. All right? So we've got to keep the corner clear . . . Because if you get too big of a crowd there, you know . . . they're going to think they own the block. **We own the block. They don't own the block, all right? They might live there but we own the block. All right? We own the streets here. You tell them what to do.**

The words belonged to a New York Police Department (NYPD) lieutenant rallying his Bronx-based troops. Lawyers from my organization, the Center for Constitutional Rights, obtained them from one of several whistleblowers who sought to document and expose the vast, punishing, and racist "stop and frisk" policing practices that had enveloped neighborhoods in New York. As a revealed secret, this moment made for powerful courtroom drama, particularly to the journalists covering what some considered the civil rights trial of the decade. But to the city's Black and Latino communities, the ideology of the Bronx lieutenant was no surprise: just as the mayor, Michael Bloomberg, liked to brag that the NYPD represented the eighth largest *army* in the world, these communities had long regarded the NYPD as an occupying force, constituted to surveil, harass, and control.

Yet thanks to a court case and the movement that both spawned it and then grew around it, this Bronx lieutenant did not have the last word. Through a remarkable fifteen-year-long campaign of activism, community organizing, and committed lawyering that was tethered and accountable to communities most impacted by policing, the case would shift the NYPD's bellicose, authoritarian, and abundantly racist narrative. And, in that time and place, people could claim back ownership of their streets.

*

The struggle of Black and Brown people against racist and abusive policing in the United States is a story that is hundreds of years old, and it has by no means concluded. Iconic of the legacy of racist police brutality is the subsequent, May 2020 murder by casual choking of George Floyd at the hands of the Minneapolis police. This, along with numerous other murders of Black people, led to nationwide protests in support of the Movement for Black Lives. But it is important to understand—and even celebrate where appropriate—victories against repressive state practices, even if they are limited in the grand structural system of racist oppression. The story of the challenge to NYPD's racist stop and frisk practices is one of them, and worth retelling.

Here is how it began.

On a cold February night in 1999, four white members of the NYPD Street Crime Unit were patrolling a Bronx neighborhood on foot and approached a Guinean man in the vestibule of his apartment building. As the man reached in his back pocket for his identification, officers unleashed a hail of forty-one bullets, riddling his body. Outrage over Amadou Diallo's murder galvanized an already robust police accountability movement that had been mobilizing to challenge police violence—led by then-mayor Rudolph Giuliani's latent racism and authoritarianism—and the NYPD's culture of impunity surrounding the racialized policing of minority communities.

Diallou's killing made notorious the NYPD practice of "stop and frisk," which had emerged from a controversial 1968 United States Supreme Court decision, *Terry v. Ohio*. This decision held that an officer could restrict an individual's liberty if the officer had "reasonable suspicion" that criminal activity "may be afoot." *Terry's* radical new regime upended the two-hundred-year-old requirement that police stops or arrests be supported by "probable cause"; now both the *quantum* of proof and the *basis* of suspicion were significantly loosened in favor of law enforcement—at a point in time when political fortunes were being made imposing "law and order" through control of Black and Brown urban neighborhoods. This broad new authority to suss out crime before it happened repurposed municipal police departments, not least the NYPD during the law-and-order tenure of Mayor Rudolph Giuliani. They used it to patrol some neighborhoods with renewed aggression and in effect to take ownership—as the Bronx lieutenant would put it—of streets where crime was high. The license, as Amadou Diallou's case revealed, was lethal.

Soon after Diallou's murder, the leaders of the active police accountability movement approached the Center for Constitutional Rights (not the other way around) to file a legal case to support their political activism. CCR brought *Daniels v. City of New York* in federal court, arguing that NYPD was engaged in systematic racial profiling in violation of victims' constitutional rights to equality, and was systematically violating individuals right to be free from unreasonable law enforcement searches and seizures. Four years of litigation later, in 2003, we reached a settlement that in retrospect was modest in its scope and force. The NYPD agreed to disband the Street Crime Unit and to adopt a policy against racial profiling. It also agreed to a provision that, for the department, would turn out to be a poison pill: to turn over to CCR the quarterly stop and frisk reports, known bureaucratically as a form UF-250, which, for every recorded stop (and frisk), contained demographic and racial identification and the purported reasons for the stop, manifested in certain predetermined and often vague checkboxes (e.g., "suspicious bulge," "furtive movement," "fits description").

Despite the *Daniels* settlement, stops and frisks rose exponentially, nearly 700 percent over the ensuing decade, and in a racially discriminatory manner, even as crime rates dropped. When we decided to bring the *Floyd* case in 2008, we had observed an important lesson about political legal dynamics that made the *Daniels* settlement disappointing: between the time when we filed *Daniels*, at a peak moment in the police accountability movement, and the time of the settlement, the 9/11 attacks happened.

Law enforcement generally—and the NYPD specifically—had become lionized features of our legal and political landscape; scrutiny and even accountability seemed secondary, if not off-limits. Demands for a better settlement and that it be monitored robustly had been quieted in the post-9/11 atmosphere.

As we developed *Floyd* in 2008 then, we had to be mindful both about constructing a legal case and leveraging it to support a political movement. This meant, for example, matching the legal claims with the communities' needs. A claim asserting a violation of a person's privacy interests—called an "unlawful seizure claim"—was not enough. The way communities were experiencing stop and frisk was not merely as physical intrusion grounded in eighteenth-century principles of personal privacy. These communities experienced the massive escalation of stop and frisk as a racialized occupation; police were flooding their communities and harassing people because of race. Therefore, even as it was enormously difficult after years of regressive jurisprudence to prove a violation of equal protection principles—that is, to show that the city was systematically engaged in *intentional* discrimination—CCR was obliged to bring that claim to court, and to try to prove it.

And if we needed to serve the movement's narrative aims in this way, we also had to respect the movement's choice of storyteller. CCR does not abide by the classic impact litigation strategy that seeks the most socially palatable plaintiff (someone whose stature renders them *undeserving* of ill-treatment) to speak for the case. Rather, we try to foreground people most impacted by a practice, who can then be spokespeople for the movement and eloquent voices for the injustices all suffer, not just the putatively deserving. This often means selecting activists, rather than "ideal victims," as plaintiffs. David Floyd was precisely that person, and the way this litigation has become known—*Floyd*—is an embodiment of this principle.

*

A generation before George Floyd's murder would further ignite the Movement for Black Lives, David Floyd had been a leader of the Malcom X Grassroots Movement, a prominent community-based police accountability organization, in the Bronx. He was also a leader of Copwatch, organizing a community-based confrontation with the police centered around know-your-rights trainings and videotaping police activity. And so, when he took the stand in March, he represented himself and the broader police accountability movement of which he was a part. As an activist, his testimony was both personal and political; he spoke both about the facts of what happened, and imbued his organizing work with additional legitimacy.

David Floyd testified to being stopped twice, unlawfully, in his own neighborhood, including one while jiggling keys to the door lock of his own building. Asked what this stop meant to him, he said: "It was, again, the humiliation. I felt like I was being told that I should not leave my home . . . [and] that I need to *stay in my place*, and my place is in my home." The NYPD tried to show him they not only owned the block, but they also owned his residence. And, in his testimony, he sought to take it back.

He also drew a connection between unrestrained police power in street encounters with Black residents—which his participation in *Floyd* sought to end—and killings of Black people: "They are carrying guns. It makes for a dangerous situation. And you know, whatever it looks like, an irresponsible person with a gun is dangerous." In this testimony, David thus both presaged the Black Lives Matter Movement's call for accountability for police violence and indirectly drew a line from Amadou Diallou to himself; from the former movement to the current one.

Another of our most powerful witnesses, Nicholas Peart, came to us from our relationship with a grassroots youth empowerment organization, Brotherhood Sister Sol. If David Floyd's name was most associated with the litigation, Nicolas Peart became the face of the trial. He was a soft-spoken and thoughtful young man, by age twenty-four the legal guardian of his siblings due to the death of their mother, and he testified to four illegal stops and frisks that made him feel "criminalized [and] degraded." These occurred in the Bronx, Harlem, the Upper West Side, and in Brooklyn, while he was getting milk for his family, coming home from the gym, visiting his grandmother, and celebrating his eigteenth birthday. For Nicholas, these actions signaled the NYPD's attempt to control where he was permitted to go and how he could feel in the city. Nicholas underscored what many witnesses told the court: that the police made him feel powerless, and more so because they were, until then, unaccountable. But he also testified that the case afforded him an opportunity to shift power from the police to his community: "I chose to become a witness in this case because I wouldn't want my brothers to go through a situation of being stopped by the police. I wouldn't want them to go through that."

Finding the right plaintiffs was one key part of the trial preparation; working with the community was the other. Mindful of the limitations of the *Daniels* settlement and the need to amplify a litigation strategy outside the courts, CCR contributed to organizing the reemergence of a police accountability movement. In 2009, CCR and other established NGOs helped to organize and resource Communities United for Police Reform (CPR)—an entity that served as the umbrella for up to two dozen grass-roots social justice and police accountability organizations in New York. This structure facilitated communication, collaboration, and accounta-bility between the lawyers and communities on the ground. CCR could talk directly to CPR, which disseminated our information and proposed strategy to its constituent groups—and vice versa. Through this symbiotic partnership, the litigation would support the movement and the movement would support the litigation.

For example, the discovery and expert report process from the litigation brought out powerful evidence about police abuses we would regularly pro-vide to the movement, which we would in turn amplify and organize around. With the accumulated 4.4 million UF-250 forms in hand and the treasure trove of data they contained, our expert statistician demonstrated an expo-nential rise in stops, their obviously racially discriminatory implementation, and the utter lack of crime-revealing efficacy. This hard data dramatically undergirded the legitimacy of the movement's narrative; it served as an edu-cative and mobilizing tool for community leaders to explain to their consti-tuencies about what was actually happening (no, we are not crazy). And, of course, it caught the eye of the media and put the NYPD on the defensive.

In addition, through the CPR coalition, the movement also played a critical role in identifying desired outcomes from the trial. Lawyers are frequently directive to clients about what is best—and often least imagina-tive—to ask for from a court. But in an impact litigation case that did not seek damages and could have far-reaching effects for the people of New York, CCR knew it had to consult intentionally with our movement part-ners to identify what remedies we would demand, should we win.

And so, about three months before the trial start, CCR and other foundation partners convened a two-day meeting between the lawyers, the community coalition, and the leaders of a police accountability movement in Cincinnati that CCR had previously worked with. In the Cincinnati case, the activists had persuaded that court to order a "collaborative process" with facilitated input and exchanges between community members leading to direct recommendations for police reform from impacted communities. Now, at the end of our meeting, the lawyers and CPR conferred at length and formally agreed *together* on what remedies we would demand from the court should we prevail: these would include a collaborative process modelled on the Cincinnati experience to include relevant community stakeholders in identifying and implementing needed reforms. Heeding CPR's goals, we put those requests in writing to the court a month before trial started.

*

Just as the litigation buoyed the movement, the movement sustained the litigation. By the trial date, in March 2013, the movement against stop and frisk was roiling to a boil. It had arranged mass marches of thousands of people. Multiple civic organizations and advocacy groups were deeply critical of the NYPD leadership and Mayor Bloomberg for their full-throated "law and order" rationale for stop and frisk. The daily papers regularly featured stories about the practice and with a critical lens that could not have escaped the court's attention. The movement to reform stop and frisk was everywhere outside the courtroom, but the CPR coalition's leadership worked to bring it inside the courtroom too.

The CPR coalition sought to pack the court with members of their communities, and the judge and the NYPD certainly took notice. Each day of the trial, the CPR organizers sought to feature a particular constituency affected in one way or another by the NYPD—public housing residents; LGBTQ youth; Muslim, Arab, and South Asian communities; mothers affected by police violence; high school students and youth organizers. Members of these groups would watch the drama of the NYPD on trial, and often hold a press conference outside the courtroom during the lunch break. Many of these groups were not working specifically on legal questions related to stop and frisk as such, but they could nevertheless use the trial to draw attention to a range of intersectional dimensions of abusive policing in New York, and how it affected them—thereby leveraging the courtroom proceedings to support the broader movement.

More powerfully, their presence in the courtroom—what I call the "power of watching"—permitted them to bear witness to an organized story of police malfeasance; a form of accountability itself. For many New Yorkers living in Black and Brown communities, a police officer was a menacing source of danger, with power to ruin your day, or your life, arbitrarily and without accountability. But in the courtroom, communities watched lawyers proving day after day that police officers lied, didn't understand the law, covered up abuses, and overtly engaged in racial profiling without concern. I recall tall, strong officers almost slinking off the stand after a particularly skewering cross-examination by the plaintiffs' lawyers.

One example stands out. When the highest-ranking uniformed NYPD officer, Joseph Esposito, took the stand, the gallery was filled with many public housing residents. On the stand he denied ever hearing complaints from community members. An audible gasp from the audience followed, which the federal judge, Shira Scheindlin, clearly noticed, because she turned to Esposito and asked him directly: "So you never heard complaints from housing residents about this?" This movement-initiated exchange caused the judge, in her comprehensive decision finding the city liable for discriminatory policing, to state that she found that Chief Esposito was not credible on this point. The community was.

As the NYPD became exposed day after day to these communities, as truth confronted power and the NYPD's seemingly impenetrable armor was pierced, the sense was palpable, in the courtroom, that power was shifting from the police to the public.

In this forum, the people recognized they could win.

*

If "the power of watching" was one way the community entered the court, "the power of testifying" was another. "I want my day in court," is a powerful phrase that operates as a shorthand for transcendent social values. The phrase also captures the basic human quest to tell one's story and, because a wrongdoer is typically sitting in the courtroom, it offers a witness the opportunity to confront the powerful with the leveling power of truth. Because, in *Floyd*, the victims of stop and frisk that took the stand were, in most cases, part of the movement for police accountability, their testimony became testimonials from—and justice for—the movement.

The old saying that the adversarial process is a search for truth is laughably simplistic, particularly given the structural power imbalances infecting so many trials. Yet, in the rare event of a fair contest, a trial can be an enormously powerful forum to produce evidence and "prove" the truth in a way that changes public opinion and political power dynamics in the real world. And the facts Judge Scheindlin found to be true, in a comprehensive 180-page opinion (with 783 footnotes to the record), *proved* in particularized, detailed, and documented ways the narrative communities had been telling for decades. The sheer weight of evidence decimated the NYPD's arrogant defense of its practices. David Floyd, and the movement he represented, had won. The decision, issued on August 13, 2013, ruled that the city had been engaged in widespread and systematic racial discrimination and unconstitutional search-and-seizure violations; it rocked the city, sitting on the front page of every newspaper and leading on national and local news stations. CCR hosted a press conference— packed to the gills—that featured our clients.

The judge's conclusion that communities were being unlawfully targeted by the NYPD was dramatic on its own terms. But in a separate forty-page ruling, Judge Scheindlin ordered sweeping reforms to remedy the systemic constitutional violations she identified. Critically, she acceded to our request for a process like the Cincinnati collaborative process, and identified a number of stakeholders (including the CPR coalition) to participate in a broad, facilitated process to identify needed reforms she had not already contemplated or ordered. She called it a "Joint Remedial Process." In so doing, she directly credited the agency and expertise of the movement (and specifically the CPR coalition, which regularly filed amicus briefs highlighting community concerns) she saw mobilized inside the courtroom:

> Community input is perhaps an even more vital part of a sustainable remedy in this case . . . If the reforms to stop and frisk are

not perceived as legitimate by those most affected, the reforms are unlikely to be successful. *Neither an independent Monitor, nor a municipal administration, nor this Court can speak for those who have been and will be most affected by the NYPD's use of stop and frisk.*

*

The city and the NYPD, ideologically and politically invested in stop and frisk, did not take the judgment lightly. They huffed and puffed, called the judge biased against the police, and promised that crime would soar. The city appealed the ruling and sought immediately to suspend its effect. Worryingly, the panel of three judges hearing the appeal revealed itself to be overtly hostile to the substance of the decision, to the judge, and to the movement. In an unprecedented move, the appeals panel actually removed Judge Scheindlin from the case, reducing her brilliant, scholarly opinion to a hysterical fit of "bias." The appeal judges made it clear, in preliminary proceedings, that they would reverse the decision at the first opportunity they got. This was one of the most shocking and disheartening episodes of my legal career; we then battled furiously to get the full appeals court to reverse this unprecedented abuse of judicial power.

But while we fought inside the courts, something arguably more important was happening in the streets. In November 2014, Bill DeBlasio was elected mayor, in large part based on a robust campaign pledge to reform stop and frisk. He well knew he owed much of his electoral success to the very same police accountability movement that supported the *Floyd* litigation. As the new mayor, he would be deeply accountable to their demands—including a many other than reforming stop and frisk.

In their long list of demands to the new mayor, can you guess what the movement made as their number one demand? They had been so credibly invested in the *Floyd* litigation, treated as partners inside and outside the courtroom. They had seen the capacity of a litigation to advance their strategic organizing goals. They had a stake in creating and participating in the Joint Remedial Process. And they trusted the legal team. And so the CPR coalition and the broader police accountability constituency made "Drop the Appeal" their number one policing priority for the new mayor. As a movement lawyer, I had never previously witnessed activists so invested in a litigation that they would prioritize it over their own non-litigation advocacy goals. The mayor listened, and obliged, taking it out of the clutches of the dangerous court of appeals and sending it back down for the reform process ordered by the court.

In so many ways—including this most direct and concrete one—politics changed the law and law changed politics.

The people used the courtroom to help leverage their power, and, in that moment, to take back their streets.

*

I have shared this *Floyd* story as an example of strategic and successful movement-lawyering partnerships, which is in no way intended as a triumphalist narrative about ending state-sanctioned violence more broadly. The constant spate of subsequent killings of Black people in New York City and virtually every city in which police interact with Black people makes that evident. Similarly, given the seeming irrepressibility of police violence, the current movement's call for change looks different than it did a decade ago: it is no longer to "reform" the police in the way the *Floyd* litigation had sought to do. Movement activists rightly argue that transformational change is not possible, and that communities should pursue a strategy to "defund the police," or a "divest/invest" strategy. This would limit the ostentatious resourcing of militarized police forces—and accordingly, their interactions with communities—and shift resources to valuable community-based projects centered around the health, education, and safety of communities. And the reality is that while the remedial process in *Floyd* has indeed decreased the frequency and violence associated with street encounters and enhanced police accountability, chronic racial disparities persist. The ultimate struggle of the people to take back their streets is ongoing, even as fundamental change remains elusive.

Still, the Floyd story is compelling on its own terms, and holds powerful lessons for future lawyers and activists alike. Despite the NYPD's thirty years of ideological commitment to over-policing Black communities on the grotesque premise that they are more inclined to commit crime, the Floyd litigation was able dismantle the racist narrative undergirding the city's stop and frisk policy. *Floyd* discredited the once long-standing baseline for policing by documenting—through witnessing, narrative testimony, evidence, and judgment—it's irreducibly racist foundation. The Black abolitionist and scholar Frederick Douglass reminds us that "Power concedes nothing without a demand; it never has, it never will." At a minimum, the Floyd campaign offers a powerful model of how to structure and build the corresponding citizen power to successfully make such a demand.

Further Reading and Listening: Elizabeth Hinton, *From the War on Poverty to the War on Crime: The Making of Mass Incarceration in America* (Harvard University Press, 2017); Alex Vitale, *The End of Policing* (Verso, 2017); *Slow Burn: The L.A. Riots*, podcast, 6 parts, Slate, 2021. The full decisions of *Floyd v. City of New York* are available at ccrjustice.org.

Five Key Ways a Legal Strategy Can Help a Movement

BAHER AZMY

What I knew in theory about social change became visible to me in practice through my experience in *Floyd v. City of New York*. Meaningful and durable social change comes not from legal rulings, which are inherently vulnerable over time and contingent on political forces in the longer term; it comes from social and political movements that center communities most impacted by an injustice as the agents of the change they demand. Law and lawyers have significant limitations in advancing ethical and meaningful social change, for a host of reasons. They are traditionally more privileged than their clients, and don't share the same life experiences. They are compelled to proceed according to a strict procedural regimen of rights as have been defined by previous courts, and that don't take into account broader contexts of social or economic injustice. And courts are conservative: judges in a country such as the US are deliberately trained not to impose radical changes on society from behind a bench, in part because judges are not politically accountable. And as we saw in *Floyd*, they are sometimes chastened by higher courts when they do.

None of the above means that the law is feckless. It is one tool, which can be deployed powerfully when social justice lawyers start from a modest premise about the law's role in support of movements. Here are five key ways:

1. Judicial commands and relief from state violence.

Courts can issue orders enjoining unlawful and harmful conduct. This is how they were most heroic in the Trump era: repeatedly enjoining the Muslim Travel Ban (until the Supreme Court permitted it); enjoining multiple orders revoking Temporary Protected Status for hundreds of thousands of immigrants; blocking other orders seeking to end asylum on the southern border. Even short of ushering in systemic change, law can serve as harm remediation: lawyers can stay executions, prevent evictions, and delay deportations. Lawyers can form a layer of resistance protecting vulnerable people from continuing applications of state violence.

2. Evidence and movement building.

Litigation can compel the production of evidence that is useful for movement partners to advance their advocacy. In *Floyd*, the statistical data and evidence of profiling obtained in the litigation developed a broader public narrative about stop and frisk. And communities could organize around emerging proof that the evidence bore out subjective experience, i.e., that the NYPD was targeting *them*. In a related context, the Center for Constitutional Rights (CCR) often uses Freedom of Information Act litigation explicitly to obtain information to share with advocacy partners to advance their own advocacy and organizing goals.

3. Public education and debate.

Litigation can *force* a public debate on a question. In the US in particular, litigation can be titillating to the media and the public, thus it can be tailored to shape public opinion or to catalyze a public dialogue. CCR's litigation challenging the detention of terrorism suspects at Guantanamo without legal process did just that in 2002 when we "dragged politics into the courtroom," as the radical lawyer and law professor Jules Lobel put it. By 2008, the litigation and the robust advocacy it spawned produced a political and legal consensus that Guantanamo should be closed. Similarly, the legal and political challenges to stop and frisk have conclusively recast the once-lauded practice as racist and ineffective.

4. Recognition and storytelling.

The legal process puts the client's own narrative centerstage, which is a form of empowerment. Every legal case has an opportunity to state a headline and tell a story. The headline itself distills the power struggle: Plaintiff versus Powerful Defendant. In the Guantanamo cases, it is a demand to be heard by demonized clients, within US institutions through the invocation of higher law. This recognition strategy can be combined with a movement support strategy when organizing partners are the ones named as a plaintiff, highlighting their role as part of a major litigation, giving them a reputational boost that, in turn, has helped it with fundraising and capacity building.

We employed a similar strategy in supporting a daring LGBTQ advocacy group, Sexual Minorities Uganda (SMUG), by naming it lead plaintiff against Scott Lively, a radical anti-gay US pastor who led a conspiracy to persecute sexual minorities in Uganda. SMUG and its organizing goals set the terms of confrontation against their US-based persecutor, not merely an abstract legal principle, and put Lively on the defensive on his home turf.

5. Resistance and hope.

Litigation can be a form of resistance that breathes confidence and resilience into a movement. Even though we know we are unlikely to formally succeed, CCR frequently challenges officials engaged in torture in the War on Terror; or unlawful (but rarely judicially remediable) military actions in Central America, Pakistan, or Yemen; or a company moving its factory out of a city dependent on it. Even where we believe we may not win we and our partners can model confrontation and resilience. Authoritarians, as they reemerge all over the globe, depend on despair, lies, and apathy. As we saw in Guantanamo and numerous challenges to the Trump administration's authoritarian cruelty, litigation is a form of resistance. It can represent a radical act of hope and of strength.

Law, Revolution, and the Rights of Detainees in Lebanon

GHIDA FRANGIEH

At 10 p.m. on the night of Saturday, January 18, 2020, at the end of what we had come to call "The Week of Anger," I was among a group of Lebanese lawyers who entered the main Police Detention Center in Beirut. We were attempting to access a group of over forty detainees arrested arbitrarily during the protests in the city. It was to be one of toughest lessons yet in my career-long battle to ensure that people held in custody had the right to access legal counsel—as guaranteed in Article 47 of the Lebanese Code of Criminal Procedures, but seldom respected on the ground.

There had been mass protests all over Lebanon since beginning of the "17 October Revolution," when hundreds of thousands of us had taken to the streets to protest the corrupt political class that had been ruling since the end of the Lebanese Civil War, and that had caused the country's economic collapse. The protests had brought down the old government, but four months later, there had been no progress toward establishing a new one. And so we were still on the streets, demanding the appointment of a government of independent experts to see the country through the transition.

In addition to our severe public debt, the banking system had also collapsed—my parents are among the millions who lost their savings—and the uprising was not only against the political class stealing public funds and their destructive economic policies, but also against the banks stealing private money too. For a whole week, people gathered in rage, in public places all over the city. It started, on Tuesday, January 14, in what became known as "Red Bank Night."

The Central Bank has its headquarters on Hamra ("Red") Street, as do several of the major commercial banks, which is how Red Bank Night got its name. On that first night, only the banks were targeted, but still, the police alleged looting and violence against its personnel, and responded with the heaviest hand yet, conducting mass arrests. When we protested the following night, demanding the release of Red Bank Night detainees, they took sixty more into custody.

This escalation continued throughout the week, culminating with what became known as "the Saturday of Anger." My colleagues and I had formed the Lawyers' Committee for the Defence of Protestors, and by the time we arrived at the detention center on Saturday night, we were exhausted, emotionally and physically. I had the responsibility of running the committee's hotline with a group of volunteers, and all week long we had been fielding desperate calls from protesters, their families, and their friends. With the scant information we had, we had spent hours racing across town, from hospital to hospital, trying to gain access to injured protestors before they were forced to give possibly incriminating statements to the police, and to ensure they got adequate care. Negotiating access to emergency rooms in hospitals is not, of course, part of a law student's training; but it seemed to me that on that night, hospitals were turned into police stations, while the police station was turned into an emergency room.

I say this because when we entered the cell at the detention center that Saturday night, we encountered one of the scariest things I have seen in my career: red faces and dead eyes everywhere. Almost all of the forty or so detainees were covered with blood and marks from their beatings. After debriefing them and checking their physical condition, our first advice would have been to prepare them to give statements. But as soon as we began talking with them—each lawyer gathering a small group—it became clear what had happened: while we lawyers had been told to wait for our clients, statements were actually being taken from them, without the benefit of our counsel.

We had, in fact, been at the detention center for two hours already, and the commander had graciously offered my colleagues and I food and drink while we waited, lying to us that the detainees were not yet there. Exhausted as we were—we are human beings too, after all—we had accepted the mankoushi (Lebanese pizza), and it was only now, when we entered the cell, that we realized we had been deceived. The result was that most of the detainees had actually renounced their right to be seen by a medical examiner, despite their injuries at the hands of the police. They too had been deceived: told that they would have to pay for a doctor, or that getting a medical examination would delay their release. Not only did this deny them their rights per Article 47, but it was a calculated attempt to discourage them from obtaining medical and legal evidence of their abuse—which was, of course, the authorities' intention. (We later managed to get them medical examinations).

Counseling the wounded detainees that night, I understood my mission more clearly than ever: not just the enforcement of Article 47, but its popularization too, so that all Lebanese, protesting or not, would understand their rights if taken into custody by our increasingly authoritarian security forces. The defense rights of Article 47 were some of the results of the criminal justice reform of 2001, in Lebanon's attempts to free itself from Syrian control. As a result, there is a plaque in almost every police station engraved with the words of the law: on it you can read your right to see a lawyer and a doctor, and advice that you cannot be arrested without judicial order. But this is too often ignored by the prosecution and law enforcement officers: as always, in Lebanon, these rights have only been accorded to those with power and influence. But now the revolution put a magnifying glass on the reality of our country's inequalities.

For years, I had been defending marginalized people, such as refugees and queer people. These kinds of rights violations were thus familiar to me, and to my clients. But now, with the uprising, everyone was experiencing it, middle-class Lebanese people too. Professionals were involved: a lawyer was beaten up and detained while protesting; well-to-do parents were calling the hotline, desperate for information on their kids. When violence is limited to a minority, people tend to shut up. Once it reaches a certain level, everyone feels concerned about it, and that's when change can happen. The politicians are feeling it; the judges are feeling it too—their kids are in the streets, in the prisons.

At my organization, Legal Agenda, we like to say that "the law is too important to be left in the hands of lawyers alone," and I do believe something shifted in Lebanon, due to the collective action of our uprising. Now we get calls on the hotline asking us, "Can they do this under Article 47?" or

"What does Article 47 say about such and such?" The number forty-seven has become a number of meaning in Lebanese civil society in the months since October 2019. This is in no small part a result of the way we lawyers were able to work collectively during the revolution—not an easy task, given the way lawyers usually work individually, and given their egos too!

We saw the result of this in the Week of Anger, when we were able to gain access to detainees by referring directly to a circular issued by the Lebanese prosecutor general (a judge) a few weeks earlier. In it, he had specifically confirmed the terms of Article 47, and this was precisely because his hand had been forced by the action of Lebanon's legal community. This shows how important it is not just for lawyers to become part of broader movements, but to act collectively as a profession within these movements, as lawyers themselves.

It so happened that the annual elections for the officeholders of the Beirut Bar took place shortly after the October 2019 uprising. In Lebanon, every significant appointment—from politics to unions to finance—is as a result of trade-offs between the political parties that used to be at war but that now run the country as a cartel using power-sharing arrangements between the different sects as a pretext. One of the major ways they exercise their power is through the boards of professional unions, which they control. The legal fraternity was no different. But this time, as a result of the uprising, the candidate who won the most votes in the elections for the Beirut Bar was the main independent candidate in the race, a human rights lawyer named Melhem Khalaf.

Khalaf had been part of our Lawyers' Committee for the Defence of Protestors ever since we formed it in the summer of 2015, during what was known as the garbage crisis, when Lebanese first came onto the streets: the way waste management worked was very representative of political corruption in the country, and during the crisis, when garbage wasn't being collected, it was as if you saw and smelled this corruption on the streets, and you felt it on your body with the insects biting you. It became very physical, and for about three months there had been protests that led to hundreds of detentions.

Now, in late 2019, as we witnessed the state using the same tactics of arbitrary mass arrests during protests, we reconstituted the committee, building on our earlier successful experience of collective work in 2015. Then, as now, the security agencies—acting on political orders—intended to punish protesters and intimidate them off the streets. They were simply "disappearing" detained protestors by refusing to disclose their locations, and denying them the right to make a phone call or meet a lawyer. In the first days of the revolution, a distraught father had actually attempted to set himself alight outside a police station in Beirut, shouting, "Where's my son?" The other protestors prevented him from harming himself, but the image remained stamped in all our minds—and motivated our actions in the Lawyers' Committee from then on. Our immediate responsibility was to ensure that the right to protest was protected and that detained protestors—often youths—were kept in the light of day and of judicial process, as was their right. We were in exceptional times and the political equation had shifted: These young protesters were on the front line to defend our country and the future generations from the corrupt criminal ruling political class. They were defending us all. So we had to defend them.

On November 19, 2020, two days after Melhem Khalaf was elected, twelve protesters were detained, and denied access to their lawyers. The lawyers called Khalaf, who came down to the station himself: "No police station will ever be closed to a lawyer again," the head of the Beirut Bar said to the media, standing outside the building. Khalaf went on to engage the Bar's board on the issue and suddenly, for the first time, we had our professional association protecting us and our clients' civil rights, rather than working against us or leaving us without any backup as had been the case before.

It was due to the above shifts in the Beirut Bar's position that the prosecutor general was compelled to issue his circular confirming detainees rights under Article 47, in December 2019. But the circular was double-edged, for it also laid down a policy that had not, previously, been put in writing: that lawyers were explicitly not allowed to attend to their clients while they were being questioned.

There was nothing about this in the law itself, and so we set about challenging it. Finally, in September 2020, Parliament passed an amendment to Article 47, explicitly permitting lawyers to attend interrogations.

The amendment strengthens other defense rights too, such as the state's responsibility to cover the costs of medical examinations.

Following in the footsteps of lawyers from previous generations, I have been fighting for Article 47 to be adhered to for most of my adult life: the breakthrough was finally created by the 17 October Revolution. An amendment like this was only possible due to the dynamics and strength of its legal movement: protesters and lawyers camping outside detention centers through the night; detainees insisting on seeing their lawyers; the Bar rallying to the cause; parliamentarians as well as some judges coming on board too and seeing it through. The rights enshrined in this law had been popularized to such an extent that all those involved in drafting the amendment accepted that it had to be strengthened.

*

Law is a tool for me, not a career.

I decided to become a lawyer, in part, because of the work I had been doing in Lebanon, with refugees. After graduating from law school in France, I returned to Lebanon to work with Frontiers Ruwad, a refugees' rights organization. I was working on asylum claims, drafting the court briefs myself, and I found myself frustrated by the lack of conviction the assigned lawyers had for their clients' cases. They had little understanding too about how to argue against refugee deportations in courts and how to reconcile international human rights principles with our national laws.

My interest in the rights of people in custody stems from a determination to reject the extreme social and legal exclusion that arises from the deprivation of liberty. More specifically, it arises from my work with refugees. Particularly in the Middle East context, refugees can be held in detention for years without any rights being accorded them, under the pretext of the "threat" of terrorism.

After I passed my bar exams, one of my first cases as a lawyer was an Iraqi refugee in detention, a man I will call Hamed, whose only crime seemed to have been that he was playing cards, with two of his friends, outside the house of a prominent politician. Because Hamed's voice sounded a bit feminine to the police—it turns out he was in transition—they asked the judge to order anal examinations for all three detainees. This was a highly invasive practice, still used in Lebanon at the time as in so many countries globally, purportedly to ascertain whether the act of sodomy had been committed, and then prosecute them on the basis of an obsolete law criminalizing "intercourse against the order of nature." By the time I had access to Hamed, the judge had already ordered this examination. I was furious that someone would be subjected to something so inhumane just because a policeman suspected an effeminate voice, and I insisted on being present for his interrogation after the procedure, as per his Article 47 rights.

But this was 2012, long before the 2019 uprising, and the police denied me access. And so I stood on the other side of the door, trying to listen to the interrogation, trying to play my role as observer to ensure he was not treated violently. I could hear very little, and after Hamed was released, I asked him how it went. "He actually beat me up," Hamed said. "He put his hand over my mouth so that you wouldn't hear anything."

The interrogator was using violence to get Hamed to confess about his private life, but luckily he did not succeed: I like to hope that my presence on the other side of the door encouraged him to resist. He was not charged and we were able to close the case. But I remained outraged—about both the violation of Article 47, and about the anal examinations. And so Legal Agenda initiated a public debate with legal and medical professionals to identify scientific arguments criticizing these anal examinations, which we dubbed "the tests of shame." We argued they constituted an invasion of privacy that amounted to torture, and that they had no legal or medical value. A few months later, the police raided the Plaza Cinema in a poor district in Beirut, alleging it was a gay hangout, and arrested thirty-six men. All were subjected, as Hamed had been, to anal examinations. The publicity around this triggered public outrage, with one major TV channel even dubbing Lebanon "The Republic of Shame." Legal Agenda took on the case of the men, which we saw part of a broader advocacy campaign, led by Lebanon's LGBTQ movement, to create a public outcry against this inhumanity. We managed to get both the physicians' professional body and the justice ministry to issue circulars prohibiting the examinations. This was one of my first experiences of the power of collective action—a movement—in bringing about change: Lebanon banned anal examinations of suspects outright.

If Hamed's case sparked my interest in defending people arrested on the grounds of suspected homosexuality, it also redoubled my commitment to ensuring the enforcement of Article 47. I realized how arbitrary the Lebanese justice system was, particularly against the most marginalized groups. You are completely alone with the police throughout the first stages of the investigation, and whatever statement you make under those conditions cannot be negated—unless there is a medical report that says you were beaten up. Which, of course, there hardly ever is: because they don't always allow you to see a doctor.

A few years later, in 2015, we were informed of another gay refugee, a Syrian I will call Samir, who had been tortured just because the immigration official did not like the way he looked. When the official confiscated Samir's phone and saw suggestive messages from other men, he beat him with electrical cables, threatened to rape him, and left him standing naked in a bathroom for hours. It is hardly surprising that Samir confessed to having sexual relations with men. Without any consideration of the illegality of Samir's confession, the prosecutor on the case then pulled in two Lebanese men Samir had been texting with. When these men were released after questioning, they contacted Helem, the LGBTQ organization, and reported that Samir was still in detention, severely beaten and pissing blood. That's when I was called in. I ran around like crazy for forty-eight hours, trying to get a power of attorney, to get judicial authorization for a medical examination, to get the examination done—with attempts at every step of the way to stop me and slow me down.

I kept on thinking about what would happen to Samir if there weren't organizations like Helem and Legal Agenda to take up his case, and a community of human rights lawyers to work on his behalf. Eventually, with Samir, I got myself in front of a judge and argued that his statement should be annulled: not just because of torture, but because homosexuality should not be considered a crime. The result: *we* got fined for abusing our right of defense, according to the Code of Civil Procedures, which limits the right to litigate by its "good use"! We filed a torture complaint and, finally, in 2019, we manage to get all charges against Samir and his two friends dismissed. I felt devastated, though, that he had been subject to this abuse before I was able to intervene on his behalf—and that, as with Hamed, he was given no indication of what his rights were while in detention. Samir was powerless, and dispensable. He could have disappeared for weeks or been deported, and no one would have even known.

My work with refugees like Hamed and Samir also led me to what I knew would be one of our biggest fights: with the Military Intelligence (MI), over "forced disappearances." I saw the danger of this through my work with Syrian refugees, because of the way MI handles terrorism cases. If you are suspected of terrorism, it's as if you have no rights whatsoever, and increasingly—particularly during the revolution—these methods were being used by MI to arrest protesters, to investigate Lebanese civilians and to torture them, with no accountability.

*

In November 2019, we received messages on the Lawyers' Committee hotline that a group of about sixty protestors had been detained by MI in Tripoli, in the north of the country. They were accused of violence against soldiers during the protests. After a fight to get them released, forty-six were handed over to the police, but ten were unaccounted for: all of them were under twenty-five, and two were minors. Their parents were extremely worried especially given the signs of beatings on those released; I brought in the child protection authorities, but not even the social worker officially responsible for the protection of minors could get any information.

And so we decided to use a new legal tool in our kit: the 2018 Law on the Missing and the Forcibly Disappeared. Legal Agenda had been very involved in advocating for, and drafting this legislation, on behalf of families of people who disappeared during the fifteen-year Lebanese War (1975–1990). We had litigated and advocated on behalf of these families, to try to get information about their loved ones, and now we saw that we could use this new law to find out information on protestors in custody. We argued that if you refused to allow detainees to exercise their rights you were forcibly disappearing them—and that this warranted an investigation by the prosecutor general. So we submitted a claim of enforced disappearance and torture in order to either trigger their immediate release, or at least disclose their location and allow them to exercise their rights.

We had already used this strategy to force MI to release three protestors, all well-known participants in the uprising. Now I went again to the prosecutor general with a similar claim for those missing from Tripoli. He disclosed their location but at first refused to allow them to exercise their rights under Article 47. I convinced his assistant—who had young children herself—to ensure at the very least that the minors contact their parents. Five minutes later the parents contacted me, crying, "He's alive! He's alive!" I had set up a WhatsApp group: I remember the feeling of relief in being able to change the name of this group from "Disappeared" to "Detained at Central MI."

In April 2020, during the national lockdown ordered as a consequence of the COVID-19 epidemic, there was a similar case of mass arrests in Tripoli, again involving a large number of youths and minors, who "disappeared" from a protest against increasing inflation after some threw stones and Molotov cocktails at military vehicles. After submitting an enforced disappearance claim, and with the support of the Bar, we were able to get unprecedented access to them, at Central MI, a special detention center located inside the Ministry of Defence that had previously been barred to lawyers.

But although our presence might have lowered the violence against them, I knew it would not prevent it. "Am I still going to be beaten?" one of the minors asked me.

I looked at him and saw a bruised face and torn shoes. I knew he had gone through hell for several days and I was the first person he saw who didn't want to beat him up. How was I to answer? In the months I had already spent documenting the treatment of prisoners since the 17 October Revolution, not a single one had come away from the MI without a beating. Would the visit of a lawyer for the first time change anything? This was one of the hardest moments of my career.

The boy was weeping. Was he able to hear the truth—that he probably would be beaten? How should I protect him, or prepare him? I chose my words carefully: "They should not be beating you. But if they do, it is your right to ask for a doctor."

In the next three days, we worked harder than ever to ensure these youths were seen by a medical examiner and brought before a judge at the military court within the four-day legal limit. Then there was an outbreak of COVID-19 in the court, so it shut down—and I insisted, successfully, that there be a Zoom hearing, since the legal deadline had passed. At the time of writing, in early 2022, the case was still ongoing—and has become part of our broader campaign of advocating for civilians not to be tried in military court.

We started this campaign during the 2015 garbage crisis, and had successfully managed to transfer the cases of those arrested out of the military court and back to the regular courts. Since then, we have successfully challenged the military court's jurisdiction over those arrested during protests several times—most famously in the 2020 case of Khaldoun Jaber, a well-known journalist, kidnapped from a protest by undercover MI operatives because of his social media postings, and so badly beaten that he lost his hearing in one ear.

In addition to good organization and coordination among the lawyers, the campaign relied on two key components essential for movement lawyering. First, effective documentation: At both Legal Agenda and the Lawyers' Committee, we have made a point of documenting all detentions and violence during protests. This has helped us understand the policies and modes of operation of different security agencies and to be well prepared for military trials, for instance by having medical reports proving torture and ill-treatment. Second, public advocacy: We knew that we had some public support about the military court's overreach, and so we published material to inform the debate, explaining how the court did not guarantee a fair trial to civilians. We also invited the media to monitor and cover the trials: given that the military court is traditionally closed to the public, such public scrutiny encouraged it to limit its jurisdiction over civilians or to ensure fairer verdicts. As a result, we've had a 90 percent rate of non-guilty verdicts and decisions declaring that the military court did not have jurisdiction over acts of rioting and criticism of politicians.

*

All this is part of the social revolution that has happened alongside Lebanon's political uprising: our self-perception as citizens and our rights in relation to the state. We do not yet have the system we deserve in Lebanon, but we do now have this objective: that we have the right to be protected as citizens, to live dignified lives, to be governed efficiently and healthily. A key part of this is building the narrative of our successes, small though they might be: for example, in ensuring that Article 47 is entrenched, or in winning the right for civilians to be tried in regular courts, not military ones.

Then came August 4, 2020. A terrible blast, the third-biggest non-nuclear explosion in history, destroyed half of Beirut and resulted in massive-scale damages with more than two hundred killed, 6,500 injured and 300,000 displaced after their homes were destroyed. This is when most Lebanese, traumatized by the scale of the destruction, saw their relationship to those in power shift completely. Our authorities had stored 2,750 tons of a highly explosive material, ammonium nitrate, in the capital's port for six years. They all knew about it, including the judges and the head of the security agencies that had arrested and prosecuted so many hundreds of protestors over the previous year. They had used all their resources to crush the uprising but took no action whatsoever to protect the city and its port. We do not know why exactly, but we know those in power only acted when it served their private interests. Corruption had now become fatal.

The realization dawned that our corrupt regime was also a murderous one, and its murderous nature became even more evident when, four days after the blast, the security forces used live ammunition on a mass protest, injuring more than seven hundred grieving protestors. This was unprecedented. One of our committee's lawyers was shot in the heart while documenting the protest; fortunately he survived. Many others were blinded. Of course, we lawyers too lost our homes and offices in the blast, and many of us have mobilized to ensure we get justice. An investigation was launched, and this raises questions still unanswered at the time of writing. Will our judiciary be able to challenge the impunity of the regime that has ruled the country since the end of the war, and hold senior officials accountable? As such, the blast trial, and how we mobilize for it, will be our country's chance to build a fairer and more transparent and independent justice system, and the lawyers' movements will be at the front lines of this battle.

At the time this essay was first published, in early 2023, the trial remains stalled—by a form of "lawfare": suspected senior officials refused to submit to the investigation, claiming they have immunity from prosecution and challenging the legitimacy of the judge. We have now mobilized to deconstruct these legal narratives that aim to obstruct and evade justice. Once the trial finally begins, we hope that as well as providing justice, it will provide the platform for victims to tell—and hear—a story of their collective trauma; a story that will be inscribed, by the trial, onto the record and into our history. I am a firm believer that lawyers and activists must be storytellers too: we must tell the stories of our legal battles, because we don't want the experiences to be limited to those who fought these particular battles, especially if the victims are not willing or able to speak up. We need as many people as possible to know of the sacrifices that were made by others, so we can mobilize around them, build on them, and prevent them in the future. We need to show that, even if we haven't yet been able to achieve our goals at the political level, even if we know that our rights cannot be protected without real political and economic change, our collective work can improve our civil rights, and change our relationship to those in power slowly.

Meanwhile, the uprising—and the Lawyers' Committee in particular—have done something critical, in our society, to change the status of lawyers. The traditional view is that a lawyer is the one who steals your money or who protects the interests of people in power. But now the perception of those people involved in the uprising, at least, has altered. I don't use the term myself, but we are often called "the lawyers of the revolution," and I think that reveals the way public attitudes have changed: that we are not the agents of power, but part of a bigger social movement. We are building on the work of several generations of lawyers before us who have fought for our rights. But we too are Lebanese. We too have lost our income and our homes, we too have been betrayed by our banks and political leaders, we too have been injured during protests or the blast.

At the start of the uprising, when people consulted me on whether they should post something on social media or organize a protest, I joked: "It's a revolution, don't consult the lawyers!" The laws, after all, are drafted by the very people we are rebelling against, and are often used against us. But at the same time, the law is a very powerful tool to use against those in power, and to help elaborate efficient resistance and civil disobedience strategies so everyone can act with knowledge of the legal risks and with an informed decision to assume the consequences. It would be a mistake to disregard it.

No revolution will be "authorized" by law. But the law, if used cannily, can create revolutions.

Further Reading: Lama Karame, "Cause Lawyers in Lebanon: A Preliminary Profile," 2016; Ghida Frangieh, "Beirut Court of Appeal: Sexual Orientation Is Not Punishable," 2019; Ghida Frangieh, "Lebanese Uprising Enshrines Defense Rights for Detainees," 2020; Ghida Frangieh, Nour Haidar, and Sarah Wansa, "How Lebanese Authorities Weaponized Arrests to Suppress the Right to Protest," 2020; Nizar Saghieh, "Lebanon's Face-Changing Opera," 2020; Nizar Saghieh, "Lebanese Court Removed Judge Who Sympathized With Beirut Explosion Victims," 2021; Nizar Saghieh, "Lebanese Protesters' Trial Becomes a Trial of the Regime: The Judge Breathes the Same Stench," 2021; Ghida Frangieh, "August 4th Investigation: Challenging a Regime Rife with Impunity," *Al-Rawiya Magazine*, 2022. All available at The Legal Agenda, english.legal-agenda. com.

What it Means to Be a "Human Rights Lawyer" in Putin's Russia

PAVEL CHIKOV in conversation with MARK GEVISSER

This conversation took place in 2021, before Vladimir Putin's invasion of Ukraine. At the time this book went to print in late 2022, the invasion was in full force, and all political dissent in Russia had been stamped out. In a postscript, Pavel Chikov reflects on human rights law within the shadow of this tragedy.

Mark Gevisser: What does it mean to practice human rights law in an authoritarian system?

Pavel Chikov: I like to joke that I entered human rights when Vladimir Putin became the head of the state of Russia, in 1999. Since then, we've both being doing the same job, with different success rates. What this means, for me, is that I have restricted experience, working only under Putin's regime in Russia, in contrast with older human rights activists and lawyers who can compare our situation with the Yeltsin era of the '90s, when things were much more free. In a way, that gives me more energy, because I don't have this memory of a time when things were better and access to public institutions so much easier. All I have are these twenty years of Putin, with degrading institutions, first and foremost of the judiciary itself. We don't have hopes and expectations right now in Russia. "Things are only going to get worse" is a slogan we have been living under for quite some time.

MG: How, and why, did you begin your practice as a human rights lawyer?

PC: After law school in Kazan, my home city, in the self-governing territory of Tatarstan, I got an internship to the state prosecutor, a very good post for a law graduate, but something of a dead end professionally. I saw an opportunity in the human rights world, so in the beginning, it was a professional decision, in part. Also, my father is a professor of biology, a scientist, and I think this influenced me in terms of wanting to see the truth; to know how everything works. In 2001, a group of us, all young lawyers, set up the grassroots Kazan Human Rights Center. In the beginning our main task was research. For two years we conducted surveys and studies of police, penitentiary officers, courts, justices of the peace, bailiffs. We wanted to understand how the criminal justice system worked, so we interviewed homeless people, sex workers, and so on, about the contacts with police, about possible brutality and bribes and corruption. This is not the kind of thing you learn how to do in law school!

I had just returned from a graduate program in public administration at the University of North Dakota, and it is here that I learned about political science, sociology, and research methods. This prepared me for the kind of content analysis of judgments we would undertake—looking at three thousand judgments on criminal cases, or analyzing interviews of two thousand prisoners, or five hundred policemen. Only after we understood that did we move to the next stage, which was working on individual cases. We began with police torture cases, because our evidence showed that this was a severe problem. We got our first conviction in 2004.

We were put under severe pressure. Our offices were searched. My parents found a grenade next to their apartment. Our dog was poisoned. There was a criminal case against my deputy. It was something like a cold shower that time, and it made me very angry—we were just lawyers, doing our jobs—and I channeled my anger into fighting police abuse even harder.

What differentiated us from the other human rights organizations was, precisely, the legal perspective. Several people in my team had a background in law enforcement—a former police officer or prison officer. From the beginning, we were very effective. We were a very local organization working only in Kazan, but we decided to have a spokesperson. We were very active in the public sphere, in the media all the time, very high profile.

MG: Was this a strategic decision?

PC: We were all in our early twenties, and it was mostly about vanity and becoming well-known! But looking back twenty years later, I can see how it was the beginning of a lifelong litigation strategy. I was trying to force the local police department to deal with us. I wanted to prove to them we young guys were serious and effective: we can put dozens of policemen behind bars, so you better sit down and talk. We definitely understood the power of media as a tool. It's one thing to put a policeman on a torture case; it's quite a different thing when dozens of journalists are sitting in the courtroom and writing about it.

And of course, this was a tool to attract more cases to us. Let me give you an example. In 2012, a man was raped—to death—with a champagne bottle, while in custody in Kazan. This was on International Women's Day, which in Russia has the custom of men buying women presents, and it was with the remains of one of these that the victim was raped. He was transferred to a hospital, but he died. We approached the family to represent them, but they declined: they were trying to negotiate, and settle the case. Of course, in the likely event that the police did settle, it would all be outside of public view, and there would be more rapes, more deaths. It was clear. We had to find someone else who was willing to go public. So we put out a call in the media, saying, "Has anyone else suffered from these officers in this particular district? Come to us."

We got *twenty* responses, raped in several ways, not to death, but with pens or pencils or bottles. It created a huge stir publicly; the federal [national] prosecutor visited Kazan, and instructed that criminal investigations be opened on all torture complaints from the previous three years. We represented fifteen of the complainants who had contacted us; thirty policemen were found guilty on torture cases.

We had been getting convictions of police torture since 2004, but now it escalated. In 2012, there were 150 in Tatarstan! And for the following years, the same number, and the same since then. There was a huge growth of these criminal cases, and a lot of investigators and judges learned how to deal with such cases. Here is the point. Once such investigations became a well-known and regular practice, it had an effect. By 2018, police had almost stopped torturing in Kazan.

In 2005, based on our success in Kazan, we set up Agora (the Inter-Regional Association of Human Rights Organizations), a national network of human rights lawyers. Now, some years later, we have data showing clearly that the levels of police torture are lower in those regions where lawyers are working on these issues.

MG: So you see your role as proactive. You don't wait for a client to walk into your office . . .

PC: We make public calls very frequently. This is a form of mass mobilization around human rights abuses, something like political mobilization, which is less possible in nowadays Russia. An example: in November 2020, we called publicly for families to come forward if their relatives had died due to COVID-19, because of the lack of medical care. Within a few weeks, we received more than thirty cases. This is a regular way to gather information, especially when it is a hot issue.

MG: If media and public advocacy is a key part of your work, how does the increasing censorship of the Russian media affect you?

PC: I spoke about the degradation of the judiciary and parliament in Russia. We are definitely seeing a degradation of the media in Russia too. There are a lot of obstacles in the way of distributing information in Russia right now, and it's only getting worse. But one of Russia's own leading activists showed us a solution: the opposition leader Alexei Navalny, in the way he developed his own social media resources and tools. Look at Navalny today: he is a huge media holding himself. He can reach his audience without any intermediaries.

So I have a Telegram channel, a bit smaller than Navalny—thirty thousand subscribers, most of whom are journalists—and it's very easy for me to get word out. I used to have a press secretary that dealt with press releases, but I no longer need one. It works very effectively, particularly when we have high-profile cases, like Pussy Riot, whom we defended, or Telegram itself, when we acted on behalf of it against the Russian government. Those cases are huge, and they take up a considerable amount of our time. But they are a very small proportion of the daily work we do, and this presents one of the problems with social media. When all eyes are on us, it's great, because everyone is interested in the case. But most of the time we are having to compete with Instagram superstars, and we cannot rely on the high-profile cases, which maybe happen once a year. If human rights issues are not on the top of the agenda, it is really hard to develop and grow a social media profile; to get noticed on social media.

MG: And of course the Russian government would like control over social media too. I'm thinking specifically of your Telegram case.

PC: Currently in Russia, there are dozens of ways you can be persecuted for information that you publish, no matter who you are. Writing and publishing facts has become very risky. This creates a culture of self-censorship too: if you step out of the comfort zone, you immediately face a whole lot of trouble.

So this raises the issue of privacy, and the state's power to spy on your communications. We dealt with this in the Telegram case. Telegram is a messenger platform, developed by Pavel Durov, a kind of the Russian Mark Zuckerberg, because he created the Russian equivalent to Facebook, VKontakte, which has a hundred million users right now. When he was forced to sell VKontakte at way below market value, he left Russia and set up Telegram, which now has about five hundred million users around the world—about ten percent of whom are in Russia. Telegram is the gold standard for privacy, because of the end-to-end encryption technology it uses. But in 2017, the Russian government adopted a law obliging the distribution of information to be registered, and on this basis, the FSB, the Russian security service, demanded the encryption keys from Telegram. When Telegram refused, it was fined and banned, and Pavel Durov asked us to represent him in Russian courts.

We have had four cases on behalf of Telegram in Russia, including in the Supreme Court against the FSB, and we have lost every single one of them. We had no expectation of victory in the courtroom, and neither did Durov. He wanted us to appeal the banning, for the sole reason that this would buy him time to develop a way to hide traffic in order to escape the ban. In the end we got him seven months before the technical guys from the government were allowed to try to intercept Telegram. But they were too late. The new technology was in place. We had lost the legal battle, but in fighting it, we had bought time to win the technical one.

The Kremlin asked Google, Microsoft, Amazon, and Apple to get rid of Telegram traffic from their servers, and to drop the application from its app stores. So we initiated a huge international campaign. I came to the American Civil Liberties Union, which helped get a letter signed by seventy international human rights organizations, and this was put on the desk of Tim Cook, Sundar Pichai, Jeff Bezos, and Bill Gates. They refused to comply with the Kremlin's request.

In the end, we went to the European Court of Human Rights, because we wanted a precedent-setting ruling on balancing national security issues with privacy in communications. There has not yet been a significant judgment on this, anywhere, and a lot of lawyers in the tech field are now looking to the Telegram case, given the concern that many governments have about end-to-end encryption: this is the first time in history that states have not had technical access to all communications, be it regular mail, or telephones, or internet. In June 2020, the Russian government said that they would stop trying to ban Telegram. We assume this is to preempt the ECHR judgement. But even without that judgement they had lost: they had no power over Telegram, which continues to operate, with safe end-to-end encryption in Russia and around the world.

MG: It's interesting to see how your career has developed from defending abject people on the ground—criminal suspects, sex workers, and other ordinary people subject to police violence—to tech billionaires like Pavel Durov. But in both instances, it seems you are setting out to make an example, to Russians, of what their rights are—to security from police, to privacy on the internet—and to keep the notion of rights in the public eye. Is this what guides you to what you call "hot issues"?

PC: There are so many reasons for doing that. Here is another: It motivates new lawyers to come to our network, and currently we have a hundred lawyers working on about a thousand cases. Even despite the degradation of the judiciary and politics I have been talking about, lawyers are coming, lawyers are willing to work. Why? Because, because we're well known, we have this reputation. "Look, these guys are working on the high-profile cases. They are working on serious cases. They are getting so much publicity for it."

MG: Never more so, I suppose, than with Pussy Riot in 2012 . . .

PC: The influence of that case, through the public—and *international*—media outcry was huge, in discrediting the Russian government, and it was definitely part of our role to incite this outcry. The Pussy Riot case was very contradictory in Russia—it was hard to raise much public support for feminist punks dancing in Moscow's main cathedral. This changed when the girls were imprisoned: twenty-year-old mothers of small kids, facing two years in a Russian jail with a blessing of Putin himself—he publicly approved the punishment. Publicizing this played as much a part as our legal arguments, in getting the girls moved to a better prison, charges being dropped against one of them, and then their early release.

But we can play it the other way too if we need to. There was a case in 2013, for example, where we were defending a young drug trafficker in a Moscow jail who had health issues that meant she couldn't go to the toilet without medical help. The result was that she did not go to the toilet for three months while she was awaiting trial. The judge approached our lawyer before the sentencing and said, "I will release her and put her on probation, so long as there are no journalists in my courtroom." The publicity was important, but our primary concern was our client. So we had specifically to go to each journalist covering the case, asking them not to show up in the courtroom. We succeeded, in part, because we work well with the media and so some kind of trust has developed precisely *because* of our high profile. We need to know when to make a case loud—and when to turn down the volume.

MG: But that's exceptional, right? It seems to me that it's very much part of your identity to make a noise through your cases—not for the sake of noise itself, but to influence public opinion.

PC: We are struggling to keep ourselves and human rights on the agenda, and this means trying to sell our values to the public differently. So we look for topics that are going to promote the concept of human rights and legal activism in Russia, such as domestic violence, which has been a hot topic for the past couple of years, or environmental rights, where people are getting more interested and active, feeling ready to protest or even fight with the police.

Let me give you another example of how we have seen this approach work. We were the first lawyers in the country to provide legal aid for street protesters in December 2011, after the parliamentary elections—the ones led by Alexei Navalny, where he was first arrested, for fifteen days. Since then, we have worked on several thousand cases during the last nine years, and we have seven hundred cases before the European Court of Human Rights from protestors alone—mainly over administrative arrests and small fines. Why do we bother? It is because by fighting these cases, we notice that the knowledge of the laws and the rules has been growing all the time. Protestors have learned that they have a right to call a lawyer, what the procedure of booking them should be, and this is very impressive, because now the lawyers and the organizers can rely on the protestors, and expect a certain behavior from them. And when there's a newcomer who *doesn't* know the rules, he's immediately obvious, and the others can educate him on the police bus. This popularizes legal knowledge. It spreads through the community.

MG: How proactive are you in spreading this legal knowledge?

PC: In some instances, its by word of mouth. In others, where specific organized groups are mobilizing, for example HIV activists protesting for access to antiretroviral therapy, they come to us in advance, and ask for trainings. We do tons of these seminars; it's part of our daily work. But it only works in some sectors. For example, in police torture, you can't work with a particular target group, because anyone is vulnerable. It's random and arbitrary in a country like Russia.

MG: Is another reason for having a high profile, that it gives you some kind of immunity?

PC: Perhaps at the local level, but if the feds decide to make trouble for us, no one can help. If Putin himself says, "Who is this? Do something with them," we have no chance. Agora was registered as a "Foreign Agent" in 2014, which has the implication of being a spy, and this presented a challenge too, in terms of where we could work and how we would get funded. Luckily we were taken off the Foreign Agents list after just a year—but in the interim, to deal with the problem, we became more international, setting up an office in Bulgaria, and working in other former Soviet states. So the challenge became an opportunity.

I am determined not to be a victim.

MG: But there are some things beyond your control, in an environment like Russia. You might be made a victim.

PC: We guard against what the tech industry calls "zero-day" risk: the possibility we will be attacked by something unanticipated. If you know what is going on and what is happening with someone in the field, you can adjust, you can adapt. Managing the risks of working in human rights in Russia is a part of our daily business, in every sphere—people, communications, funding, clients, documents, reputation. We have thought, of course, about what will happen to Agora if some form of physical violence happens to me or to anyone in the team. We are prepared.

MG: Are *you* prepared, personally?

PC: The price we pay doing this kind of work is the personal risk of being attacked and criminally persecuted everyday. You have to be okay with that risk. This is something I came to terms with only quite recently. I mean, I am a *lawyer.* I work in the legal profession. Like a criminal lawyer, or a judge, or an investigator or police. But if I'm criminally prosecuted, that's the end of it, for me professionally. You, Mark, can continue being a journalist even if you have a criminal record, but for me, for any lawyer, it's over. So I used to be very nervous about a possible criminal case, on any trumped-up charges, and what it would do to my career. Until I understood I had to make a choice. Go for it and accept that risk, or quit and do something else. I made the first choice and, immediately, psychologically, everything became easier.

Of course there's a price to taking such a risk, and the way you offset it is by taking pleasure in every success you achieve, in your professionalism. Especially if it's a political case, where there's an activist found not guilty and an investigation terminated, or released from custody. This gives one a lot of motivation, and energy, to continue, particularly with everything bad, and getting worse. You think, "Sometimes I can win even in such a shitty environment."

MG: Pavel, we are resuming this conversation in July 2022. What are your thoughts about the themes we have explored above, five months into the Russian invasion of Ukraine?

PC: We have been extremely busy during these first months of the war, working sixteen hours per day. More than twenty thousand people applied for our help—anti-war street protesters, critics of the government in social media, journalists, people looking for psychological assistance, conscripts and their parents. Thousands of Russians have been arrested and fined for protesting against the military action in Ukraine. A package of military censorship laws was adopted in March and more than three thousand people have been prosecuted for publicly opposing the Russian army and the president. We have cases of Russian national guard officers and soldiers who refused to go to Ukraine and were fired. Truly speaking, the main message we wanted to send to the Russian public, to Ukrainians, and to the world is this: this is Putin's war, his and his close circle of old men from the Soviet Union and KGB. But twenty years of police state, a decade of violence against the dissent in Russia led to the total fear and loss of faith in ourselves in Russia.

As to the future, it is almost impossible to predict. A lot depends on the military situation in Ukraine, on the possible peace agreement, on social protests inside Russia, or on a possibility of a coup in the Kremlin. So far things have been deteriorating rapidly almost every day. If the trend continues I don't see me and my team working on the ground in Russia even by the end of the year. We are one step away from massive repression. Still, I am still in Russia, and personally safe so far.

Law, Information, and Power:
On Being Julian Assange's Lawyer

JENNIFER ROBINSON

My very first conversation with Julian Assange was about West Papua.

It took place in September 2010, at the London home of one of my mentors, the human rights barrister Geoffrey Robertson KC. I had been invited over because things were about to heat up for WikiLeaks, and for Julian, its founder. On the heels of the Collateral Murder video and the trove of leaks it had published about the Afghan War, WikiLeaks was about to release the Iraq War Logs and the US diplomatic cables—revealing more evidence of war crimes and human rights abuses by the US and other governments around the world. Geoffrey thought I might be interested in joining the team representing Julian. WikiLeaks's alleged source, Chelsea Manning, had been arrested and was awaiting trial, and the Pentagon had created the WikiLeaks Task Force, with a rumored international operation to track down and imprison Julian to stop him from publishing any more information. When I walked into Geoffrey's kitchen, Julian was sitting at the kitchen table working on his laptop. I apologized for being a little late, explaining that I'd just been giving a TV interview about West Papua. Before we could exchange any other pleasantries, he was off, talking intensely about the region's history and politics and the geopolitical interests driving the colonization and oppression of the West Papuan people.

I was taken aback that he knew anything all about this small contested territory, occupied by Indonesia, far off most Westerners' radar. West Papua is only three hundred kilometers north of Australia, but most of my compatriots know very little of its history and confuse it with its independent neighbor Papua New Guinea. Journalists have been banned from entering West Papua and academics have difficulty getting access so there is very little available information. But Julian knew a lot.

By the time I met Julian I had been working with Benny Wenda, the leader of the West Papuan independence movement, for almost a decade. As a twenty-one-year-old Australian law student, I found myself in West Papua volunteering for a human rights NGO, having stumbled upon the injustice while living in Indonesia. I learned how the territory, a former Dutch colony, had been handed "temporarily" to Indonesia in 1962 on condition that the West Papuans be given a referendum on independence in 1969—a referendum that never happened. Indonesia refused to give the territory a free and fair vote and has since brutally oppressed the West Papuan people and suppressed its liberation movement.

In 2002 I worked on Benny's trial when he was being held as a political prisoner, facing false accusations. When it was apparent he would not get a fair trial and would likely be killed, I helped him and his family flee the country and get political asylum in the United Kingdom. It was a tough but important lesson for a young, aspiring human rights lawyer: politics can trump the law—and due process.

I never thought of myself as a "movement lawyer" back then. In fact, I had not yet heard the term—and I had no conception of what it meant, as a lawyer, to try to build power in a movement through the law. But looking back, I see that it was my role. If helping the Wenda family flee just seemed like the right thing to do, so too did helping them build their international campaign and establish the international law position to support that campaign. But for their right to self-determination to be given effect, decision-makers and their governments needed to get behind the cause. I've learned that it's often not enough to have a just cause; you also need politics on your side. And for this to happen, the world needs to know about the injustice. We need to know about it to be able to act to change it. That was why I was in that TV studio talking about West Papua on the night I met Julian: I was a lawyer, but I understood that it was part of my job to speak out publicly about the injustice of Indonesia's unlawful occupation.

That first meeting with Julian was to change my life. Since then, I have come to understand that what I witnessed in West Papua prepared me for my work for WikiLeaks. Both causes show that being cut off from information allows injustice to fester.

At the core of the West Papua economy is the US-owned Freeport gold mine. In 2002, two American teachers from the international school for mine staff were killed while out for a picnic. The Indonesian authorities and the mining company alike blamed the liberation movement, although we discovered evidence that the Indonesian military was behind their murders. When we tried to make this evidence public, an American diplomat intervened and essentially told us to shut up. I still had naive faith in diplomats; I was shocked that the US would care more about the continued operation of this mine and its relationship with the Indonesian military than about finding out the truth and seeking justice for the murder of American citizens. This gave me an early insight into what everyone would later learn through WikiLeaks: this is how US diplomacy operates. I came to understand how diplomats are part of the culture of secrecy that covers up wrongdoing. I also came to see the way power—colonial, imperial, capitalist—relies on secrecy and control of information. Soon I would learn how those in power could be so threatened by the free flow of information that they would go to extraordinary lengths to criminalize and demonize my new client.

When I started representing Julian and WikiLeaks, I really didn't think about my job as serving a movement. I saw it as defending an individual and advising an organization, the traditional role I had been taught in law school. But then I saw how this person, with nothing more than a backpack and small, effective groups of volunteers, could shake the world's superpower to its core, with revelations about war crimes, human rights abuse, and corruption. Fighting Julian's extradition from the UK to Sweden and then the US, I witnessed the way the power of the US and its allies was being used to cast him as "a high-tech terrorist" and a threat to freedom when, in fact, his work was designed to facilitate freedom: freedom of speech and the public's right to know. I cared deeply about these freedoms myself, understanding how important they were for everyone and for every social movement. I also understood, and then witnessed, how WikiLeaks and its work was itself part of a global movement—a transparency movement—which served so many other social movements around the world. From West Papua's self-determination movement to Brazil's Landless Workers' Movement (MST) to the Arab Spring to the anti-war movement

to the human rights movement, Julian's work with WikiLeaks was celebrated around the world and seen as a tool for change.

*

From a straightforward civil liberties point of view, I found the WikiLeaks
work fascinating. Julian's due process rights were being trampled upon,
first by Sweden and then by the US and UK, and a range of other extrajudicial measures were being applied to undermine WikiLeaks and stop
its publications. Long before meeting Julian, I had seen how important
the publications were for human rights accountability. The release of the
Guantanamo torture manual and assessment reports proved, for example,
that detainees were being mistreated as a matter of policy and had been
locked up for no good reason at all.

But it wasn't until Julian began talking me through the Iraq War logs
that I understood WikiLeaks's political mission and its importance for the
anti-war movement. "If lies can start a war," he said to me, "and we all
know that lies started that war in Iraq, then the truth should be able to stop
it." It was a lofty statement of principle and a line he would repeat later at
the huge Stop the War protest in London; it was a line later proven to be
right. As the result of those WikiLeaks publications and others detailing
US war crimes and human rights abuse, the Iraqi parliament withdrew its
immunity agreement for US troops (which protected US forces from criminal prosecution). The US eventually withdrew from Iraq—ending the war
and US occupation.

Soon after the high-profile publication of the Iraq War Logs, Julian
told me about the quarter million diplomatic cables WikiLeaks was about
to publish in partnership with media organizations around the world. It
would demonstrate the true nature of US imperialism, he said. But he knew
it might result in an unjustified and perhaps even unlawful backlash toward
WikiLeaks and toward him personally. "The Americans are going to chase
me to the end of earth and make life hell," he said to me, "but I have an
obligation to the source who gave WikiLeaks this material, and to the public, to make it available." I was struck by his commitment to free speech
and, without hesitation, I said I would defend him. I had no idea what I was
getting myself into.

The backlash was swift, and beyond anything I had imagined. Julian's personal bank accounts were shut down. WikiLeaks was denied access to its servers. PayPal, Mastercard, Visa, and other service providers were pressured to drop WikiLeaks, cutting off the organization from donations. WikiLeaks also came under a massive "denial of service" attack: a coordinated effort to force it offline. The response was astonishing—people around the world started mirroring the data on the WikiLeaks website to make sure it could never be taken down. It was then that I first marvelled at the power of collective action in resisting censorship by a superpower and its allies. I began to understand the global movement in the tech community of which Julian and WikiLeaks were part.

The US government began to try to discredit the information being published by WikiLeaks, using disinformation to vilify it and Julian. It alleged that that Julian and WikiLeaks "had blood on their hands" because of the publications—even though, ten years on, it was unable to produce evidence in the extradition case that anyone was ever physically harmed because of WikiLeaks' publications. A connected smear was that WikiLeaks had been "reckless" and "irresponsible," and "dumped" information online, when in fact WikiLeaks had engaged in a careful redaction process with its media partners: the *New York Times*, the *Guardian*, *El Pais*, *Le Monde*, *Der Speigel*, and a hundred other media organizations worldwide.

Under President Trump, the US government decided to charge Julian under the Espionage Act. This was the first time in US history that a publisher would face prosecution, as it was common cause that publishers and journalists were considered to be protected by the First Amendment. And so, to make its case, the Trump administration needed to paint WikiLeaks as somehow "other" than mainstream media organizations. But as we had warned since the beginning, it would be impossible to distinguish between what WikiLeaks did and the daily work of other media organizations, which was to receive, possess, and publish classified information in the public interest. The *New York Times* itself raised the so-called *"New York Times* problem": that by prosecuting Julian the US would be criminalizing public interest journalistic practices. This, ultimately, would be the reported reason the Obama administration chose not to indict Julian, but the Trump administration took a different approach. Mike Pompeo, then CIA head, gave a speech in April 2016 claiming that WikiLeaks was a "hostile non-state intelligence agency"; Pompeo warned that the First Amendment freedom would not be a "shield from justice" for Julian.

After 9/11, the US had deliberately and effectively deployed semantics to justify previously unthinkable and unlawful conduct. For example, the phrase "enhanced interrogation techniques" was used to enable the use of torture, and "unlawful enemy combatants" to justify unlawful detention in Guantanamo Bay. A few days after Pompeo's speech, I happened to be on a public platform with Professor David Kaye, who was then the UN special rapporteur on freedom of expression, and I predicted what would come next: by strategically using this nonsensical language, the CIA head was laying the groundwork to justify the prosecution of a publisher and journalist under the Espionage Act. Sadly, I was right: within a week, the attorney general, Jeff Sessions, stated that it was now a priority to prosecute Julian. An unprecedented indictment followed, seeking to put Julian in prison for 175 years—the rest of his life.

Julian had sought asylum in the Ecuadorian embassy in London in 2012, after he lost his final appeal against extradition to Sweden: the Swedish, British, Australian, and US governments refused to seek or offer assurances that Julian would not face extradition onward to the US from Sweden. Sweden had issued an international arrest warrant in late 2010—just as WikiLeaks began publishing Cablegate—seeking Julian's extradition to question him in relation to allegations of sexual misconduct, despite the fact he had offered to answer their questions voluntarily and there had been no decision to charge. The Swedish prosecutor was found in an appeals court to have breached her duties; she finally travelled to London in 2015 to question Julian and decided to drop the case; the UK changed its laws to prevent extradition requests being abused in this way.

As a matter of international law, Julian's asylum in the Ecuadorian embassy protected him from extradition to the US, once he was charged in 2016, but it was not clear that the British authorities would respect this. They didn't. One evening in 2012, not long after Julian had sought refuge in the Ecuadorian embassy, I spotted a headline on Twitter: "Ecuador is not a colony of the UK," quoting the country's president, Rafael Correa. I scrambled to find out what was going on: the British government had sent a diplomatic note to Ecuador saying that if it did not turn Julian over to UK custody, it would withdraw the diplomatic protection of the embassy, meaning that the police could enter the embassy and arrest him.

Within the hour, I had a panicked call from WikiLeaks staff at the embassy saying that a large number of police officers were outside and there was concern they were preparing to raid the embassy and take Julian into UK custody. While I was on the phone frantically trying to convey to the WikiLeaks team and the media that this would be unlawful, hundreds of protesters were turning up outside the embassy in response to the news. I tweeted the Crown Prosecution Service rules about embassy premises and the legal process the UK would have to follow to remove diplomatic protection, and I gave media interviews. It was important to arm the media and protesters with the information about the UK's international obligations to respect the sanctity of the embassy, about Ecuador's right to grant Julian asylum, and about the legal process the UK had to complete before entering the embassy (which could not possibly happen in one night). I emphasized the dangerous precedent the UK would set for its own embassies and diplomatic staff if these laws were violated. I was doing what I could in the circumstances to protect my client: to build the narrative to protect him by highlighting the applicable international law and pointing out the adverse consequences for the UK.

The story about the potential police raid was making headlines around the world. An online live stream was set up by activists outside the embassy, which I followed from home along with my Twitter feed. Social media can be a democratizing force—allowing protesters and activists to convey information directly to the public that the media might not report—and a tool for organizing. I watched this happen, toggling between multiple calls—with Julian too, inside the embassy. The global solidarity was remarkable: those who couldn't turn up in person to protest were organizing to deliver pizzas to the protesters outside the embassy. There was also humor: at one point I enjoyed a brief laugh with a WikiLeaks staffer when iconic London black cabs started turning up outside the embassy with signs saying, "Julian Assange for the airport."

The moment passed and Julian remained safe in the embassy, at least for a while. The outcry reminded me of how much global support there was for Julian and for WikiLeaks and how inspiring it is to see people mobilize so quickly in response to the threat of unlawful government action. It also reminded me of the truth of the concept of movement lawyering to which I had been introduced by another mentor, the legendary American human rights lawyer Michael Ratner: "It takes an activist, a lawyer, and a storyteller to bring about positive social change." As Julian's lawyer, I worked together with the activists to inform their advocacy and the movement to push back on unlawful action. This continues to be an important part of my work: providing a counternarrative for the world's understanding of who Julian is, what he did, and why his actions are protected by the law.

*

Julian's fight against extradition has claimed the lion's share of publicity about him, but it has been only been part of the work. In effect, we have been trying to use the law to push back against a superpower's abuse of power. We have filed cases in the Inter-American Commission and Court of Human Rights; together with Ecuador, we even considered going to the International Court of Justice. We obtained a ruling from the UN Working Group on Arbitrary Detention, declaring that the UK's refusal to let Julian leave the Ecuadorian embassy without fear of arrest and US extradition amounted to an arbitrary deprivation of liberty under international law. The UN decision was critical of the UK and Sweden for refusing to acknowledge Julian's asylum in the Ecuadorian embassy, and the failure of due process in Sweden that had undermined his right to be presumed innocent and left him in a legal black hole. As always, there is an interplay between the legal work and public advocacy: even though the UN ruling was not enforceable in the UK, it was important for our broader advocacy efforts. The UK routinely demands that other countries comply with the rulings of the UN Working Group, as it did in respect of Myanmar's detention of Aung San Suu Kyi. It was really effective, as a political advocacy tool, to be able to point out the ongoing injustice of Julian's situation and the hypocrisy of the UK's refusal to comply with the UN ruling in Julian's case when the UK criticizes other governments for refusing to do so.

Ultimately, our legal efforts to protect Julian from arrest were unsuccessful. In early 2019, a new Ecuadorian administration agreed to hand

Julian over to the UK, and thus the US. We made an urgent application to the Inter-American Commission of Human Rights for provisional measures to prevent this, but the commission refused the application, claiming that Ecuador's obligations under international law were enough to protect Julian. The commission was wrong: Ecuador revoked Julian's asylum without warning—an action that Ecuador's own Human Rights Commission said was unlawful—and British police were invited into the embassy in London to arrest him on April 11, 2019. I had been preparing to visit Julian when I received the call: he had just been arrested and bundled into a police van. There was nothing our legal team could do to stop it.

Within hours, Julian was served with a US extradition request in relation to WikiLeaks publications in 2010 and 2011. The Trump administration had crossed a new legal threshold and had indicted a publisher in a precedent that could be used against the rest of the media. Julian was charged under the Espionage Act for receiving, possessing and publishing US classified information: the Guantanamo Bay files, the Afghan and Iraq War Logs, and the US diplomatic cables. He faces 175 years in prison.

It was the most unsatisfying "I told you so" I have ever delivered. For years, I had felt like a broken record, warning about the precedent that would be set for all of the media by the criminal investigation and prosecution of Julian, cajoling media organizations to defend their own interests by standing with Julian and with WikiLeaks. Finally, with an administration in power that called the media "the enemy of the people," the mainstream media—much of which had repeated and propagated the government othering of Julian and WikiLeaks—got on board. Editorials from the *New York Times* and the *Washington Post* decried the indictment as criminalizing public interest journalistic practices. One wonders whether, had the media taken a more proactive and robust stance earlier, the indictment would have become politically impossible.

Since 2019, the injustice has been stark. I have been visiting a publisher in a high-security prison in the UK, where he was facing extradition to the US and 175 years in prison for the very same publications for which he had been nominated for the Nobel Peace Prize and had won journalism awards the world over.

*

We only had "our day in court," as they say, ten years after this all began. In 2020, we fought the US request to extradite Julian in the high-security court attached to Belmarsh prison, built to try terrorists, and later in the storied Old Bailey, London's Central Criminal Court. For Julian, a huge part of WikiLeaks' mission has been to provide the public with the information it needs to overthrow authoritarian regimes, to end unlawful wars, to highlight injustices around the world (including in West Papua), and to ensure the public's right to know. And so, in court, we argued that his publishing efforts were protected by the right to free speech and driven by legally protected political opinions on transparency and accountability, the need to highlight and expose the US's hypocritical support for politically aligned authoritarian regimes, to end unjust wars, and to expose government human rights abuse and interference with citizens' rights through surveillance.

We presented evidence of how WikiLeaks material had been effectively used in human rights litigation. For example, in Pakistan, the WikiLeaks material was part of the litigation against CIA extrajudicial killings and drone strikes, and was fundamental in shifting public opinion on the use of drones there and elsewhere. Khaled El-Masri, a survivor of US extraordinary rendition and torture, gave evidence about how important WikiLeaks revelations had been in his successful case before the European Court of Human Rights. We also gave the example of how I had cited WikiLeaks cables before the International Court of Justice in support of our arguments about the unlawful occupation of the Chagos Islands by the UK and the US, and about how the UK Supreme Court confirmed the admissibility of the cables as evidence, which will mean the cables are and will continue to be cited in common law courts around the world.

We showed the court how WikiLeaks publications have ensured that people have the information they need to make democratic choices and to hold governments to account. For example, Amnesty International credits Julian and WikiLeaks as being a catalyst of the Arab Spring: the publication of US cables about Tunisia and Egypt, which revealed that those corrupt regimes did not enjoy US support, emboldened the public and the opposition, triggering the revolution. We also debunked the propaganda that WikiLeaks had "dumped" material: to the contrary, WikiLeaks had introduced state-of-the-art digital security and encryption into journalism and engaged in a security and redaction process on each of the publications with its media partners around the world.

American legal experts who gave evidence in Julian's extradition trial explained how the unprecedented prosecution would mean the end of national security journalism, and establish a new legal frontier which would endanger all journalists, everywhere. We called Daniel Ellsberg, the celebrated source of the Pentagon Papers (which revealed the way the US government had lied about the Vietnam War), to testify in Julian's defense. He compared the unlawful actions taken against him by the Nixon administration with the unlawful actions taken by the Trump administration against Julian. Ellsberg's powerful point was that when he was prosecuted under the Espionage Act, the case was thrown out with prejudice due to unlawful actions taken by the Nixon administration—and those unlawful actions paled in comparison to what was happening to Julian under the Trump administration. We had already presented evidence of these extraordinary measures in court, including unlawful spying on Julian inside the embassy—on his medical appointments, his legal meetings, and his lawyers. I had personally been named as a target. The operation went so far so as to go through trash bins to obtain DNA from his baby's diaper and discuss the possibility of poisoning Julian (we learned this thanks to a whistleblower). Ellsberg also described how he too had been vilified by the US government, and cautioned the court and the public on its attitude to Julian: history would vindicate Julian, Ellsberg said, just as he had been vindicated.

One moment during the trial provides a telling insight into Julian, and how he puts the bigger principles before his personal interests. The US was adamantly opposed to Khaled El-Masri, a victim of US rendition and torture, giving evidence in person; this would have been the first time he would have told his story in any court. In the end, a mere summary of his evidence was read into court. Julian was outraged. Despite having already been warned by the judge about speaking in court except through his counsel—and being threatened with removal from the court and having the case heard in his absence—he shouted out, "I will not allow a victim of torture to be censored! I've told my lawyers, my instructions are, he will not be censored!" Julian risked his ability to participate in his own case to try to ensure that a victim of torture would be able to tell his story in court.

On January 4, 2021, a judge blocked Julian's extradition to the US, but not because his case was political or because it threatened free speech around the world. District Court Judge Vanessa Baraitser found that Julian's extradition would be oppressive given the US prison conditions he would face, the decline in his mental health after a decade of persecution, and the fact the medical evidence showed Julian would very likely kill himself if extradited. The evidence showed that Julian would be sent to a supermax facility in the US, where he would be placed under draconian Special Administrative Measures (SAMs), which would further isolate him from his loved ones and his legal team. While we were relieved that judge blocked his extradition, the decision reached the right outcome for the wrong reasons: Julian's extradition was barred, but the judge rejected all of our free speech arguments, setting a terrible precedent for all media workers in the UK.

The US was quick to appeal the decision—and shift the goalposts. Unhappy with the outcome, it offered a conditional, diplomatic assurance about prison conditions to get around the judge's decision. Amnesty International and others have pointed out how US assurances have not been respected in the past and cannot be trusted. Further, the assurance in Julian's case was equivocal and could be reversed if Julian committed "any future act that met the test" for the imposition of SAMs. Since the trial judge's decision, we had learned—thanks to a Yahoo News investigation based on interviews with US government sources—that the unlawful actions of the US were even worse than we had known. The CIA had planned to kidnap and assassinate Julian in London; this was the same agency that would decide on Julian's prison conditions were he to be extradited.

Despite this new evidence, the appeal courts found that the US assurance could be accepted and Julian could be extradited, despite the suicide risk. We sought leave to appeal to the Supreme Court, the highest UK court, arguing that the assurance came after the judge's decision and therefore could not be properly contested at trial. But the Supreme Court refused to hear it. The decision on whether to extradite Julian was in the hands of the UK Home Secretary.

On 17 June 2022, the Home Secretary ordered his extradition to the US. We filed appeals and, at the time of writing, we await the US government response. We continue to raise arguments about free speech, abuse of process, and the political nature of the case to try to stop the extradition. So our decade-long legal battle continues. Julian has already spent more than three years in a high-security prison because of the US extradition request—and our ongoing appeals mean he will, unjustly, be there for years to come—unless there is a political decision to put this case to an end. There is a huge amount of public support for Julian: in October 2022, thousands of people joined a protest in London and formed a human chain around the British Parliament to demand his freedom. As I walked around the human chain to thank people for coming, it became clear to me that people turned up because they understood the way Julian's case affects them and their rights. The protests will continue – and it is time those in power start to listen.

This story is about an injustice served on one man by two governments that claim to be global leaders in human and civil rights: the US and the UK. It is a story about the denial of his human rights, his liberty, for protected actions he took in the public interest. But in truth, this story has never just been about Julian and WikiLeaks—for him, or for me as his lawyer. While he is the lightning rod, the mission he has pursued through WikiLeaks is far broader, as are the reasons for the backlash. He is being targeted as a figurehead of a movement for transparency and accountability, as a deterrent to any other whistleblowers, editors, and journalists who might publish what the powerful don't want you to know.

*

As I reflect on two of my most well-known clients, my work on the case against Julian has not been so different from my work on West Papua.

As counsel to Benny Wenda and the West Papuan liberation movement, I have been working to use international law to build power in their movement. For almost two decades, Benny and I have been building the international law case for self-determination. In 2018, fifteen years after I had left West Papua in despair, I stood up in the International Court of Justice for the island state Vanuatu (which has long supported West Papuan independence) to argue for the legal principles to ensure West Papua's claim for self-determination against Indonesia. We had intervened in the advisory opinion proceedings about the Chagos Islands in the Indian Ocean, in which Mauritius claimed the UK had excised the islands unlawfully to make way for a US military base (WikiLeaks documents demonstrating US and UK imperialism were cited by numerous states in submissions to the Court in support of Mauritius). The case raised legal issues directly relevant to West Papua's status and we intervened to ensure, through our submissions, that West Papua was protected. It worked: in a blow to American imperialism and British colonization, the ICJ gave its opinion in favor of Mauritius, and through the law it laid down, West Papua's claim is supported and protected. This does not necessarily mean the UN General Assembly is going to vote to ensure that Indonesia gives West Papua a proper referendum to determine its future, but it's an important result on which the liberation movement can stand, and continue its campaign.

As it has been with Julian, a large part of my job as Benny's lawyer has been to simply do whatever I can to protect him, so that he can carry on his work for the benefit of the West Papuan people. After his escape from Indonesia, I helped him obtain asylum in the UK. When Benny was subjected to an Interpol "red notice" by Indonesia in 2011, meaning that he could be subjected to arrest and extradited to Indonesia, we challenged it before the Commission for the Control of Interpol's Files—and we won. Many countries were using the Interpol system to pursue activists in exile, and Benny's was the first case using Interpol's own constitution to challenge such abuse. The work we did for Benny allowed him to continue to travel for his work for the movement, and it created a precedent for many other dissidents around the world. We have used the law to build power in the West Papuan movement and to defend the movement's leader from arbitrary and unlawful state actions. Similarly, in Julian's case, our legal team is using all the legal avenues available, to defend and protect him, and to establish a precedent that we hope will protect others in the future. By doing what *we* can to protect Julian's ability to do what *he* does for the benefit of the public and the transparency movement, we have been trying to protect the space for other journalists, publishers, and whistleblowers to do the same.

In this work, I have learned that the law is a language of power and it is a lever, but it is not the only lever. The law has been essential in ensuring that Benny Wenda has been protected from Indonesian persecution. The law is also an essential support for West Papua's claim to self-determination. But in the end, it's not enough that we are right as a matter of international law. We need people to protest and for the politics to change. And for the politics to change, we need the law to help build a narrative, through our public advocacy, that will bring more countries at the United Nations on board to give effect to West Papuans' rights. We have also used international law to show that Julian's treatment by the UK, the US, and Sweden has been unlawful, and this has been a powerful tool in our public advocacy effort. We have set out the legal dangers of the prosecution under the First Amendment and now have unanimous support from free speech organizations, human rights organizations, and mainstream media organizations.

But even if we ultimately win the extradition case in the British courts, that won't protect Julian from extradition in any other country than the UK. If the US does not drop this case, Julian could still face extradition from any other country, including from Australia, should he return home. Ultimately, the resolution of this case once and for all may be political: a political decision by the new US administration to put an end to a case that should never have been started and that sets a dangerous precedent for press freedom.

Further Reading: On WikiLeaks: Julian Assange, ed., *The WikiLeaks Files: The World According to the US Empire* (Verso, 2015); Tariq Ali and Margaret Kunstler, eds., *In Defense of Julian Assange* (OR Books, 2019); Nils Melzer, *The Trial of Julian Assange* (Bloomsbury, 2022). On West Papua: Carmel Budiarjo and Liem Soei Liong, *West Papua: The Obliteration of a People* (Tapol, 1988); John Saltford, *The United Nations and the Indonesian Takeover of West Papua 1962–1969: The Anatomy of Betrayal* (Routledge, 2006); Pieter Drooglever, *An Act of Free Choice—Decolonisation and the Right to Self-Determination in West*

Papua (One World, 2009); Jason McCleod, *Merdeka & the Morning Star: Civil Resistance in West Papua* (UQ Press, 2015). Cases: *El-Masri v. the former Yugoslav Republic of Macedonia* [2012] ECHR 2067; R *(on the application of Bancoult No 3) v. Secretary of State for Foreign and Commonwealth Affairs* [2018] UKSC 3; *Legal Consequences of the Separation of the Chagos Archipelago from Mauritius in 1965*, Advisory Opinion, ICJ 534 (ICJ 2019), February 25, 2019; *Re Assange's Application (No. 2)* [2018] 2 WLUK 274; *United States v. Assange* [2021] EW Misc 1 (MagC); *United States v. Assange* [2021] EWHC 2528 (Admin); *United States v. Assange* [2021] EWHC 3313 (Admin); *United States v. Assange* [2022] CO/150/2021.

Building Spaces of Hope:
Working for Indigenous Peoples' Rights in Mexico

ALEJANDRA ANCHEITA

I will never forget my first visit to Unión Hidalgo, the indigenous Zapotec community in Oaxaca we have been working with since 2011. The community had signed individual land lease contracts for the development of a wind farm and I was startled by how ashamed the leadership felt about it, once they realized they had been tricked.

Unión Hidalgo is on the Tehuantepec isthmus, where the wind speed is very high; it is therefore an area that had attracted the attention from a big number of multinational energy companies. Some members of the community believed they could earn extra income renting their land while still maintaining the right to work on it. But they soon realized this was not the case. They no longer had access to their own land and, when they tried to nullify the contracts, they found the legal process expensive and complicated; in order to take action, they needed to travel to the capital and have a lawyer. By the time they contacted our organization, ProDESC, there was already one wind park being built on their territory and more than twenty-seven in the region. At that moment the elders of the community wanted us to challenge the project, developed by the Spanish company Renovalia, and to stop another one in the works by a Mexican subsidiary of the French energy utility EDF. With this new project, fields of windmills would encircle and lock up the community, shutting down any room for decision-making on how, where, and when to develop in a sustainable, self-determined manner. If the EDF project came to be, it would probably force them to leave their territory.

At that first meeting in May 2011, I watched in dismay as the elders almost cried with shame. They told us that they felt they had been tricked, and now feared they had sold out the younger generations. They felt helpless for not realizing what the corporation was up to, and embarrassed that they had not been clever enough to understand the magnitude of what they were signing away. As I always do in such a situation, I told them how there were communities like them all over the world. There is a global trend of corporations dispossessing communities of their land: they were not the only ones to feel tricked.

The Unión Hidalgo community had contacted us because of the work we had done for another Oaxacan community fighting wind farms, and also in the north of Mexico, where my organization was suing the Canadian mining company Excellon, on behalf of an *ejido*. An *ejido* is an entity that owns agricultural land communally on behalf of a community: in the state of Durango, the *ejido* of La Sierrita had entered into a land lease agreement with Excellon. The Canadians took advantage of the community with unfair clauses and with no obligation beyond the leasing agreement, so the *ejido* wanted to cancel the contract. As one elder said during a meeting with the community: while money is nice, "if we don't have any environmental clauses and social clauses in the contract, in fifteen years we will have nothing!"

And so in 2008 ProDESC started advising La Sierrita in order to renegotiate the contract under fair and equitable conditions. As a consequence, Excellon had no choice but to sign a new contract that included environmental and social clauses for the sake of the community. For the next years, the company fulfilled their financial obligations but neglected the environmental and social clauses, breaching the agreement. In 2012, the *ejido*, with ProDESC legal counseling, started litigation against Excellon. It was not an easy process, since we had to overcome many challenges that demonstrated how pro-corporate interests were embedded in Mexico's institutions. From the court to the local police, many advocated for the company—even though La Sierrita was comprised of their own fellow citizens.

It took four years, but we finally won the cancellation of the contract. This was a huge loss of face and capital for the Canadian corporation, given that it had already started the extraction process. In the meantime, my organization and I were demonized. Several newspapers ran articles saying that we were the single greatest threat to development in Mexico, and even *El Economista*, one of the most influential financial journals in Mexico, called me nothing less than "the devil's advocate."

There were death threats, and vigilante action outside our office, and I was frequently overwhelmed by feelings of uncertainty and danger. A little later I became pregnant with my son, and I could not but think of my own father, a human rights lawyer himself in the state of Chiapas, who defended Indigenous peoples' rights against landowners. He died in unclear circumstances in 1984, when I was eight years old.

It was only when I was at law school myself, a decade after his death—in the heat of the Zapatista rebellion of the mid-1990s—that I really began to understand that my father had died because of his work and commitment to social justice. We students provided support to the peasant insurgents, and this came to define our worldview: before long, I was in Chiapas myself, working as an activist. This made my mother anxious, and she wanted me to understand what was at stake if I continued on this path. She spoke to me for the first time about my father's funeral, and how loved he was by the communities he served. People walked great distances just to attend the ceremony, and they told my mother that they saw him as one of the only honest lawyers who worked with them. But the price he paid for this commitment was very high.

It had been a different era, of course: he did not have the rule of law to work with, as I do now; nor a judicial system, which is governed by an excellent constitution. Still, I often think of my father in relation to my own work. The contrast between his story and mine suggests a distinction between the lawyer as leader and the lawyer as organizer. In my work, communities have often expected a leader: a man with all the answers. I decided from the start that this was not going to be my position. I am not interested in re-creating those patriarchal power relations. I want to build a collective. My father was a lawyer as leader partly because he was a man. I am a lawyer, a woman, and a community organizer who is not interested in using law in a traditional way. My approach is collective and not everyone understands that, communities and other lawyers alike.

At the height of the La Sierrita conflict, I was already very visibly pregnant—something, frankly, I had concealed in the early stages, in part because I didn't want people to typecast me as hormonal and unpredictable.

But at a human rights forum we ran in the community there was no hiding it anymore: I was only weeks away from giving birth. We had invited communities from all over the country, academics and agrarian and law experts, and we were discussing the extractive industry and the damage this industry causes. The people attending were very surprised that I was still working, given my state, and some even admonished me for this. But they treated me with such respect and kindness. I had been working with them for nine years, after all, and in the nature of the way ProDESC works, we had become close. They were more than "clients."

One of the elders told me my unborn son could be part of the next generation of lawyers helping communities like theirs in future. On the one hand I found it very beautiful, that they were thinking of my son as a seed of hope, probably not for them, but for future generations of people living in communities and being threatened by corporations. They were imagining a heritage of seeking justice, not just from my father through me and then to my unborn son, but more broadly in society. But on the other hand, I thought, *Oh no! I want my son to have a chance to choose his own life, perhaps as an artist or a dancer, where he doesn't have to work the craziest hours and risk his life!*

*

My legal team and I learned an important lesson at La Sierrita, one I was now determined to apply at Unión Hidalgo: We have come to term it "preventive litigation strategy." By the time we won our victory at La Sierrita, the scars were already deep in the community and on the environment, given the extraction that had already taken place. In the future, I resolved, we would need work with communities to stop such damage before it even began.

At ProDESC, we have come to see litigation as only one step. We balance it with another: effective community building, in an effort to generate resilience. These cases often go on for years, after all. We start the process by conducting what we call a pre-diagnosis. We check which violations are occurring (land rights, labor rights, freedom of association and collective bargaining) and assess what internal problems there might be. We also spend time doing community organizing, finding out about the current internal structures of decision-making, and discussing what changes the community might want in the future. Our primary concern is that the community becomes stronger, as a collective.

And we do not always measure our success by legal victory. At Unión Hidalgo, after all, we were not able to prevent the development of Renovalia's wind power project. But after four years, in 2016, the Agrarian Court in Tuxtepec, Oaxaca, gave us an important victory, by recognizing the communal ownership of the lands in Unión Hidalgo and the application of the Agrarian Law to the case. We would not have been able to win this victory, were it not for what we had achieved while preparing for all those cases we lost: the recovery of communal life within Unión Hidalgo, and a much greater awareness, in the general public, of the existence of the *comuneros* and their plight.

Once we had this victory in the Agrarian Court, we had the legitimate authority to question the legal merits of EDF's wind power project. The company had argued that the lands were private and therefore could be subject to private leasing. But now, with the recognition of the *comuneros'* legitimacy to bring cases before a tribunal, the company did not have the last word. The first thing we did with this legitimate authority was to challenge the development of the project: a thirty-year license to generate electricity had been granted to the company by the Energy Regulatory Commission without the proper consultation mandated by law.

The "consultation," such as it was, had been done immediately after a terrible earthquake on September 7, 2017, with many members of the community still mourning their dead families. The houses were destroyed, the schools were destroyed, the market was destroyed, they didn't have potable water: it was a really bad situation. We showed how the local government and EDF's local partners came with medicines and trailers to "help" the community, but only in exchange for moving forward with the "Indigenous consultation" to speed the construction of the wind farm. A district court in the state of Oaxaca found that this was a violation of one of the requirements of an Indigenous consultation, which is that it must be free of coercion or violence. We won the case, and the district judge set clear standards for the development of a free, prior, and informed consultation in Unión Hidalgo.

Of course, this victory was just a stepping stone to other battles. When the Indigenous consultation began again, the company intervened in a way calculated to silent critical voices, and even to spark violent conflict: by co-opting assemblies held in the community as part of the consultation process, as reported by community members. Its approach was to create new committees of people from Unión Hidalgo, sympathetic to the corporation, as legitimate actors participating in the consultations.

Of course, there are different opinions at Unión Hidalgo, as there are in any community. You could summarize it as "economic development" on the one hand, and "self-determination" on the other. The younger people are more interested in developing the wind parks: they left the countryside to go to the cities anyway and are convinced that leasing the land is a way out of poverty. The older people grew up working the land and have a deep relationship with it, with the wind and the trees and the water. It is part of their identity. These different perspectives either divide a community or make it stronger. Unfortunately, companies take advantage of such diversity, and they push people to antagonize one another. A divided community is less likely to be successful when demanding the respect of their human rights.

But antagonism, when strategically channeled, can be a powerful tool. In the Unión Hidalgo case, the company and the government argued that some groups within the community were troublemakers. Part of the work ProDESC did in this case was to unify the community under one objective—defending their land and territory from the wind farm corporations trying to make a profit from them. We achieved that as part of a long process within the community, in which we analyzed the main causes of their human rights violations and identified the people who were behind them. It mostly came down to a few stakeholders: some government actors, the company that was building the project, and local gangs involved in drug trafficking. With this collective recognition of the causes, ProDESC managed to unite the community and channeled their antagonism instead toward those responsible for the human rights violations from which everyone suffered.

A big part of ProDESC's responsibility, in Unión Hidalgo as elsewhere, was to act as a clearinghouse of information. We were very involved in informing different media outlets, our allies, and our followers on social media about the situation. But we also realized we needed to buy some time for the community to organize itself, and after some research we saw that we could do so through the Organization for Economic Cooperation and Development (OECD)'s Guidelines for Multinational Enterprises, applicable to both Mexico and France as member states.

We argued that EDF had violated OECD guidelines regarding human rights due diligence, because it did not take into consideration that Unión Hidalgo is both an agrarian community, like La Sierrita, and an Indigenous Zapotec community, protected by Mexican and international law. We filed a complaint before the OECD's National Contact Point in France: partly because the National Contact Point in Mexico was not responsive, and partly because the responsible company was French and we wanted to build solidarity in France against the EDF's overseas activities. Other human rights organizations became interested, and in 2018, a trade union delegation of French EDF workers visited Unión Hidalgo to witness what their employers were doing abroad.

This awareness and solidarity was particularly important, because we were depicted by some media and also some conservation organizations as working against something "good"—a green initiative saving the planet! We have had to emphasize that we are not fighting against the transition to sustainable energy; we are fighting against the imposition of an industry that does not respect human rights. Any investment that is going to be good for the future must adhere to international principles of human rights. Communities like Unión Hidalgo are not against green energy either; they are against being evicted from their own territory, and not being consulted about what happens on their own land. We must remember that green energy is mainly a business that is earning corporations a huge profit that is not shared with local communities.

With this in mind, we made the point of bringing a community leader with us when we went to Paris in June 2018 to follow up on the complaint and attend the OECD Forum on Responsible Business Conduct: Guadalupe Ramirez, a wise and sharp old woman and an active part of the committee of resistance against the wind parks in Unión Hidalgo. She is also particularly respected because she inhabits the traditional role of

goola: a woman in charge of the most important festival in the community, Las Velas. Dressed in her magnificent embroidered vest, she took her
responsibility seriously in Paris, and explained what the real effect of this
"green energy" would be on her community. I could speak to the technicalities—how the situation was violating the national and international legal
frameworks for responsible business conduct, and what corporate and state
obligations were—but she could give it a human face. Far away from her
home, Guadalupe and her words brought attention to what is important not
only to Unión Hidalgo, but all over the world where Indigenous communities do not have the platforms to make their voices heard.

We went as far as we could with the OECD mechanism: structural
deficiencies and conflicts of interest within its members did not provide
substantial remedy, so we decided to step out of the procedure. Still, the
National Contact Point identified important breaches in EDF's human
rights due diligence, even if only weakly addressed in its final statement.
Back in Mexico, the newly reconstituted "Indigenous consultation"
carried on. In October 2020, together with ProDESC and our partner organization, the European Centre for Constitutional and Human
Rights, community members filed a lawsuit against EDF for breaching
its legal obligations regarding human rights due diligence related to the
wind power project: Unión Hidalgo stands to be the first Indigenous
community in the Americas to bring a multinational company before
French courts. One way or another, we have succeeded in suspending the
construction of a wind power project with the actual engagement of the
effected community, and have ensured that it has the leading voice.

When colleagues and community members get impatient, I have to
remind them (and myself!) that this is a long game. It took us four years
just to win the right to challenge EDF on behalf of the agrarian community. Our goal now is to continue helping develop the resilience of Unión
Hidalgo for the long battle ahead. And so we carry on: supporting the community to organize, to claim its rights in courts, to advocate for its situation
in national and transnational forums, and to get the attention of the media
about the case and their demands.

*

In my work, my thoughts have often circled back to my father. He was of a generation of lawyers who were less protected in their work and had to operate in a very solitary way. Mexico is different now: things are a little more democratic, and electoral politics do play a role in how campaigns work out. Politicians want to be reelected, in other positions or even as advisers of transnational corporations, so sometimes they side with the community. Given this shift, I wanted to work differently from the way my father did: to create an organization and approach issues collectively. When a public face is needed, I have no qualms stepping into the foreground, but often one needs to step back and develop more layers of leadership. This allows for more people to be involved in the defense of human rights in a proactive way, with the certainty that they will continue even when the leader is gone. Developing different layers of leadership ensures the continuity of collective work and allows new generations of human rights defenders to take a space within the broader movement.

Lawyers always want to win, and I imagine this was as true for my father as it is for me. I'm very strict with the lawyers on our cases: working collaboratively with communities does not mean losing the rigor you need to win the case. But litigating such cases in a country like Mexico—weak in human rights and strong on interests of corporations—is complex. You're not going to win the case just because you're an excellent lawyer. And in this context, we must conduct a power analysis: winning the case is important but building power in the community is even more so. Indeed, if we lose a case, we have the commitment to continue organizing.

Many lawyers, especially in Mexico, question my approach and find it strange. I question it myself: you have to do so, in order to rethink your strategy and evaluate the impacts. I have been struck by the way that lawyers from countries where there have been strong human rights movements—such as South Africa, Brazil, and India—seem to understand instantly. These global networks are important, particularly for human rights lawyers from the Global South. European lawyers are attracted to my approach, but they don't consider adopting it themselves, even when they are working in situations with similar power dynamics, such as in Syria or Papua New Guinea. The power dynamics inside the human rights movement are rarely analyzd, and as defenders and activists we need to be wise to how we reproduce dynamics of subordination or discrimination between each other or with the people that we work with. This imbalance of power can hamper a collective project between lawyers and organizations from the Global North and Global South. Addressing it is part of the solution, as is constantly engaging in negotiations of understanding.

My own work, and my reflection on my father's work, highlights the distinction between lawyer as leader and lawyer as organizer. I think by being the latter we have a better chance of giving communities the necessary space to fight their own battles while still playing a supportive legal role. Still, it is never one or the other: you must be both leader and organizer to create meaningful and lasting resistance to the global trend of corporations eroding community rights. Doing this work in a country like Mexico is also a challenge when you are a woman and a mother. The level of violence against female human rights defenders is out of control and, alarmingly, that violence could also reach our families. In 2020 alone, eight female human rights defenders have been killed, and nine more suffered assassination attempts among other cases of intimidation. In the community of Unión Hidalgo, one of the most prominent female leaders defending the community's land and territory was almost kidnapped.

Having my son was one of the most important decisions of my life. His arrival changed my perspectives about life: about my past, my childhood, and my father's activism, as well as his death; about my present as a human rights defender; and about my future, as a mother. I completely understand how committed my mother was to my future, as her daughter, and now to my son's future, as her grandson. I now have to balance my personal decisions with my political ones. One of my responsibilities as a mother is a commitment to build spaces of hope for him and others, and to believe that it is worth fighting for a dignified life.

Update: In June 2022, after a thorough pressure campaign, the Mexican Federal Commission of Electricity finally and definitively cancelled its energy supply contracts with the French corporation EDF. The wind park will not be built. Three months later, in September 2022, Oaxaca's First District Court ruled that all of the community's land is collectively owned. This is a pathbreaking precedent, because it means corporations may no longer sign individual land leases with private entities when building wind parks in the region. Taken together, these two victories for Unión Hidalgo mean that governments can be pressured into doing the right thing, if there is a strong movement from communities to sustain the fight. Legally, the precedent definitely diminishes power inequalities between indigenous communities and corporations. Now, these communities can even ask for the dismantling of existing wind parks if they have been built under unlawful, individual land leases.

Further Reading and Viewing: On the Union Hidalgo conflict: ProDESC, *Wind Resistance*, YouTube, November 2021; ARTE.tv, *Winds of Anger*, YouTube, December 2021; ProDESC, ECCHR & CCFD-Terre Solidaire, *Vigilance Switched Off*, June 2021, avaliable at ecchr.edu; ProDESC & GI-ESCR, "UN Experts call on all EDF's key stakeholders to uphold their human rights obligations in the development of a wind farm in Unión Hidalgo, Mexico," 2021, available at prodesc.org.mx. On human rights violations and renewable energies: Business and Human Rights Resource Center, *Renewable Energy & Human Rights Benchmark*, June 2020. On gender justice and the transition to renewables energy: The Global Initiative for Economic, Social and Cultural Rights, *Renewable Energy and Gender Justice*, December 2020. On genuine transnational collaborations: Alejandra Ancheita and Carolijn Terwindt, "Towards Genuine Transnational Collaboration between Human Rights Activists from Global North and the Global South," Forschunsjournal Soziale Bewegungen, September 2015.

The River Brings Oil: Working for Indigenous Peoples' Rights in the Peruvian Amazon

MARISSA VAHLSING and BENJAMIN HOFFMAN

Marissa

February 2012

I should have expected rain like this. We *were* in the middle of the Amazon. But when we had set out in the *peke-peke* canoe an hour earlier, the sky had been spotless and the sun unforgiving. I thought we could make it from town to the village before the sky did anything dramatic. I was wrong.

"Ben, did we bring a dry bag for the documents? The ink is running. I guess this is what we get for planning ahead."

"Yeah, back here. Just roll the papers up and hand them back. Glad we actually get a chance to use this thing and I haven't just been carrying it around for nothing. Always prepared!"

I passed Ben the rolls of poster paper that we had populated with our workshop agenda and presentation points earlier that morning. We were on our way to Nueva Chacra, an Indigenous community in the Peruvian Amazon struggling with the presence of Bain Oil, an American oil and gas company, on its traditional lands.* The company's subpar infrastructure and careless practices had resulted in continuous spills into community streams and tributaries. Fish were dying. People were getting sick, and studies showed elevated levels of lead and cadmium in people's blood. In response to complaints by the people of Nueva Chacra about the spills, Bain Oil had built a defunct internet tower for the community. It wasn't clear that the tower had an electricity source to power it so that it could work, but there it stood, a testament to the company's "goodwill."

---

* Although this account is based upon real events and conversations, we have opted to give the community and the oil company fictitious names so as to protect the confidentiality of the stories, perspectives, and strategies that its people shared with us.

Over the previous few years, the people of Nueva Chacra had worked with a number of Peruvian and international NGOs to try various strategies to force Bain Oil to improve its practices, with limited success. There had been online petitions, know-your-rights workshops, international campaigns, multi-sectoral governmental dialogues, and complaints to international development banks that funded the oil company. Anthropology students had visited the community to study the situation. And more than one ayahuasca tourist had gotten lost in the area after wandering over to check out the scene. ("We usually give them a family to stay with in the village until they realize who, and where, they are; we teach them to cook or fish, and when they are ready, they simply leave," one of the village leaders had explained.)

Ben and I, two white lawyers from the United States, were traveling to Nueva Chacra at the invitation of its leaders to pitch a new idea: litigation against Bain Oil in its home court in the United States. We were working with EarthRights International, an organization that uses training, campaigns, and legal strategies to help affected rights-holders hold corporations and governments accountable for human rights and environmental abuses. We had supported other Indigenous peoples in the Amazon to sue US companies in their home courts, and the abuses we saw here were a variation on an all-too-common tragic theme: oil company enters, thinks no one is watching, thinks it has a god-given right to profit from exploiting land people have called home for generations, thinks the Peruvian government won't care (it doesn't), and employs some combination of trickery, sabotage, and misrepresentation to try to force the local Indigenous community leaders to put up with it. We were hoping litigation might be a powerful strategy to break this pattern.

This wasn't our first time visiting Nueva Chacra; for the past few years we had been getting to know them and their history, learning about the strategies they were using to try to bring the company to heel. At the end of the day, the only thing that ever really seemed to make the company blink was when the people of Nueva Chacra "took the wells." This typically involved dozens of community members shutting down the oil wells and setting up camp nearby to ensure the workers didn't come back to restart them until the community's demands were met. The reason it worked was because it affected the only thing the company cared about: its bottom line.

Like taking the wells, litigation would affect the company's bottom line. But it might do more: because it could result in the company paying reparations for the harms the community had suffered, it could force the company to internalize the environmental and human costs to its current business practices, rather than just pushing all of those costs onto the people of Nueva Chacra. And the company might actually adopt measures to prevent future harms instead of continuing the status quo. More broadly, the general state of corporate impunity would be challenged, and all companies engaging in similar practices would be on notice.

At Nueva Chacra, Bain Oil had been stringing the people along in a "negotiation" process, promising the men work clearing brush in exchange for use of their land for oil extraction. The terms were laughable and the people knew it. The amount of money the company was offering in total, 40,000 soles—about $15,000 USD—was barely enough to cover the purchase of the protective gear needed to carry out the work. The leaders of Nueva Chacra demanded that Bain Oil pay for an independent study of the environmental harms its spills had caused, but the company countered that it would do so only if the study also calculated the positive "social impacts" conferred by Bain Oil onto Nueva Chacra. In other words: only if the study accounted for the cost of the internet tower the company had provided.

"According to that logic, the company will be sending the community a bill!" I had exclaimed out loud when I had first heard about the company's offer.

We both grew quiet as the canoe left the main waterway and started approaching the outskirts of the village. Thatched roofs clustered together began appearing over the top of the riverbank and a large sign bore the name "Nueva Chacra" with the initials "CCNN" signalling that it was a *comunidad nativa*, or native community.

Ben gestured to the water. "See, when it rains like this, the tributaries flood and the rainwater mixes with the runoff from the oil wells. This is what the *apu* was explaining to us," he recalled, thinking back to a conversation we had had with the elected village leader. "A rising tide lifts all oil. Look over there."

I looked. We were now approaching one of the tributaries closest to the village and there was a sheen on the water as it churned toward us. Fishing boats clustered near a stairway that descended to the river. Women washed clothes from the back of the boats while children splashed nearby. Moments later, we had to duck our heads as our *peke-peke* passed under oil pipes that were dangling overhead.

"Wait, so, whenever it rains and the river is high, these pipes are basically at canoe level in the water? And any villager that is out on the water risks getting clotheslined?" I asked.

"Guess so. And here I thought we had to be on the lookout for snakes and shit."

"But isn't the rainy season half the year?"

"Yup."

"Can't the company just loop these pipes through its nonfunctioning internet tower instead? That would at least get them out of the water."

"Ha."

*

Ben
February 2012

"We need your advice on how to argue for better terms in a labor contract that the company is offering us."

Marissa and I were taken aback and exchanged a confused glance in response to this comment from Juan, a highly respected figure in Nueva Chacra. Was this really the community's priority? What about a remedy for the company's continued pollution of the rivers—isn't that why we were there? Didn't they want to talk about litigation?

We glanced around at the faces of the forty men and women gathered on benches in the large, covered meeting space for our workshop, trying to gauge their reaction. While Juan was not a formal member of the community's elected leadership, his opinion carried weight, as he had spent years building connections in the closest major city and had started several economic initiatives in the community. Juan's kindness, and his perfect Spanish, made him an easy and valuable ally in our early visits to the community. This was an important response to get right.

Before we could respond, the rain picked up again, and soon we were unable to hear anything over the loud crashing of the heavy showers against the corrugated metal roof. Some children ran by the meeting place, clothes completely drenched, laughing and oblivious to their mother's shouts for them to take cover. Glancing at the sky, and anticipating that the rain could last a while, several of the women got up and started passing around bowls of *masato*, a milky fermented cassava drink consumed throughout the region. Marissa and I took advantage of the natural intermission to put our heads together and think through a response, interrupted only by the occasional sip of *masato* we accepted.

Juan's intervention had come at the end of a short presentation we had given, drawing on our experience as US-trained lawyers, on how US corporations make decisions and what motivates their actions. I had started the presentation with the idea that most corporations will do whatever it takes to maximize profits, and likely even feel legally obligated to their shareholders to do so. That said, there are limits on company action imposed by law and social pressure. When affected communities, or the state, effectively mobilize those limits, the company will attempt to behave well to avoid costly litigation, fines, or protest actions. Those limits are not effective, however, if the company believes that the punishments are not severe, or that there is systemic under-enforcement. In those situations, the company will prioritize profit and often behave poorly, which likely explained, at least in part, what was happening here.

Marissa then discussed how it was now up to the community to increase the pressure on the company's US executives to recognize and fix the problems. Marissa explained that there were lots of ways to apply such pressure—and that litigation was one of the most powerful. Nonetheless, she continued, a company like Bain Oil is likely to use different strategies to try to undermine litigation, including running out the statute of limitations on legal claims, offering a cheap settlement with technical language to try to buy off the communities, and dividing the community from within.

It was when we had finished our presentation and asked for any comments or questions that Juan had stood up from his spot on a bench in the back of the hall to ask for our help negotiating better terms for their labor.

Juan's question didn't come out of nowhere. We already knew about the 40,000 Soles that the company offered to clear brush near company pipes, without providing uniforms or safety equipment—and we knew that lack of safety equipment had contributed to some community members being harmed on similar projects in the past. "We don't want to be cheated, and if the company will do everything to minimize their costs as you just told us, 40,000 Soles is too low," Juan said. "Are there laws that we can use to justify higher wages? How much do other communities receive? We don't have much experience yet with these types of labor contracts."

Now, under the cover of the rain, Marissa and I debated how to respond. "It sounds like he is proposing a form of *acompañamiento*," I suggested, referring to the type of lawyer-client relationship common in Peru where the lawyer "accompanies" members of the community in each of its struggles, regardless of the subject matter or the lawyer's opinion of the strategy, to help strengthen the power of the community to achieve its goals. Here, the people of Nueva Chacra felt vulnerable with the arrival of the foreign oil company, and their lives had changed in a variety of ways. They frequently felt at risk of being cheated, whether it was about compensation for environmental and health harms or labor contracts. Providing legal support and advice as the community adapted to the presence of the oil company, even if such support and advice was limited to matters of employment contract negotiation, *would* be an important means of working with the community to amplify their power.

This resonated with our law school lessons about some forms of "community lawyering." It was our mutual commitment to this type of lawyering—particularly with respect to corporate accountability for environmental and human rights—that had helped solidify my friendship with Marissa as classmates during law school and that had led us to work together with EarthRights. And it was certainly an affirming experience, less than a year after graduating, to be riding in that *peke-peke*, surrounded by the lush Amazon forest, confident that we were finally implementing that model of lawyering we had learned about.

"But would we really be serving EarthRights' and our own goals of defending human rights and the environment if we help them obtain a labor contract with the same company that has been polluting their water?" Marissa asked, taking the question right out of my mouth.

"And a contract that might actually *facilitate* oil extraction, and do nothing to address the frequent spills, which are very dangerous to their health?" I added. Marissa and I both paused to think.

In that moment, our broad goal of building power in the community felt at odds with our more specific goal of pursuing a particular notion of justice for environmental and health harms. Of the many things Marissa and I had discussed in canoes over the past year, this was one of the big questions: When is it appropriate to limit our support, and what is the impact of the act of drawing such limits on community power?

We had been introduced to the people of Nueva Chacra by local partners and Indigenous federation leaders because they thought, given our experience suing US companies, we might be able to work with them to develop a new strategy to address the company's pollution. But, as we could have anticipated, the people of Nueva Chacra had a variety of goals, including some that were, understandably, of a much higher immediate priority—like the improved employment opportunities and economic income promised by a better labor contract.

We would have a lot to discuss on the canoe back upriver. But Juan needed an answer right now, as did the forty other men and women looking to us, once the rain died down.

We decided to be practical, rather than philosophical. "We have only recently opened an office in Peru," I started, "and without a Peruvian lawyer on staff familiar with these issues of Peruvian law, we are limited in the type of advice that we can provide. We are US-trained attorneys with expertise in US and international law, and although we wish we could accompany you in every strategy we simply don't have the knowledge to be able to provide legal advice on this issue at the moment."

Marissa then jumped in: "With our current resources, what we can offer is to work with you to bring international litigation about the environmental harms if that is what you are interested in. The hope is that this will strengthen your position. For other issues, we can connect you with other NGOs and allies to assist."

We had directly and intentionally taken a step back from *acompañamiento*, offering the community a much more limited menu, to address a limited set of goals. We felt frustration that our limitations prevented us from providing the type of integrated advocacy in which we deeply wanted to engage. But we also felt a certain amount of comfort in being honest about these limitations, as it helped us engage in a frank dialogue with the community about our own vision of justice and the strategies that we were prepared to help support.

We went on to describe what the process of litigation against the oil company in the United States would be, explaining the costs and benefits, possible outcomes, various challenges, and how such litigation might contribute to changing corporate behavior. It was a strategy that we believed in, that we thought could contribute to strengthening the community's power to advance change. But we recognized that litigation is not always the right strategy for every community, and we expressed a commitment to do what we could to support other strategies for accountability (within our noted limitations) should the community decide not to litigate.

We left Nueva Chacra that afternoon with the agreement that the community would discuss our presentation internally, and we would return, several times if necessary and useful, to seek to arrive at a joint strategy, informed by the different experiences and knowledge that everyone could offer, to advance a shared vision of justice. In the meantime, Marissa and I would work to build a network of allies for this community to ensure that they had necessary collaborators for strategies beyond our capacity or interest to support.

*

Marissa
May 2012

Three months after that meeting when Juan asked his difficult question, we were back in Nueva Chacra's meeting space, sitting with the five male community representatives, including the *apu* (elected leader). The *apu* was a quiet man. He listened more than he spoke; and when he did speak, he gestured gently with his hands as if he was warming them in the sun. We were back, specifically, to discuss the litigation strategy, and they told us that the whole community had met in *asamblea* (assembly) to discuss the idea of litigation, along with a variety of other possible strategies.

"How long would litigation take?" the *apu* asked in Spanish, smoothing out a fresh page in his notebook. "And if we sue them, would the company still hire us to clear their paths?"

We answered as best we could before the leaders turned to each other and began to discuss the matter in their own language. We couldn't understand more than the occasional Spanish word thrown here and there.

I glanced at my watch. They had been talking for about twenty-five minutes, and didn't seem anywhere near ready to come back to us. And so when Juan's wife, Leonia, came by to make sure that both Ben and I would be staying for lunch, I politely excused myself and left with her. We walked toward the group of women preparing food—*caldo de gallina*, a hearty chicken stew—for everyone to be served at the end of the meeting. I asked the women about the various ingredients, and about the health of the local chickens and herbs. Several of the women complained that the quality of the plants used for the herbs had decreased with the frequent oil spills. They also said that many chickens had been growing sick. More than a few women expressed concern about the priority that several male leaders seemed to be placing on the labor contract when they and their children were suffering rashes and respiratory problems from exposure to the oil.

After some time, I rejoined Ben and waited for the group of men in the meeting house as they continued to discuss and debate what to do with the oil company, and presumably, what to do with us. I watched as no-see-ums, tiny little black flies, circled my wrist, looking for an entry up my sleeve. Suddenly, the group grew quiet. The *apu* stood up to address us. He was carrying a waterproof folder containing various *actas*—meeting minutes— from recent meetings. He set the plastic folder on a chair and approached us. Ben and I waited.

"We would like to show you something," he said in Spanish. "Come with me."

Ben and I followed the *apu* out of the meeting hall and down a path that wove through the thatch homes of the community. It had been raining, but the sky now seemed clear. Children were emerging to examine the puddles.

Dogs shook the rain from their coats. We passed the internet tower on our way. A gray lifeless thing; an alien amid this thriving green place.

The *apu* kept walking. We followed.

You never know when you will end up going for a hike, I thought to myself as we walked deeper and deeper into the jungle. I thought wistfully back to the water bottle I had left on the bench of the community meeting house.

We walked for some time. I was glad for my rubber boots. They were the most useful purchase I had made since moving to Peru. Finally, we stopped. The *apu* turned to us and extended his hand, gesturing to the plants and trees around him.

"These are our *chacras*," he said, using the Spanish word for a small plot of farmed land. He pointed to little plots of cultivated crops surrounded by dense jungle. I recognized cassava and plantain but struggled to make sense of the dozen or so other crops—vines and ferns—some with leaves larger than my outstretched hand. "We live from these plants as we live from the river. But they are no good now. The water is bad, and it poisons our plants. These plants are also our medicine. But they no longer have the power to heal."

Ben took a bandana from his pocket and tied it around this neck to absorb the sweat that was running down his face. "How long has it been like this?" I asked.

"Since the company came."

"How far are we from the river?" I asked next.

"As far as we have walked," the *apu* responded.

At least a few miles, I thought.

Ben and I exchanged a meaningful look; it was the type of look exchanged between two lawyers worried about facts. The polluted water wasn't close to these plants; causation might be hard to prove.

"Are there any oil pipes running through here?" Ben asked hopefully (in the way a lawyer comes to see bad facts as "good").

"No, they are all back down near the river."

How were we going to explain to the *apu* that the law might not recognize this impact as related to the oil pollution, at least not in terms of a tort claim?

"If we bring a lawsuit," Ben began, "the company might argue that something else might be responsible for the crops not growing, and they might point to the fact that the wells are far away."

The *apu* paused for a moment and then spoke: "You know that all of this is connected, right? The river floods during certain months of the year. In the past, the river would leave nutrients that nourished these crops. No longer. It now brings oil."

"We can argue that, but we want you to know that the company will challenge whether the oil is responsible for the crop failure. Our legal system doesn't always recognize all harms, even when there has been an injustice. It's a shortcoming." Ben explained.

"I can tell; that's why the company thinks it can do whatever it wants here."

He turned quietly and led us back toward the center of the village.

"About the lawsuit," he began. "We don't think it's going to work. We still want to be compensated for the harm to our environment. But we also want to push the company to give us better labor contracts, and we are worried they won't work with us if we sue them. The company is our neighbor. And the company is our only opportunity for work when our *chacras* no longer produce."

"Does this decision have anything to do with what we just said about the impacts to those crops being difficult to argue in court?" I asked.

"No," said the *apu*, with a slight smile on his face. "We decided this days ago, during our community meeting. But I wanted you to see our *chacras* anyway so that you would understand how we live; how everything is connected. Maybe your legal system doesn't see it; can't see it. But you can."

"So what will you do?" Ben asked. "We can connect you with labor lawyers that we know in Lima," he offered.

The *apu* stopped and turned back toward us. "We will do the only thing we can do; the only thing that works: we will take the wells."

*

"Do you think it will work?" Ben asked me. We were back in the *peke-peke*, motoring toward town.

"Probably. In any case, taking the wells will take less time than getting past a motion to dismiss."

"I wish we had a criminal defense lawyer on staff in the Peru office. And a Peruvian labor lawyer."

"And an agronomist. And an epidemiologist. And a nurse." But Ben had a point, the strategy did have its risks, and the people of Nueva Chacra could find themselves in jail. With the government's blessing, the oil company had drilled those wells and was basically pumping out money. By taking the wells, and impeding the company's access, the men and women from the community would be shutting down production, but likely violating certain laws to do so.

*

Ben

August 2012

"This is a good thing!" Marissa insisted, as we sat down over *cremoladas de aguaje* in our favorite smoothie shop in Pucallpa. Juaneco y Su Combo began playing from the speakers overhead and she was tapping her foot to the electro-cumbia.

"I still don't know," I replied. "I just keep on thinking that the community is making a mistake in not litigating."

"But look at what they have done since they took the wells!" Marissa insisted. Several months had now passed since they had done so. At first, Bain Oil's response had seemed promising. Rather than calling in the government to take them back by force, the company had agreed to convene a multiparty negotiation involving company representatives, the government, and the community. The company had even agreed to fund an assessment of the environmental and social harms caused by the spills and allowed the community to select the expert.

Now, however, Bain Oil was contesting the validity of the expert's findings and had put forward its own study contradicting nearly every conclusion. The people of Nueva Chacra still maintained hope that the government would intervene and put a thumb on their side of the scale. But in the most recent negotiation session we had just attended, the government seemed reluctant to take a position with respect to the competing studies and appeared a little too sympathetic to the company.

Debriefing later with the community representatives, we once again made a case for how litigation might increase their leverage in these negotiation sessions, but we were told that the moment was not yet right. "Let's see where the negotiations go first, *doctores*," the *apu* told us. "We can always consider litigation later."

Marissa scooped out the last bite of her *cremolada*. "You're missing the positive. We haven't forced the community to take any action they don't want to take. We aren't 'those lawyers.' And we have respected the community's worldview without imposing our own. Remember that it was the community's strategy that brought the company and the government to the table in the first place. Give them some credit. We have a lot to learn from them as well."

As was usually the case, Marissa was right. But I still couldn't shake the discomfort.

"I'm worried though that this negotiation process is just a colossal waste of time. Do you really think the company is ever going to agree to pay reparations for the environmental harms without any additional leverage? Will the leaders end up just accepting better terms on the labor contract so that they don't return to the community empty-handed? You know better than I do that not everyone in the community will be satisfied with that outcome."

Marissa nodded. I knew she was thinking back to the women who were cooking the *caldo de gallina*; she had told me all about it. "I guess we will just have to wait and see."

I pushed forward. "Were we too equivocal in expressing our support for litigation? Did we hold back our convictions out of a misguided, maybe even patronizing, effort not to undermine 'community agency'? Did we not make a strong enough case?"

Marissa shook her head. "No. We were *honest*. Litigation comes with both costs and benefits, and we had to discuss them all. And remember, when they asked for our opinion, we didn't shy away from telling them that we thought the benefits of litigation outweighed the costs. Whether we agree with their decision or not, the community is enacting its own vision and shaping its own future. And now they are better prepared to consider litigation in the future."

"Is it really 'the community' though? It seems like a lot of decisions are made by just a few male leaders."

"Well, if the community disagrees, those leaders will change." Marissa and I both smiled, recalling the several changes in leadership even in the relatively short time we had been supporting the community—changes that often coincided with periods of greater or lesser interest in exploring litigation.

*

February 2014

The rumble of the *peke-peke* still felt familiar, even several years later. I smiled, thinking about my colleagues from law school staring at their computers all day in in their tall concrete towers, missing out on this life.

Having saved up some vacation time, we were on our way back to the same village to visit Juan and Leonia and the other community members with whom we had kept in touch over the years. Juan had developed a small sustainable farming center that received frequent visitors and volunteers eager to learn about local plants and medicines; Leonia had organized many of the women from the village in a collective to create and sell intricately embroidered fabric *telas* and other Indigenous artisan crafts.

In the end, the question as to whether to litigate became moot: the statute of limitations for the strongest claims expired. We didn't force the issue, and the community chose instead to continue its negotiations with Bain Oil. They managed to obtain some concessions from the company with respect to labor contracts, but there never were full reparations for the harms they had suffered. Nonetheless, we didn't hear news about any other major oil spills stemming from the company's operations, so the whole process clearly had had an impact on the company's behavior.

Marissa turned sideways in the *peke-peke* to make it easier to chat. I saw her mind at work, and I smiled, recalling many similar conversations in the past.

"What's on your mind?" I asked.

"This feels right—going back to see them," she said.

I knew what she meant. Despite our continued misgivings about some of the community's decisions and priorities, it felt good to be going back, and to be welcomed back, and the community appeared to be doing well.

"Do you still think about their decision not to litigate? And those labor contracts?" I asked.

"You know I do, but I don't really feel that discomfort you once described. So many NGOs propagate—and fundraise off—this romanticized idea that supporting Indigenous peoples and their supposedly uniform 'way of life' is the antidote to all the ills of civilization—ills that Westerners have mostly caused. They are not necessarily wrong, but their theory assumes that all Indigenous peoples and communities want the same thing. And it assumes that Indigenous people are static, unchanging, and uncomplicated. But they aren't. And neither are we. This work is always complicated. It is figuring out how to manage the complications with respect that is important."

I nodded and let Marissa's words sink in as the *peke-peke* rounded another bend in the river.

Further Reading: Marissa Vahlsing and Benjamin Hoffman, "Collaborative Lawyering in Transnational Human Rights Advocacy," *Clinical Law Review*, vol. 21, no. 1, Fall 2014; Sarah Knuckey, Benjamin Hoffman, Jeremy Perelman, Gulika Reddy, Alejandra Ancheita, and Meetal Jain, "Power in Human Rights Advocate and Rightsholder Relationships: Critiques, Reforms, and Challenges," *Harvard Human Rights Journal*, vol. 33, 2020; Susan Farbstein, "Perspectives From a Practitioner: Lessons Learned From the Apartheid Litigation," *Harvard International Law Journal*, vol. 61, no. 2, Summer 2020.

Holding China Accountable for Environmental Pollution at Home and Abroad

JINGJING ZHANG

The first time I really understood what it meant to be what we now call a "public interest lawyer" was outside the appellate court in Fuzhou, in June 2005. I had flown to the capital of Fujian province as part of the legal team in a landmark Chinese class action environmental case. We were representing 1,721 plaintiffs, farmers from the town of Shuangxi in the mountainous agricultural northwest of Fujian Province, many of whom had developed skin diseases and other medical conditions as a result of the toxic waste being dumped into the river by a chemical factory. Our clients had won in the city court, and the factory was now appealing the judgment. Now, outside the Fujian Provincial High Court, about fifty of them were waiting for us, having traveled overnight by bus from their village with their community leader, a barefoot doctor, as the Chinese call traditional healers. Almost before the group could even greet us, they started engaging animatedly about the technicalities of the case, giving us lots of advice about how we should run it, full of talk about "compensation" and "environmental data" and what happens in "appellate court."

It was three years after I had first travelled to Shuangxi, and I realized how empowered my clients had become, through their fight for justice. They had come to understand what the law meant, and how they could use it to protect their own rights. They had become the owner of their laws—I could even say the owner of their power. They were furious with the company for appealing the verdict, but I sensed something else alongside the anger: I would call it confidence. I could not suppress my own smile: all around me were *citizens*, not subjects. It felt like a first for China, and whether we won or lost, I knew I had done my job.

As it turned out, we used the appeal case to request an even higher compensation than the city court had awarded us—and we received an extra 400,000 renminbi ($60,000, an unprecedented amount in China). Once divided, this was not a lot per family, but we also secured a court order compelling the factory to clean up cadmium-laden waste dumped on the farmers' lands. We obtained a precedent in Chinese law! Most important, we got 1,721 plaintiffs who understood their rights—and had experienced for themselves the way power can shift when you have information, and when you know how to use it. It was exhilarating.

When I began studying law in the 1980s, I had a very different, very Chinese, understanding of what "law" meant: a tool of authority, not the people. Certainly, my Tiananmen Square generation was interested in politics, but we were taught that the law was there to *serve* politics. We studied law so we could get into politics and make "the right decisions" on behalf of the people; we would become prosecutors and judges, and have the power to make these "right decisions." It was only in 2003, when I joined the Center for Legal Assistance to Pollution Victims (CLAP-V) at the China University Political Science and Law, that I came to understand what it meant to be a public interest lawyer.

In ways I didn't quite register at the time, my own father laid the ground for this. As a university student in the 1960s, he had been very outspoken, and had criticized Mao Zedong's position on collectivization and the Cultural Revolution. He and his friends were reported to the government, and labeled *you pai*: enemies of the people. He was forced to give up his career as an engineer and assigned to work as a laborer for twenty years at the chemical plant where I grew up. This was a tragedy in his life, but it opened the door for me in two unexpected ways. The first of these was that, when I was awakened in the 1980s, I could look back at my father's life and make a decision about how I was going to fight for the truth.

The second was that my father's punishment exposed me, in my own life and my own childhood growing up around the chemical plant, to the dangers of environmental pollution. I don't know if this is what got me to apply for the job at CLAP-V, but I do know that when we received a call our hotline from the "barefoot doctor" reporting about what was happening in his village in Fujian, I felt an immediate empathy with these people, because I recognized what they were going through, from my own childhood experience.

In fact, it had been during my teenage years, in about 1986, that I had seen a very small news report about Greenpeace's ship *Rainbow Warrior*. There was no environmental movement at all in China at the time, and I was so touched by this—this group of brave people putting themselves at risk to save the planet. My mother was a doctor, and she had instilled in me the value of helping others; then, when I read about *Rainbow Warrior*, I had this teenage-girl idea: "I need to be a hero too. I need to save something."

Here I was, finally, twenty years later, outside the court in Fuzhou, with a more adult understanding of my work as a legal activist: quietly helping others to find a path to the citizenship that is their right.

*

This has become work that has taken me out of China and all over the world. Although Chinese industry is being compelled to clean up its act back home, because of new legislation and regulations, it is simply exporting these problems abroad: investing in coal-burning plants in Africa and in other parts of Asia, for example; chasing oil in the Amazon; facilitating the destruction of forests to satisfy its demand for timber, soybeans, and beef.

And it was now mining bauxite in Guinea, to feed a similarly insatiable demand for aluminium. China was no longer able to exploit its own reserves, close to Beijing, due to new anti-pollution regulations, or to import bauxite from Malaysia, given that country's ban, on environmental grounds, of bauxite mining.

When I first traveled to Guinea in May 2018, two years after China started mining bauxite there, I was shocked. The West African country is so rich in the mineral—two thirds of the world's reserves—but people in Boké, at the heart of these reserves, still struggle to get clean tap water, and their roads are flooded every day of the six-month-long raining season each year. The mining industry is booming: heavy mining trucks run 24-7, but roads and bridges are poorly maintained. The land is so green, but around Boké the topsoil has been removed to extract the ore needed for aluminium, leaving the rock exposed, so the countryside is covered in red patches like angry open wounds.

When you speak to the people who live in the villages around these mines, you discover that this is symbolic of the pain they feel. Certainly, they were promised jobs, and some of them have found employment. But the mining excavation affected watercourses that are essential for people's livelihoods, and left scarcity in villages. Dust from the mines covers everything: people, dwellings, crops, even food inside people's homes. It has made mango and pistachio trees much less productive and has caused a reduction in air quality and possible respiratory problems for residents. The traffic of thousands of vehicles used to transport the bauxite exacerbates the dust problem, and adds the problem of vehicle fumes.

I was taken to Boké by a Guinean NGO, AMSP, whose leader speaks the local language, Susu, and I have returned several times. Here, as in Fujian, our first steps have been toward empowering people. In Boké this has meant, above all, training the villagers in documentation. If you make any requests to the company, write it down or have some way of making a record. If you see pollution, take a photograph. If a manager makes a promise to clear up a mess, make him write it down. I have also tried to use a cell phone app to test the air quality in Boké. To have power in today's world, communities need to understand the power of documentation and evidence by using the new technology. They need to be both transmitters and receivers of information.

As I did in Fujian, I am doing my best to help the villagers of Boké find a path toward full citizenship: letting them know which laws can protect them, what rights they have under those laws, how they can stand up against the corporation—and how to request the help that is their right, from the government they elected. I like the phrase "legal empowerment," as it seems to encapsulate what I do: using litigation (or the threat of it) to educate and inform a community, and to unleash the power within it. I cannot deny that, despite the fact that Guinea is apparently a democracy, this work is so much harder in Boké than it was in Fujian, because the conditions are so much worse, from education levels to infrastructure. How can you exercise your rights to citizenship, in a modern state, when you are illiterate, and you can't get around?

As I complete this essay in 2022 there is still space, at Boké, for the Chinese-invested mining company to improve its environmental performance; with myself and an excellent local partner as intermediaries, it has shown itself willing. Corporate players too suffer from a lack of information: many Chinese companies are still learning to operate in a multicultural environment, within other countries' laws and global norms. The best-case scenario would be that the company responds positively to the communities' complaints: that it drills wells, provides water to the village, reduces dust and noise. In that case it won't be necessary to go to the court. Litigation is expensive, and we would rather use it as a last resort. If there are better ways to convince the company to make or improve its environmental, social, and governance criteria, like a social media campaign, of course we would be open to it.

One of the first lessons I learned in China was that if you are a lawyer and you want to make a difference you need to be a social activist and even a political figure too. You need to know how to communicate, how to mobilize, how to inspire a community and equip it with the resources it needs to fight a long battle. These are certainly not skills I learned at law school in China. I don't see them being taught at most law schools anywhere else, either. Community lawyers seem to learn these skills from practice alone.

*

When the Chinese government announced its Belt and Road Initiative in 2013, Chinese companies started investing increasingly in infrastructure and extraction projects all over the world. After completing my masters degree at Harvard's Kennedy School, I moved to Washington, DC, in 2014 for family reasons. If leaving my country made me feel that I had lost the foundation of my work as an environmental lawyer, it opened another door for me, one that would lead me to Boké. I became interested in trying to find a way of holding these companies to account for the environmental and human rights damage they committed beyond China's borders.

I started considering how I could hold China to account for its extraterritorial obligations under international human rights treaties. According to these obligations, companies are required to account for human rights violations outside the country in which they are incorporated and headquartered. But of course, this usually happens in countries with an independent judiciary, courageous human rights lawyers, and a strong rule of law: it is not an easy job to apply the principles to Chinese overseas companies because we don't have these conditions in our legal system back home. The Chinese government is the regulator as well as the shareholder of its giant state-owned enterprises, and this dual role inevitably weakens the possibility for accountability. China also uses its "noninterference" foreign policy as an excuse to avoid its extraterritorial responsibilities. This is what I came to see: China wants the benefits and rights of doing business abroad, but not the legal responsibilities that should come along with those rights and benefits. In this way it is in violation of treaties—such as the International Covenant on Economic, Social and Cultural Rights.

I was able to test these ideas in 2015, when a Mexican environmental lawyer approached me. He was leading the efforts of a marine protection NGO, representing local fishermen in Baja California trying to stop a Beijing-based company building residential and commercial buildings near a marine protection park; he approached me to explain Chinese law to his colleagues and clients. When he won the lawsuit, I saw how I could make Chinese corporations accountable for their actions thousands of kilometers away from where they were headquartered.

Unfortunately, we Chinese human rights and environmental lawyers are rare, even more so those of us who speak some English. Because NGOs and Indigenous activists are so desperate to find ways of holding Chinese industry to account, word has spread quickly that I am doing this work, and I have traveled to eighteen countries, mainly in Africa, Latin America, and Southeast Asia. Often I am the very first Chinese person that Indigenous communities will meet, even though it is Chinese companies digging up their land. It has made me realize that there really is a firewall between China and the world: the NGOs and communities I meet really have no idea how to reach anyone in China, they don't know the Chinese laws, and they obviously don't have the language to be able to do even the most basic research, such as searching company information online. So when I show up in a place like Boké, they are very surprised—in a good way. The network is spreading, and I've had so many requests, I have needed to start my own public interest law organization.

The way I was called to Ecuador is a case in point. I was asked to become involved in litigation by local activists against a Chinese corporation mining gold at Rio Blanco, on indigenous Kichwa-Kañari land to the south of the country. I visited the site and wrote an amicus brief in which I explained that the company was in violation of both Ecuadorian and Chinese laws. On the basis of this and other opinions, the court ruled that the provincial government had to suspend its mining license to the Chinese company to extract gold and silver from Rio Blanco, as it had failed to consult as required by Ecuador's own constitution, by the ILO Indigenous and Tribal Peoples Convention (ILO 169), and by the UN Declaration on the Rights of Indigenous Peoples (UNDRIP). It was clear to me, as an observer, that the case was so viable because the community was so strong. There had even been violence at Rio Blanco: resistance from miners who, of course, feared losing their jobs. But the community stood firm. It even rejected a private payout of $18 million, which the company offered to be able to continue mining. The community understood that the contamination of its water sources, and the violation of land it held sacred, was not worth it.

In the Rio Blanco case, even the mayor of nearby Cuenca filed an amicus brief to demonstrate that the local government did not support the mining project. His testimony made a significant impact. The democratic system makes a big difference, compared to China, because elected officials see they might not be voted in again if they do not listen to the people. It is very different in China, of course, where we have to find space under the one-party system. By working internationally, I have come to understand not just the complex technical challenge of finding jurisdiction, but also the political, cultural, and practical challenge of how to present and build a case, depending on the political system and culture of that jurisdiction.

*

If I compare my experiences in Rio Blanco in Ecuador with those in Boké in Guinea or Fujian in China, I see one very important lesson, given how reliant people become on lawyers and our knowledge; how they see us as their last hope; and given how resilient they need to be during the course of a legal process that can take years. I have come to understand the importance of strong leaders *within* a community, for they connect the community to professional NGOs and lawyers. Yaku Pérez Guartambel, the Kichwa-Kañari lawyer in Rio Blanco, was such a leader; the "barefoot doctor" of Fujian was another. In Fujian, our role as lawyers was to strengthen his leadership by teaching him the laws so he could become a "barefoot lawyer" and activist too! Having such trustworthy leadership within a community means that you know you can consult the community effectively; that you can understand the dynamics and trust the intelligence you are given. This is important, because the decision-making is always difficult.

This brings me back to Boké in Guinea, and a dilemma I face as I write this essay: Should I represent one community to get temporary compensation, or should I think about the overall plan for the thousands of villages in Guinea, and try to spread my limited resources around to help all of them? As a lawyer, I have been trained to choose the case where I have the best opportunity to win. Others might be in more miserable conditions, but the case itself is not as strong in court. I have to make a decision, because one good case can have a bigger impact, which will eventually help other communities.

Of course, if you open yourself to your clients, and accept the community's determination and its leadership, you are going to have to accept that they have their own ideas—and their own dynamics and egos! The "barefoot doctor" in Fujian had very much his own idea of what a campaign should be, and we did not always agree. And because it had become *his* whole life—it was his community, after all—his limits were different from mine.

Learning to set boundaries is essential, which is not always easy for me. I often say to myself, "JingJing, you need to keep a professional distance. Don't get involved with one or two people in the most miserable conditions, look at the bigger picture." But when you think of the bigger picture, the reality of life on the ground in China as in Guinea, really, that emotional connection is very important. I feel that's what makes me different from a corporate lawyer: my clients have faces I will never forget, while their clients are faceless corporations. Perhaps that's what make it easier for them to see law just as a job, whereas for lawyers like me, it's personal: it's my vocation and my duty; my life's work.

I remain haunted by something that happened in 2005, when I was working at CLAP-V, and a maternal cousin came to me for help. In my mother's home village, the county government sold the communal land to a property developer, and the villagers were told they would be relocated without adequate compensation. When my cousin told me all of this, I threw up my hands in resignation: "I'm an environmental lawyer, not a property and land lawyer," I said. In the end my uncle and his neighbors were put in a detention facility for fifteen days, an administrative penalty just for having the audacity to travel to Beijing and attempting to ask the central government to help them. And of course they lost their land.

I take two lessons from this.

The first has to do with how powerless *I* felt at the time—because *I* didn't have the information or the networks to enable me to realize my rights and obligations, as a lawyer, as an activist, as a concerned citizen, and as a daughter to this community of dispossessed people. Just like those villagers in Fujian or Boké, I was not yet strong enough (in my case, as a lawyer or as an activist) to protect my family. It makes me realize that it's not enough for us just to build power in the communities of our clients— we have to build power within our own communities as professionals, as activists and lawyers. And this even more urgent in countries like China or Guinea than, for example, in the United States.

Which brings me to my second lesson, and my conclusion, after working in so many countries across the world. Even when regimes are hostile, if there is the rule of law then lawyers and activists could be more confident that they had a path, through it, to exercise their citizenship. But in an authoritarian country like China—where, for example, you cannot dare to criticize the government as part of your legal strategy—you have to work differently. You cannot even *call* yourself a "human rights lawyer." In my case, what little space I have to maneuver back home is because I am an "environmental lawyer." My government wants to show that it can lead the world on green policies—and it recognizes the damage that pollution has done, particularly around Beijing. Being an environmental lawyer or climate lawyer will more effectively achieve my dual goals: protecting the planet and protecting human rights.

It is difficult to find the path, but it's my life's work, inside China and beyond. My inability to help my cousin back in 2005 keeps me going, even today: from Fujian to Rio Blanco to Boké, I am still finding my own power, which means—given my vocation—my ability to use the law to help others. This is my own journey, along China's Belt and Road Initiative.

Further Reading: Manuela Picq, "Can the Law Prevail over Chinese Investments in Ecuador," *Intercontinentalcry*, July 25, 2018; Ma Tianjie, "Interview: China's Overseas Investments Face Legal Pushback," *Dialogo Chino*, February 4, 2020; Lili Pike, "China's 'Erin Brokovich' Goes Global to Hold Chinese Companies Accountable," *Inside Climate News*, June 19, 2020; Rhett Butler, "'I never give up': Q&A with Chinese Environmental Lawyer Jingjing Zhang," *Mongabay*, May 5, 2021

The Decriminalization of Homosexuality in Kenya

NJERI GATERU in conversation with MARK GEVISSER

Kenya, like thirty-five other former British colonies, still has a law on its books outlaw-ing homosexual acts between men as "unnatural offences," "carnal knowledge against the order of nature," or "indecent practices." Several countries have had these laws ruled unconstitutional, through strategic litigation. These include South Africa, India, Belize, Trinidad and Tobago, and, most recently, Botswana, in 2019. In 2016, a coalition of Kenyan LGBTQ organizations petitioned the Kenyan High Court to do the same, on the basis that it violated the rights to privacy, freedom of expression, human dignity, health, and protection against discrimination, as enshrined in the country's 2010 constitution. Despite subsequent courtroom victories getting anal examinations of suspected offenders banned and permitting LGBTQ organizations to be registered, a 2019 high court ruled against the petition, on the basis that the litigants had failed to provide evidence of dis-crimination, but gave them leave to appeal. Njeri Gateru's National Gay and Lesbian Human Rights Commission led the process. She discusses it here with Mark Gevisser, in a September 2019 conversation.

Mark Gevisser: Could you talk about your strategic litigation on the decriminalization of homosexuality in Kenya?

Njeri Gateru: My organization, the National Gay and Lesbian Human Rights Commission, works specifically to use strategic litigation toward creating a better climate for LGBTQ people in Kenya. One of the cases we've been working on has been seeking to decriminalize homosexual-ity, or what's called the "unnatural offenses" clause of the Kenyan penal code. Basically, this is a law that makes it illegal for any person to engage in anal sex, and for males to have sex with each other. This law effectively criminalizes the lives of anyone who identifies within the LGBTQ com-munity. It's been ongoing work for us: we collected evidence and provided legal aid to clients until we felt that we were in a space where we could begin the actual work of litigating in a court of law. In 2016 we filed the decriminalization petition, and we have been going through the motions in court.

MG: How did you prepare for the case?

NG: Strategic litigation is a way to carry out public interest litigation: the results of this case would not affect only a single person or a single issue, they would have direct impact on the lives of a subset of society. So to be able to do this work, and to feel that the story was adequately presented to the judges who were sitting on this bench, it was important to figure out which stories were the most powerful and who were the best people to tell them. We had a huge number of affidavits from people who identified as LGBTQ in Kenya, and we ended up with a group of six individuals, identifying all across the alphabet soup, with very different stories of how this particular law affected their lives. So it's about collecting those stories and laying them out in a way that would be most useful for the three judges who get to determine our fate to hear, and to imagine what it must be like to live as a queer person within a criminalized context.

MG: I imagine there was personal and emotional preparation too . . .

NG: Of course. And because I am both a lawyer representing the queer community, but also a member of that community too, there are two parts to this. The first is preparing yourself as a person who participates in the movement. The second is preparing the emotions of the community for whatever the outcome is of such huge litigation.

MG: Could you describe being in the courtroom on the day of the judgement, and what happened in the community then and after?

NG: It was May 24, 2019. We had been in court for three years but it was the first time that we had appeared so publicly. All of a sudden we were clutching to the hope that we were going to win this. The three judges walked in and started reading the judgment. It felt like they were playing with us. They would say one thing and then go in circles so you couldn't figure it out, whether this was positive or negative. Everyone was holding each other and you could feel when it got too tense. Then it got to a point where we started to realize: actually, guys, we're losing this.

We did lose.

In African communities, you're allowed to cry and mourn when you have lost. You are not allowed to cry and mourn when it doesn't seem like there's a direct connection to loss. But with the community it felt like we had genuinely lost something. Like there was a death in the community. We went through grief; we're still grieving. It was interesting to see how that showed up in the different people we are, and to see it in a very public gaze. Usually you mourn privately; you are held, behind closed doors. But this was happening publicly. I was holding Toto, my little friend, and when I started saying, "We're losing," I could see they were shaking. I could feel them tense up, their body going through the motion, and I remember telling them, "Babe, don't cry. If you cry they'll take a picture of you, and that's the picture they're going to plaster everywhere."

So you could see everyone sucking it in. Then news came through that a trans woman was beaten up because of the judgement. This finally got everyone to let go, after they had been holding it in so bravely. Everyone was in in tears. People had been holding it in so long, and this pushed everyone over the edge. It was chaotic. You're trying to be a leader, but you're also fucked up. You can't openly perform mourning, because that would be a betrayal of our commitment to carry ourselves with dignity.

It was a moment of emoting and not wanting to emote, not wanting to process, but having to process. But there are parts of it that were so incredibly beautiful: losing together. There was a feeling in that moment that there was nothing that could break us if this judgement didn't. It was a loss in the sense that we didn't win the case, but certainly we walked this journey together.

MG: I know you have been thinking deeply about the quality of this 'togetherness' and how it is represented through high-profile litigation . . .

NG: Before, people were organizing on different themes, highly dependent on different identities. So trans people were doing their own thing, lesbians their own thing, gay and bi men doing their thing, mainly about health. Rarely did we have moment where we all came together and embarked on one thing. "Decrim" became that one thing.

But along the way we nearly fell apart. We tried to be strategic, intentional, about building a strong organization, but the litigation almost tore it down at one point. There was a huge rift in the movement, funders were involved too, over whether it was right to spend this amount of resources on decriminalization when there were so many other issues. There was a move to get us defunded, and we could have easily gone under.

And of course, neither a win nor a lose in court will necessarily keep a movement together. In our movement, we had already had many moments of fracturing. We came to the movement knowing we're different on so many things. But we came together on this. Even when we were banding together around this thing, we did so knowing there are very many things we disagreed on. But this is the thing we agree on. The most visible thing. You can put it in a report: "The movement came together." You can put it in a picture.

Still, I could see how this picture was also an illusion. How do you describe a dignified life, a strong community, for LGBTQ people? People do things together. They go on drives, they eat meals, they farm, they visit their families. But that doesn't fit into the log frame of a report to funders. That doesn't look good in the *New York Times*. What looks good is *decriminalization*! We can put a caption under that picture: "The Kenyan movement came together!" But it might not be true. It might not be representative of the whole of our world.

MG: Can you say more about the relationship between movements and pain, and what it means for you as a lawyer?

NG: Something I often say is that movements are generally products of pain. When I think about what's at the root of the pain of queer Kenyans, and in other words for me too, it's the *law* itself. It's the law that permits all the violence and discrimination against us. And now I must go into battle to make things better by using the tools of that very same law that causes the pain in the first place! It's a complicated thing to do.

MG: Did you "win" anything, despite the loss in court?

NG: Well, firstly, the coming together I have been talking about. Before it seemed like a condition for survival to band together, but now it's because we can, because we see how it works, because we want to. That has been the most beautiful thing for me to see: the intentionality of queers banding together of their own volition.

And secondly, the presentation of a mulilayered, multifaceted experience of queer experience, and throwing that in the face of all the stories that have been consumed in Kenya. We rewrote the narrative. Queerness is no longer engaged with as an abstract. Going to court definitely raised awareness in the Kenyan public. Seeing people—members of parliament, newscasters, bloggers, everyone—state exactly where they stood in this conversation: I think that was really important, and we hadn't experienced that within the Kenyan public space before.

Being yourself publicly also changes people's perceptions. People are unable to marry their hate or their ignorance with their understanding of your humanity. That breaks a barrier. My experience is that people can read the most brilliant writing or the most brilliant theories or consume the most articulate stories and data, but fail to make sense of all of this information and relate it to a human being. Usually what changes people's minds is meeting people who are LGBTQ.

MG: Did you find support in unexpected places?

NG: It certainly helped us figure out to what extent we could rely on allies. It strengthened some relationships: for example the Kenya Human Rights Commission filed as an amicus on our case. This was a big deal. This is a governmental agency, filing on our case! Religious leaders too were mobilized. They showed up in their collars. Parents, media, religious leaders, celebrities, and social media influences: I liked seeing all these different parts come together.

MG: What next?

NG: Of course, we're not giving up. We've already filed for appeal and we are currently waiting for a hearing date and we'll continue the process of litigating from there. We're going to expand conversations around the importance of decriminalization of homosexuality: not only in Kenya, but also in other African countries. And this time, we hope that we win.

MG: What would you say to an LGBTQ movement from another African country contemplating a similar decriminalization case?

NG: All the things I've already said to you about the dangers of coming apart rather than together. Then there is the cost of leading a decrim movement, to organizations, to people. I would want to explore with them the doubts that are faced, the insecurities, the anxieties, the surveillance. The risk it causes to your partners, families, friends, the possibilities of them not standing with you.

MG: The high profile, in an environment where there is so much public homophobia, must be particularly daunting . . .

NG: Someone asked me how I deal with the fear and the danger of this work. I think I'm always afraid. But I'm not just afraid because I'm a queer person who's visibly queer: I'm afraid of dying in an airplane! I'm afraid of snakes! I'm afraid of many things. The fear is part of my experience of being human. What keeps me sane is knowing that I'm completely loved and affirmed. I have a family that loves me, and I walk a little more boldly because of that. I have a partner who's able to make me laugh, and I'm happy for that, and ridiculously blessed. And I have friends who band around me in so many ways and I lack words for them. I walk safely because when I'm around my core people, there's really nothing about me that's different from them. There's that feeling that we're in this together, even when it's tough. This happens, and then we live another day, and something else happens, and I'm grateful for that.

CASE STUDY

Financial Accountability:
The World Bank

From Narmada to Tata Mundra in India: The Activist's Perspective

JOE ATHIALY

In the summer of 2010, I was a part of a group of activists who visited Bhadreshwar, a sleepy fishing village on the Gulf of Kutch, in the state of Gujarat in western India. We had been invited by local communities affected by Tata Power's Mundra project, given that our organization monitors international financial institutions and their investments in India. The fisherfolk wanted to discuss Tata's gigantic coal-fired thermal power project coming up in their backyard—and another already built, by the Adani company. The Tatas and the Adanis are India's two most powerful industrial families, both perceived to be close to the ruling dispensation, and their new plants were part of a huge special economic zone being developed at a rapid rate around the port of Mundra—the pet project of the Indian prime minister, Narendra Modi, Gujarat's former chief minister.

In the face of such power, the villagers of Bhadreshwar were small fish indeed. And the Tata and Adani projects had the power to wreck their lives and livelihoods, to damage the breeding grounds of fish and other aquatic wealth, and to destroy an ecologically sensitive area that included the date and cotton plantations of local farmers as well as hundreds of hectares of indigenous mangrove. When we first visited in 2010, the Tata plant was in the initial stages of construction, but the fish workers' livelihoods had already been severely damaged by the Adani development.

The fish workers are Muslim, in an area dominated economically by wealthy Jains and, politically, by Modi's Hindu nationalist Bharatiya Janata Party (BJP). This is significant, because as the Gujarat chief minister, Modi had overseen carnage in which thousands of Muslims in the state were killed in 2002. It was a moment that shifted Indian politics decisively toward the Hindu populist rule we see now, which masquerades as being driven by economic development. And it had a profound impact on the fishing communities on the Gulf of Kutch, as on Muslim communities all over the country.

This was part of a bigger trend. In the name of "development," there has been the systematic weakening of communities already marginalized and vulnerable because they are poor, Indigenous, religious minorities, or dependent on natural resources. These very citizens have had their rights to free speech and consultation shut down in a deliberate attempt to limit their power to resist. In the 2002 Gujarat carnage, this process might have been orchestrated by a Hindu political party or gang; now, with Tata and Adani in Mundra, it is by huge corporations. But for a community like Bhadreshwar, the effect has been the same: profound disempowerment and impoverishment.

At that first meeting in 2010, the fish workers were astounded when we told them that the Tata Mundra project was partially funded by World Bank's private sector arm, the International Finance Corporation (IFC). The World Bank Group has poverty alleviation as one of its primary goals—and is bound by its own regulations to meaningful consultation with affected communities. How was it possible, the villagers wanted to know, that a project like this could come up without any consideration of its effect on their livelihood; without so much as a courtesy visit?

In the years of India's economic boom there has been a development mantra that is all-too-often unchallenged: "someone has to make the sacrifice, for the great common good." But who decides which communities must make the sacrifice, and who will benefit? And are the people compelled to sacrifice even consulted, or compensated?

For two decades I have been involved with a movement that defined these questions in India: the Save the Narmada Movement, first as a full-time activist and later as a supporter. It was established to stop the building of the Narmada Dam in central India, which would displace or severely impact over a million people. Now, as I sat and listened in Bhadreshwar, I realized that the fisherfolk here were facing the same issues as the villagers along the Narmada River: someone else's development priority, and profit motive, was threatening their land and livelihoods, their very lives. They had no say in the matter.

*

In October 2018, eight years after I first visited Bhadreshwar, I found myself standing in line to enter the grand US Supreme Court. I was with Bharat Patel, the head of Association for the Struggle for Fishworker's Rights, representing the fisherfolk of Kutch. When we got there at 7 a.m. there was already a queue round the block, from people waiting since 4 a.m. for seats, to hear the oral arguments being presented that day. When a guard saw the badges we had been given by our lawyers at EarthRights International, he ushered us through. It was only then that the significance of our presence there dawned on me: here we were, two Indian activists representing some of the most marginalized people in our home country, being listened to as petitioners in what was arguably the world's most powerful court, against the world's most powerful financial institution! The shanties of Bhadreshwar were a different world from the court's pomp and splendor: Would the community ever be able to challenge an institution like the World Bank?

We were asking the court to review the findings of two lower courts: that, as international financial institutions, the World Bank and the IFC were immune from judicial scrutiny in US jurisdictions and hence exempt from any claims for damages caused by their investment. We had gone to these lower courts in the first place because of our lack of success with the IFC itself, which we had approached on behalf of the fisherfolk through the corporation's own accountability mechanism, its Compliance Advisor Ombudsman (CAO).

In 2011, we assisted the fish workers' association to submit a mountain of evidence to the CAO. We recorded a rise of three to five degrees in the temperature of the water, together with high chemical content and increasing acidity due to the project's effluent, detrimental to fish eggs and larvae. We documented the way large stretches of mangroves, dry-land forests, and biodiversity-rich creeks had been destroyed for the construction of the inlet and outfall channels, and how access to fishing farms and grazing grounds had been blocked or diverted, forcing villagers to pay more for their transport and resulting in a considerable delay for women returning from the markets after selling fish. We were also able to present evidence of a substantial reduction in fish catch, as well as of health risks due to pollution. Most of all, we showed how the IFC had *violated its own rules* by neglecting to consult the fish workers at all.

The IFC countered that it had not taken the fish workers into account because these people did not actually own the land around the *bunder* (port) and were thus not "affected parties": in fact, the IFC alleged, in its submission to the ombudsman, that the fish workers did not even live permanently in the villages on the Gulf of Kutch! The truth is that these communities only left the *bunders* to go inland for three months a year, during the monsoon: for the rest of the year, the *bunders* were their permanent homes, their sole means of livelihood, and where there children went to school. It was laughable to claim otherwise—and for me it was a lesson in how corporations just assume that because they are wealthy, their lies will not be challenged.

The CAO's findings, published in 2013, were the most scathing the body had ever issued, validating nearly every issue the fishing communities raised. It found that the IFC had committed serious supervision failures and significant policy breaches: failing to consider the risks to a vulnerable religious-minority population, compromising on marine and air quality standards, and failing to do proper compliance on the plant's seawater-cooling project.

But, we discovered, the CAO was toothless. It does not have any implementing power, nor can it make recommendations. It can just document the violations. The IFC dismissed its findings, and issued no remedial action. Even the World Bank president Jim Kim, known for his alleged commitment to poverty alleviation, stood by his IFC staff and their Indian client.

And so we made a decision to go to court—on the World Bank's home turf, in Washington, DC. Given that the institution was domiciled in the United States, we wanted to argue that it could be sued for damages according to its country's own laws. We had an immediate reason: to be able to sue for damages for the fisherfolk of Kutch. But we also had a long-term motivation: powerful institutions such as the World Bank wield disproportionate power to influence and change the course of economies. When they are privileged with immunity, they tend to believe they are above the law.

For years, there have been a number of efforts to challenge such immunity, and learning from these attempts helped us successfully, this time.

Finally, in February 2019, the US Supreme Court ruled in our favor. We could proceed with our suit.

*

A few weeks after this victory, we returned to the Gulf of Kutch to celebrate with the fisherfolk, in a bright white tent festooned with pink ribbons looking out across the water toward the hulking power plant. Hundreds attended, not just from the fishing villages themselves, but from all over India. We had a very special "chief guest": the inspirational Medha Patkar, who for decades has led the struggle of villagers against the Narmada Dam project, which by now has displaced tens of thousands of people.

"Friends, it is your strength which gave us this victory," Medha said in her address. "Some say it is a small victory, some say it's a big victory, but I think it's the biggest victory, because this has laid a foundation on which further victories could be built."

This statement had special resonance, coming from Medha: the victory we were celebrating that day had been built on the Save The Narmada Movement (NBA)'s extraordinary victory nearly thirty years previously. The Narmada project had also been funded in part by the World Bank, which in 1985 approved a $450 million loan toward its construction. Medha and people from the affected villages led several Gandhian nonviolent actions on the ground; the World Bank looked the other way even when the state responded with violence, from beatings and arrests to the bulldozing of houses. Six thousand people marched toward the dam site to demand a review of the whole project. When police stopped the march at the state border, the protesters held a sit-in at a remote village at the peak of winter. Seven key activists, including Medha, went on an indefinite fast.

Twenty-two days into the fast, the World Bank announced the formation of an independent review committee, known as the Morse Commission. Medha and her fellow activists sparked what would become a global movement demanding more transparency and accountability from the World Bank, and it was successful. In 1993, the World Bank set up an inspection panel, the first legal accountability mechanism for international financial institutions, later replicated in nearly all other such institutions. This was later adapted by the IFC as the Compliance Advisor Ombudsman.

It was thus particularly powerful to have Medha present at our 2019 celebration. And it had a moving personal resonance for me, given my own history. I had first visited the Narmada valley in 1994, as a twenty-five-year-old member of a youth movement from my native Kerala, on a two-week "exposure tour." The NBA had already won its victory against the World Bank, but the government was proceeding anyway with other finance, and people like me were being pulled into the movement from all over India to prevent the project from going forward.

The NBA, and Medha in particular, had an uncanny ability to draw you in, and before I knew it, my two weeks had expanded to three months. In September 1994, I was one of the seven activists who occupied a house in the village of Manibeli during the rainy season, refusing to leave while the water behind the dam rose. This was an annual protest action of the NBA: to declare the lowest-lying house in a vulnerable village to be a "Satyagraha House"—after Gandhi's nonviolence movement—and to occupy it as the monsoon rains began, in defiance of the flooding of the villages behind the dam wall. All sorts of activities would happen in the Satyagraha House—cultural events, political meetings, lessons—attended by sometimes hundreds of people, in a season lasting three or four months. This year, while many others were engaged in other actions in different villages, seven of us stayed in the Manibeli Satyagraha House until the bitter end.

By 2 a.m. the water touched the door of the mud hut, and by 3 a.m., when the water was seeping into the hut, the police came and dragged us up the hill to a makeshift camp, where we were officially arrested. It was pitch dark, and we couldn't see anything, but when the first light came at dawn about two hours later, we looked out over the village . . . and all we could see was water. I had been in Manibeli for the previous three months, so I was very familiar with the topography, and I was startled. The view had completely changed. All you could see above the water level were the tops of a few trees. There was nothing else. It was absolutely silent. There was just water.

We were in jail for seven days, and during those days my friend and I—he was also a member of youth movement from Kerala—spoke about how shaken we were by this vision. We realized, for the first time, the depth of our actions. We had been repeating what the villagers were saying, "This is our home, and this is our right to be here, and we will not move," but now it really sank in: the house that had been destroyed by the flood, the house we could no longer see from our vantage point in custody up on high ground, was *actually* someone's home, their place of birth, their land, their livelihood, and it was no more.

How could we go back to our old lives of comfort after witnessing that? After my release, I returned to Kerala briefly, but I was back in the Narmada region within a couple of months. I stayed for nearly seven years.

I was among a small team of activists taking care of technical, legal, and financial issues, as well as mass mobilization on the ground. My particular area of focus was communication and coordination with supporters of the movement. A key part of our mission was to encourage a good number of professionals—teachers, lawyers, doctors—to join the movement as supporters, and to draw on their expertise, particularly in the gathering of data and evidence. We were focused, in those years, on a petition to the Supreme Court of India, with a comprehensive case challenging the dam project. This was a gamble: an unfavorable judgement could cause the movement to fall flat. But preparing the case gave us the impetus to mobilize, win or lose. The movement had spread to a large number of villages falling into the submergence zone. Mass protests in the villages as well as the state capitals and Delhi, sit-ins, rallies, and other forms of protests strengthened people's resolve to fight the dam project.

The NBA used mass mobilization as a strategy in tandem with litigation, seeking relief in the courts from the early days of the struggle. Sometimes it helped, sometimes not. In cases related to civil and political rights the courts usually gave progressive judgements, but there was a red line: any litigation even remotely challenging the project fell on deaf ears, for developmental projects were (and to a great extent continue to be) a holy cow. While the Indian judiciary has found fault with compliance issues and violations of environmental and human rights, it has very rarely fundamentally intervened in a development project already underway. Of course, the state fought back, using the law too: at the peak of the struggle, false charges were made against leaders and members, and there were illegal arrests and detention as well as intimidation.

Finally, in 2001, after seven years, the Supreme Court ruled 2-1in favor of the government. The construction continued. The movement did not fall flat, but it certainly was a setback, given that people were sure that truth was on their side and the government had argued on the basis of false data and fabricated stories. The affected communities continue to struggle, and refuse to give away their rights. And despite the Supreme Court ruling, the NBA continued to seek relief from the judiciary on many issues. Where else can one go when the state turns a blind eye to people and their concerns?

*

The building of a dam is obviously very different from the building of a power plant. The way communities' rights have been violated, in Kutch and in Narmada, is different too: at Narmada, thousands were forcibly displaced from their villages and their land submerged in the reservoir; in Kutch, thousands were affected not by physical displacement but by the negative impact on their livelihood due to discharge from the thermal plant. Of course the struggles of the two communities are dissimilar, not least because they have been fought in such technologically disparate eras. The means of mass mobilization are different, as is the contribution to the development debates in India and the way both have influenced other political struggles. Still, as we celebrated the 2019 Supreme Court victory in the villages of the Gulf of Kutch, we saw commonalities with Narmada in the relationship between litigation and movement building.

At both Narmada and Mundra, we based our arguments in empirical data and facts that neither the World Bank nor the IFC nor the judiciary could contest. At Narmada, the door-to-door survey that NBA volunteers conducted (in hilly terrain on foot) exposed the false data of the government, which claimed that everybody in the submergence zone had been rehabilitated. At Tata Mundra, an independent fact-finding team documented each violation by the project, rendered incontestable by the IFC. There was value to such meticulous documentation: it helped the communities stay positive, even for large stretches of time while governments and other institutions refused to engage and turned a blind eye.

Both struggles had (and still have) space for any and everyone who wanted to contribute. Students, lawyers, journalists, activists, and many national organizations have become a part of these struggles. Their knowledge about law, wider strategies, contacts, and building mutually respectful relationships has been immensely helpful and has helped to sustain relationships between outside individuals and community members. Of course, this presents its own challenges: the timelines, priorities, or interests of such supporters may not always match those of the local communities. However, sustaining a mutually rewarding relationship is fundamental to many struggles that require connections between the local and global.

This was the first, vital lesson we learned from Narmada: the importance of a successful linkage between the local and global. These struggles were successful in their ability to take the movement to global platforms while maintaining local engagement. Without such a connection, we would have never succeeded in convincing the World Bank in the 1990s to review a project it had financed. Because organizations in the West consistently amplified the demands of Indian people on the ground in forums convened and led by the officials, the bank had no option but to heed these demands. Both projects had international funding and support. That made it natural for them to reach out to like-minded organizations and individuals abroad, seeking support and solidarity.

And this leads to our second lesson: the blurring of boundaries between "insiders" and "outsiders." Given how complex Narmada was, expert outsider participation was essential as we tried to navigate the complexities and bridge the gap with local communities. At Narmada, the local activists welcomed and embraced this, encouraging full-time activists or even part-time supporters to come for a small period. As I discovered myself, everyone was welcome if they contributed their time or skills; trust and confidence between "insiders" and "outsiders" was reciprocal. It has been similar in Mundra, where the complexities of the policies and procedures of international financial institutions have had to be deconstructed and demystified for people to understand and engage with these institutions.

Which leads to our third major lesson: the value of linking local struggles to bigger issues about development and accountability. We learned how powerful this linkage was at Narmada, and we applied it again with Mundra, this time connecting to international activists who not only wanted to make World Bank more transparent and accountable, but wanted to pressure it to stay away from fossil fuels investments.

In Narmada, we had been able to use the issue to question the mainstream developmental paradigm, and highlight the paradox of a rising income gap and inequity at the same time as rapid economic growth. The Narmada struggle raised the questions of what development was, who benefited from it, and who needed to make sacrifices for a supposed greater common good. We carried the notion through with Mundra, asking bigger questions: this time about the transparency and accountability of international financial institutions in an era when their influence and investments were increasing, and seemed unassailable, hiding as they were behind the veil of immunity.

Activists in both struggles invested a significant amount of time educating the affected communities not just about the project and its impacts, but also about the wider issues of rights and accountability. Participation in struggles was supported by village meetings, youth camps, and workshops. A testament to this investment is the way in which, even after thirty-four years, NBA can mobilize thousands of people for their rallies.

In both Narmada and the Gulf of Kutch, people have sought justice through litigation because the government was not responsive to human rights violations, was siding with the perpetrator, or was the violator itself. What that means is that ordinary people have been pitted against the might of the state—or, even worse, the combined might of the state and corporations. At Narmada, there were four states and the union government involved, which meant fighting against the best legal brains the government could hire in addition to the highest legal officer of the union government. In Tata Mundra, the IFC was footing the bill, on its home turf, in US courts, for the best American lawyers money could buy. These cases may survive only if local communities can find senior, knowledgeable lawyers ready to fight cases pro bono.

Narmada managed, with the help of senior Indian human rights lawyers; the Tata Mundra case depends on EarthRights International. In many other struggles, communities will lose for want of able lawyers, resources to engage lawyers, and the ability to produce solid research and documentation. And even assuming they do find senior lawyers, the challenge is to sustain such a case for so many years in a country like India, bleeding resources, energy, and time. The Narmada case went on for nearly seven years; we have been working on the Tata Mundra case for ten years already, and we know we have several more to go.

And, of course, the stakes are high. What if you lose your bid at the courts? Does it close all other avenues of negotiations? Will the state be more aggressive? Would that turn away the public support you might have garnered over the years? These questions weigh heavily on a movement deciding on whether or not to litigate.

The buffer, of course, is to root litigation within a larger strategy of political struggle.

The Tata Mundra case was finally dismissed, and so we lost our suit to hold the World Bank liable for damage to the fish workers' villages and livelihoods on the Gulf of Kutch. Still, we feel we won a major victory, just by being heard in the Supreme Court—and by getting the court to agree with us that international financial institutions such as the World Bank are not immune to prosecution in the United States. It is clear to us, already, that the Supreme Court ruling has changed the way the bank works. It is strengthening the Compliance Advisor Ombudsman, for example, and it has set up a social and environmental due diligence desk to approve any new project, alongside the normal financial viability due diligence it usually conducts. This is as a direct result of our case.

*

"This victory over World Bank has given us hope and strength to take this struggle ahead."

Budha Ismail Jam, an elderly fisherman who was our key petitioner, said these words at the March 2019 victory celebration. He was unable to come to Washington with us because he had neither a passport nor the documentation that would enable him to get one.

I listened to his words with mixed feelings. He was right, of course, and I could only salute his perseverance, and that of his fellow petitioners. But nothing, yet, had materially altered in his own life, and his own ability to earn his living on the Gulf of Kutch. I had been working with him for eight years, but we had only just won the right to begin fighting the World Bank on its own turf! Indeed, in February 2020, we would lose our first bid to hold the World Bank accountable, in the District Circuit Court of Washington, DC. The court ruled that we had not proved, sufficiently, that the harm was caused *in* the United States, and that it did not have the jurisdiction to rule on harm done beyond the United States—even if done by decisions made in the United States. Then, in 2022, the Supreme Court refused to hear our appeal, ruling that in this particular case, the World Bank did have immunity. It would be a long time, still, before Mr. Jam would feel any kind of tangible relief.

In my work around Mundra, and my work at Narmada, I have come to think, deeply, about what it means to "win" a court case, and its relationship to "winning" a struggle for the most basic human rights.

Look at the Save the Narmada Movement. It initiated a major national discussion on the viability of dams and the kind of development model that best suited India. It mobilized tens of thousands of people, from the villages themselves but also across the country and even the world, into one of the most creative and enduring mass movements of the era, a movement that has thrived from the mid-1980s until today. But at the end of the day—because Narendra Modi decided that he wished to fill the Narmada dam to its capacity as a show of his power on his sixty-fifth birthday—the affected communities lost everything in September 2019. They lost their fields, and they lost their houses. How do you think of victory, in that context?

The Modi era has been the lowest point, for civil rights in India, since Indira Gandhi's state of emergency in 1975. In Delhi alone, fifty-three people were killed in attacks on Muslims from December 2019, following protests against the government's new legislation preventing Muslim immigrants from taking up citizenship. After stripping Kashmir of its special status in 2019, the Indian state put it into lockdown, shutting down all communications; the internet was shut down in the country in many protest hot spots—more than one hundred times in 2019 alone. Prominent civil rights activists and advocates were arrested and hounded by spurious investigations: by 2020, several activists, lawyers and intellectuals had been in jail for nearly two years under the Unlawful Activities (Prevention)

Act. And two of the country's most important movement lawyers, Indira Jaising and Anand Grover, were charged with being in contravention of the Foreign Contribution (Regulation) Act: it was clear that they were being harassed in retaliation for fighting cases exposing the complicity of Prime Minister Modi and other senior members of his government accountable for the Gujarat carnage.

In the face of this, I take heart in the power of the mobilization that is happening, as I write these words, against the Modi government, and particularly its Hindu populism. I have never seen such numbers as in the student-led protests of early 2020, and I have never seen such an innovative way of protest too: the way humor and art were being used, and technology, as a means of mobilization. This kind of energy and creativity has its roots in the struggles of past decades—including in the Narmada mobilization, which set the bar for how to move beyond the regular kind of street protest and adapt it to new terrains, or contexts.

In movement building as in legal advocacy, victory (and failure) are hard to define. But as I look at how popular mobilization has shaped up in India the past few decades—the way it has adapted to different circumstances—I find the struggles of both Narmada and Mundra very inspiring.

There is victory, at least, in such continuity.

Further Reading: On Narmada: Philippe Cullet, "Human Rights and Displacement: The Indian Supreme Court Decision on Sardar Sarovar in International Perspective," *The International and Comparative Law Quarterly*, vol. 50, no. 4, 2001; Arundhati Roy, *The Greater Common Good* (India Book Distributors, 1999); also the film *Narmada Diary*, available on YouTube. On Tata Mundra: Lakshmi Sarah, "Coal-Ravaged Indian Fishers Take to the Supreme Court," *Sierra Magazine*, April 26, 2019; Barry Yeoman and Michael Hudson, "The World Bank Group's Uncounted," *International Consortium of Investigative Journalists*, May, 1 2015; Lesley Clark, "Supreme Court rejects World Bank coal case," *Greenwire*, April 25, 2022.

Narrative Justice and Financial Accountability: The Lawyer's Perspective

DAVID HUNTER

It is Halloween morning, 2018. I pass a long line of people who have been waiting since before dawn to enter the US Supreme Court. Despite the chill they are visibly excited to witness history: the case before the court today, *Jam v. International Finance Corporation,* pits a community of rural fishermen from India against one of the world's largest international financial institutions. Many in line are my friends and colleagues from Washington, DC–based environmental groups, beaming at the prospect of a victory over the powerful World Bank, of which the International Finance Corporation (IFC) is part. A few people I recognize from the US Treasury greet me as well, more reserved but just as excited: they have been monitoring the environmental record of the World Bank for nearly as long as I have. Another contingent is from the World Bank itself, some secretly allied with our efforts at reforming the bank and some decidedly not. Both sides of the World Bank team pretend they don't know me.

Next to me, in the much shorter line reserved for the litigants, are two representatives of the Indian villagers that have challenged the bank's impunity all the way here to the US Supreme Court. Joe Athialy and Bharat Patel, dressed neatly in suits and ties, are jet-lagged and nervous, but project a sense of quiet resolve. They are here representing Budha Ismail Jam, a fisherman from the Kutch region in Gujarat, West India, and other local fishermen and farmers whose livelihoods and environment have been ruined by a massive power plant built by the huge Tata company, backed by the government of India, and bankrolled by the IFC. As we shuffle into the courtroom, the men tell me they have no idea what to expect. Also in the litigants' line, more comfortable in their suits, and certainly more talkative, are the World Bank lawyers. Their idle chatter betrays their own discomfort: the World Bank has never been before the Supreme Court either.

After passing security, we are ushered into the surprisingly austere courtroom and instructed to sit quietly in the reserved section, a few rows behind the counsel tables. We sit on long wooden benches awaiting the nine black-robed justices. "We'll hear argument next in Case Number 17-1011, *Jam versus International Finance Corporation.*" The words from Chief Justice John Roberts both silence the whispers among the observers and signal counsel to begin their well-rehearsed oral arguments. The counsel representing both sides have argued before the Supreme Court many times before and seem the least nervous of anyone in the room. Their arguments are straightforward and professional, with no theatrics or fireworks: the sole question before the court is whether the World Bank is immune from lawsuits in the United States, and both sides interpret arcane legal texts to make their case.

I am conscious of Joe sitting next to me, translating the arguments into whispered Hindi for Bharat, sitting on his other side. I am part of the team advising the fishermen's counsel, and at times Joe translates between me and Bharat too. This seems, to me, an apt metaphor for the role Joe Athialy has long played in India: a bridge, working with affected communities to turn the challenges they face into effective advocacy strategies, drawing when needed on international experts like me. I marvel at the distance the two have come in search of justice: not just the thousands of miles that separate Gujarat, India, from Washington, DC, but the even larger power gap that separates all rural communities from global institutions like the World Bank.

For decades, I have also worked to bridge this power gap as an international environmental and human rights lawyer representing communities affected by large-scale projects. Now as a law professor I continue the work I began three decades ago at the Center for International Environmental Law (CIEL), representing communities that seek justice at the international level. This was a new frontier in movement lawyering at the time, given that international institutions—and international law, for that matter—do not traditionally make room for the voices of affected people or communities. In international fora, the people do not have any voice of their own: only their governments can speak for them. My work has been aimed at changing that dynamic. Sitting next to Joe and Bharat in the court, I believed that a Supreme Court ruling ending the World Bank's absolute immunity from lawsuits would be a major milestone in this decades-long effort.

After the argument, our team met for photographs on the court's iconic front steps, followed by a lunch with supporters at a nearby home. The atmosphere was notably subdued, and Joe and Bharat seemed exhausted. Some of it was jet lag and some the natural letdown from the morning's controlled adrenaline rush. But something else flattened the gathering's energy: *the fishermen had had their day in court, but their story had not been heard*. Rather, a technical debate had taken place over the meaning of three words in a seventy-five year old statute.

The World Bank's claim to absolute immunity pivoted on the meaning of these words. All parties agreed that a 1944 statute granted international organizations "the same immunity as that of foreign sovereigns." In 1944 this meant complete immunity, but Congress subsequently eliminated foreign sovereign immunity under certain circumstances. The *Jam* case could continue if the Supreme Court ruled that, when Congress defined the immunity for international organizations to be "the same as" foreign sovereign immunity, it intended the former to evolve over time as the latter itself changed.

Our superb counsel sought to keep the court's focus on the statutory language, which was our strongest argument. A majority of the court, at the time, was widely viewed as favoring corporate interests over those of individuals and particularly disfavoring lawsuits brought by foreign plaintiffs alleging harm outside the United States. The best strategy for winning was actually to *avoid* talking about the specific nature of the plaintiffs and their claims. The lawyers knew the court would be moved by the plain meaning of the statute, not the injustice visited on fishermen and farmers living eight thousand miles away.

The potential disconnect between the correct legal strategy and the plaintiffs' reality triggered some discomfort in me regarding the role of lawyers in transnational advocacy: What does it mean when we replace the passionate voices of our clients with our own polish and analysis? It is, of course, our job to *professionalize* the discourse—some would say sanitize it—to match a particular advocacy strategy and institutional context. Lawyers are well-trained in shaping our clients' stories into a legal narrative that can explain, legitimize, and validate their claims in language understood by other professionals, like those who sit on courts or run the World Bank. But when we are pushing for radical change, our voices— powerful though they are—are rarely sufficient in isolation from a broader (and louder) narrative.

In fact, in *Jam*, counsel had made a different decision when the case was argued before the lower Appeals Court. Because that court had already upheld the bank's absolute immunity in several previous cases, we knew we were likely to lose and be forced to appeal to the Supreme Court. In preparation for the Appeals Court hearing, Rick Herz, the EarthRights International lawyer representing the plaintiffs, was urged to tell the fishermen's stories to the court. This might not be enough to give the judges a reason to turn their back on decades of their own precedent, but at least the injustices caused by the IFC would be placed on the record and reported in the media. Rick highlighted the fishermen's stories, which seemed to answer the curiosity of at least one of the three sitting judges. As the judges entered the packed courtroom, Judge Cornelia Pillard was overheard asking the other two judges, "Wow, I wonder why we've drawn such a crowd?" During the hearing, Judge Pillard seemed sympathetic to the plaintiffs' plight, and, indeed, she would write a separate opinion inviting the Supreme Court to accept their case. I am certain that the connection between the abstract legal principles and the flesh-and-blood people these principles affected was partly responsible for her favorable opinion.

*

The relationship between the legal narrative inside a courtroom, legislature, or boardroom and the external political narrative had been clear from the earliest days of the global campaign to reform the World Bank. Now, in 2018, as I sat next to Joe Athialy, in court and at our celebratory lunch afterward, I could not help but think back thirty years, when a compatriot and comrade of his, Medha Patkar, first came to Washington, DC, to tell the story of the plight of tens of thousands of Indians threatened with forcible evictions from their homes in anticipation of rising flood waters behind a massive new dam on the Narmada River.

The Narmada dam had been financed by the World Bank. Beginning in the late 1980s, Medha Patkar was leading massive protests, campaigns that Joe and other activists linked to the push for reforms at the World Bank, an effort I was supporting in Washington, DC. In the Narmada Valley, thousands of people marched; back in DC, Lori Udall of the US-based Environmental Defense Fund raised the controversy with Congressman James Scheuer. Scheuer invited Medha Patkar to testify in the US Congress in 1989.

Medha's powerful testimony had almost immediate impact. Not only did the US government start to raise questions, Japanese and Dutch officials saw the testimony and their governments too raised concerns to the bank's board of directors. Shortly after, the bank constituted an independent commission to review its support of the project. The resulting report largely confirmed the villagers' claims of significant human rights violations. India would ultimately withdraw its request for funding from the bank. For several years, US congressmen who heard Medha testify cited impacts in the Narmada Valley when they tied further support for World Bank financing to environmental and social reforms. Previously closed doors at the highest level of the bank opened to me and other representatives of affected people.

Lori Udall could have relied on her own testimony of what she had witnessed in the Narmada Valley, but she recognized the value of Congress hearing directly from those more closely representing the flooded victims—and equally the value of others knowing that the Narmada protesters had been to the US Congress. Creating space for Medha's passionate testimony was the right strategic choice for the venue.

On Capitol Hill, in 1989, the voices of those threatened with being flooded out of their homes in the Narmada Valley were heard loud and clear. But in 2018, just across the road at the Supreme Court, the voices of fishermen from another part of India were silenced in favor of their lawyers. As I said goodbye to Joe and Bharat before their long journey back to India, I thought about how this difference exemplified the strategic importance of choosing the right voice and messenger in seeking justice for communities. For me, making that choice has been a matter of trial and error, and of lessons learned.

Although I did not see Medha's testimony, I felt its reverberations. The independent commission established to look into the Narmada Dam was the model and inspiration for the Inspection Panel, created in 1993 to investigate complaints raised by local people about World Bank projects. Much of my work in the years since has centered on aiding communities to "follow the money" and press their claims at the Inspection Panel, which was specifically designed to bring the voices of affected people directly to the highest levels of the bank. In this way, the arc from Narmada to *Jam* spanned much of my career and provided many lessons in how to mix campaigning and legal strategies: how to blend the power of law with the power of people.

*

"Why would these men come all this way just to lie to me?"

I was glad that the World Bank president James Wolfensohn's question was not directed to me, but to Shahid Javed Burki, the bank's vice president for Latin America. Australian born, Wolfensohn carried himself with the confidence and charisma of a world leader who had succeeded at everything he did. The men to whom Wolfensohn was referring were two middle-aged Paraguayan fishermen whose sun-weathered faces and evident discomfort in an office reflected a life spent outdoors. They had arrived the night before from small villages where the massive bank-financed Yacyreta dam threatened to destroy the livelihoods of artisanal fishermen and brickmakers.

Guiding the fishermen through the enormous, bustling World Bank lobby, I was conscious of how they stood out, in their worn but neat jeans and plain collared shirts: they noticed too, apologizing for their poor English. But as we walked in to Wolfensohn's top-floor office he ignored all the suits in the room—including the vice president for Latin America, the Inspection Panel chair, two or three other Bank officials, and me—and moved directly to greet the two fishermen, sticking out his hand and guiding them to the two seats closest to him. This set the tone: he focused intently on the fishermen as they told him of their concerns.

At one point Burki, the bank vice president, interrupted, challenging the fishermen's claims that the key project documents had not been translated into Spanish nor effectively conveyed to local communities. Burki insisted that the project documents had been translated and were widely available in Paraguay. It was then that Wolfensohn turned abruptly toward him and asked why the fishermen would lie to him. Turning back to the fishermen, he instructed the vice president personally to fix the problem in the next few weeks, or begin looking for new employment.

I am not always quieted by World Bank presidents, but I learned to hold my tongue that day. Wolfensohn respectfully welcomed me and my colleague, a Paraguayan environmental activist named Elías Díaz Peña, and thanked us for coming, but he wanted to hear from us about as much as he wanted to hear from his vice president. He made it very clear that he was interested in the unfiltered voice of the fishermen his institution was supposed to be helping. Having studied Wolfensohn closely, I understood his position: while Elias and I might have a political agenda, the fishermen themselves would speak with passion, and without pretence, of their lived experience. Although Elías and I were prepared to cite all the bank policy provisions that supported the Paraguayan fishermen, in this instance our silence better served their cause. Our position prevailed precisely because we stayed silent.

*

James Wolfensohn's attention to the Paraguayan fishermen was exceptional among World Bank officials who prefer to speak through "professional" intermediaries, either because they have no interest or no experience in meeting affected community representatives. A few months earlier, I had met Ibrahim Shihata, the World Bank general counsel, when he summoned Lori Udall and me to his office in the midst of a dispute over his powers.

"Do you know how rare it is for someone in my position to meet with someone like you?" he asked, somewhat aggressively, even before greeting us or shaking our hands. Shihata was one of the world's most respected international lawyers and by far the most powerful person at the bank: he had been general counsel for decades. He was gruff and imperious, feared by bank staff and government lawyers alike. He followed his opening salvo with "Are you lawyers?" and "Where did you go to law school?" We didn't know whether to be insulted or to laugh. Apparently satisfied with our credentials, he ushered us into his office.

I had expected the meeting to be contentious, but I had not expected to be met with such apparent disdain. Shihata, after all, had been the bank's primary architect of the Inspection Panel, which had been designed in part to satisfy benchmarks set by Lori and me. We were now in a struggle to ensure that the panel remained independent and effective in monitoring bank operations. Lori and I had recently rebutted Shihata's assertion of authority over how the panel should operate. We argued that the general counsel had an inherent conflict of interest and the panel should obtain its own legal advice. Because of our political influence (as much as our legal analysis), we were prevailing, and the general counsel was facing a rare loss in a major decision. We had received an audience, I suspected, because he wished to bully us into deference.

But I was wrong. "Why do you NGOs hate me so much?" he said as we settled on to his couch. "I have never met any of you before." Over the course of the meeting, I came to understand what I first took as insult was actually ignorance mixed with curiosity. Such was the state of civil society alienation in international law that one of the most well-respected and influential international lawyers, working at one of the most important international organizations, had never before actually met with somebody who represented fishermen, or bricklayers, or any other community members directly affected by bank-financed projects. He only met with governments, given that governments alone were perceived to represent the interests of their citizens at the bank.

But the Narmada campaign and creation of the Inspection Panel had changed things: it had given affected people and their representatives direct access to the World Bank and in time to other international financial institutions. The Inspection Panel was new and we were setting precedents with every meeting. Lori and I were also a new breed of international lawyer. We did not aspire to represent governments or the World Bank. Less interested in the development of international law for its own sake, we aimed to address injustices done to communities that had no rights to be heard in international law. It was a sea change, and Shihata's struggle to grasp this was a clear reminder of how discomforting such a sea change could be to the status quo.

The status quo is powerful, and public interest lawyers face steep obstacles in finding legal forums that will allow vulnerable communities to be heard—whether through their lawyer or directly. And as illustrated by Mr. Shihata's greeting, international movement lawyers must overcome a legal culture in which their clients are not always recognized as legitimate participants. This makes our work more challenging, perhaps, than movement lawyering at a national level, where the role of lawyers and the rights to legal counsel are as entrenched as the citizen's rights to participate, to consult, and to petition public officials. In the international context, no such consensus exists, and thus we lawyers have to fight to get affected communities in the door and then must learn when to be silent and let the communities speak for themselves.

*

"World Bank, Are You Listening?"

So read the placards of hundreds of Tibetans protesting outside the World Bank in July 2000, timed perfectly so that the protesters' chanting and drumming could be heard inside the bank just as the board of directors considered the Inspection Panel's legalistic findings. At issue was whether the bank would support a loan to China, its largest and most powerful borrower, for an ill-conceived effort to transplant fifty-five thousand ethnic Chinese to lands used traditionally by Tibetan nomads. The conflict became an international test for China's claims of sovereignty over Tibet and enflamed tensions with the United States over China's human rights record. Alleging "interference" with its internal affairs, China at one point even threatened to leave the World Bank if the project was not approved.

Now, in Washington, DC, the confluence of "external" Tibetan voices and internal legal ones had been orchestrated by my colleague Dana Clark and our partner, the International Campaign for Tibet. With high stakes and a powerful opponent, the panel's clear confirmation that the project did not comply with the bank's environmental policies could not guarantee the project would be improved or stopped. The active protests let bank management know that continued support for China's project would come with a reputational cost. Alone, neither the legal strategy nor the campaign strategy would have prevailed. But the strength and moral clarity of the Tibetan voices made the bank *want* to stop the project and the lawyers' apolitical confirmation of noncompliance gave them the political *cover* to reject the project. Faced with an imminent and embarrassing defeat at the board of directors, China formally withdrew its funding request from the World Bank. In this way, the power of law and the power of people gave the Tibetans a rare victory over their Chinese oppressors.

The same explicit blend of people power and legal power converged later that year during the World Bank Annual Meetings in Prague. Anti-globalization protests raged in the streets. Anarchists broke with the tra-ditions of nonviolent civil disobedience and rampaged through the city. Organized marchers, including bank reform campaigners, joined in the protests, chanting among other things "Get your ass out of oil, mining, and gas." A few of us lawyers and policy advocates remained in dialogue with the bank. Our threats to walk out and join the protesters moved the bank to make a number of concessions, including a review of its entire extractive industries portfolio. Close coordination between the outside protesters and the inside advocates ensured that the concessions responded to the protest demands. It would take another eighteen years of campaigning and policy work, led by Oil Change International, before the bank finally announced it would provide no further support for fossil fuels.

*

In April 2019, five months after Joe Athialy and Bharat Patel came to Washington, DC, the Supreme Court overturned decades of decisions in lower courts and held the World Bank was no longer absolutely immune from lawsuits in the United States. Mr. Jam's case and others like it would be allowed to continue; he might yet still have his whole story told, and he might still compel the World Bank to pay for the damages from its negli-gent financing.

In India, Joe Athialy travelled to Gujarat for a victory celebration, and brought Medha Patkar as a special guest of honour. "I say this is the biggest victory because this has laid a foundation on which further victories could be built," she told the gathering—evoking the long road traveled from

Narmada and the way the struggles of villagers from both the Narmada Valley and the Gujarat coast have helped affected people around the world fight against economic injustice. The Narmada campaign used the power of locally organized people to strengthen the bank's environmental and social policies and to create a space for citizen-based advocacy at the bank. These were advances that would make a "follow the money" strategy standard for the global financial justice movement. Although the *Jam* case would ultimately be dismissed on other grounds, it opened new possibilities for holding global financial institutions accountable through its success in eliminating the bank's absolute immunity.

Reflecting on the journey from Narmada to Tata, it is clear to me that while "the power of law" and "the power of people" need to work together, there is no formula for how the legal "voice" and the people's "voice" interrelate—except, perhaps, that neither is likely to bring success entirely on its own. It is a fluid situation, requiring flexibility in strategies and in the lawyer's role.

Whose voice is being presented, and how it is being presented, are context-specific decisions. Where you are advocating can also influence whose voice is chosen to fill the room. Going to the US judicial system virtually guarantees the lawyer a central role in setting the strategy and controlling the narrative. This does not foreclose broader, more direct messages from the community, but it does give the lawyer the largest microphone.

But as suggested by the above, once outside the confines of the court, the choice of who expresses what narrative may be one best made by campaigners or community leaders who have a broader perspective. Chad Dobson, the founder of the Bank Information Center and the primary architect of the Bank reform campaign, once asked me, "What difference does it make if I pay you $5,000 to write a brilliant policy brief or if I spend $5,000 creating street puppets, if I get the same result?" It hurts as a lawyer to be compared to a street puppet, but the sentiment is worth remembering. In long-term efforts for social justice reform, street puppets and lawyers are both best thought of as tools in an overarching campaign. Certainly, lawyers might be more helpful than street puppets in figuring out the campaign strategy—but we also bring risks. Lawyers thrive in legalistic venues that simultaneously professionalize the discourse and risk devaluing the community's voice. The lawyer's role is to recognize that bias and support the community's right to choose whether to tell their story through puppets, through lawyers, or through their own voice. After all, the people we represent are the ones who reap the benefits (or endure the consequences) of our advocacy. In choosing how and who gets to tell their story, they at least have the opportunity to tell their story their way and, in doing so, to gain some form of narrative justice.

Further Reading: On efforts to reform the World Bank: Bruce Rich, *Mortgaging the Earth: The World Bank, Environmental Impoverishment, and the Crisis of Development* (Island Press, 2013). On community-based advocacy at the World Bank Inspection Panel and other accountability mechanisms: Dana Clark, Jonathan Fox, and Kay Treakle, eds., *Demanding Accountability: Civil-Society Claims and the World Bank Inspection Panel* (Rowan & Littlefield, 2003); David Hunter, "Using the World Bank Inspection Panel to Defend the Interests of Project-Affected People," *Chicago Journal of International Law*, vol. 4, no. 201, 2003. Also, visit the websites of Accountability Counsel, www.accountabilitycounsel.org; the Bank Information Center, www.bankinformationcenter.org; and the Center for International Environmental Law, www.ciel.org.

ACTIVISTS ON LEGAL POWER

Jonny and Me: Three Decades of Debating the Law and Social Movements

ROBIN GORNA

Jonny and I used to tussle about this: How best to achieve social justice? Is it all about using the law to force change? Or should we focus our efforts on building movements?

We had met in London in 1987, both of us idealistic recent graduates who had landed unexpectedly in the early days of the AIDS crisis. Outraged by the discrimination swirling around us and fired up with youthful zeal, we plotted ways to make change happen. It wasn't academic: our fury at the hideous discrimination against individuals and communities was grounded in respect and friendship with many of them, people whose lives were being ruined by this wretched illness and facing near-certain death. Many were in their twenties—like us.

Although Jonny and I both spent our lives fighting for social justice, especially gender and sexuality rights, our paths diverged. I stayed mostly with social movements, working from the grassroots up. He went into law, changing things from the top. His was the more establishment direction—although a big part of his impact, and charm, was that he was never fully absorbed by it.

Thirty-four years later, in September 2021, Jonathan Cooper died unexpectedly of a heart attack while walking in the Scottish highlands with his husband, Kevin. Jonny's career had been illustrious: in 2008 he was made an OBE—the Order of the British Empire—bestowed by the Queen, for his work on human rights law. Meanwhile, I found myself working in international development, and expanding my feminist zeal to fight for sexual and reproductive rights as well as AIDS and global health.

When we first met, I had just started at the Terrence Higgins Trust (THT), the UK's new AIDS charity, and Jonny had a job at the British

Haemophilia Society. I had hoped for a life in the theater; his passion was history. Fresh out of university, we were both startled to find ourselves in such responsible roles, in the middle of an urgent crisis. His focus was young men living with HIV and hemophilia, as well as their parents—people battling with the daily indignities of their inherited illness combined with rank prejudice against HIV, the virus they'd received with their treatment. I had in my sights the rapidly growing number of (mainly) gay men with AIDS, their lovers and friends, and the generous strangers who stood by their sides. My first job at THT was to organize the Buddy service—those generous volunteers whom people leaned on when families abandoned their dying sons; when people found themselves too exhausted by the daily horrors of sitting at the bedside of one friend or lover after another, worrying that they would be next.

One of Jonny's first actions was to oversee the Haemophilia Society's work suing the government for compensation, on behalf of the 1,200 people who had acquired HIV by following the National Health Service's advice and receiving a contaminated clotting agent. In 1987, this meant near-certain death from AIDS. The state refused to accept liability, instead offering a cash settlement—about £20,000 per person. Jonny was outraged, but in the end the society decided that immediate welfare needs trumped the point of principle.

"I saw the potential of law, but where people did use it, they rarely succeeded," Jonny would later write of these early experiences, which stayed with him forever. He remembered early cases such as a young woman being told that she was pregnant and had HIV. She was pressure to have a termination and at the same time to be sterilized: she had no legal recourse. "The lack of a framework of rights showed the weakness of the common law and administrative law," Jonny later wrote. "People were left without any language of rights to articulate their grievance." Facing the constant flood of individual cases, Jonny created a coalition of nongovernment organizations (NGOs) to draft a "UK Declaration of rights for people with HIV and AIDS." He got into it the gritty detail of the Universal Declaration of Human Rights, and the European Convention that was inspired by it. He saw his path and went back to university to train as a barrister, a legal advocate.

Jonny and I saw the same horrors, the individual cases of discrimination and hateful behavior. But my response was different, perhaps because of my growing feminist consciousness. While he started to focus on the law as a solution, my focus became political advocacy, awareness raising, and movement building. I'd already started to flex my muscle as an organizer, sorting out the THT Buddies so they could provide direct help to hundreds of individuals with AIDS. Now I sharpened my skills in strategy, facilitation, and communication, finding ways for people's voices to be heard. The starting point was to help make connections: with others facing similar challenges, and with the politicians, bureaucrats, and media who could help them to make change happen. I was helping movements take off: through meetings to share stories, more formal research, seminars, conferences, media articles, and evidence sessions in Parliament, and eventually through the UN. I was connecting people, pulling them together to provide support and education. And to make a noise.

So began my debates with Jonny. To me, all this talk of declarations— the focus on erudite documents and perfect language—seemed like an excuse to delay action. Later, working in the belly of big bureaucracies, I would come to see the power of using language, "agreed text," as a hook to get things done. But back in those painful, death-filled days, I wanted action, not words on paper. The law was dry and boring.

Jonny got busy drafting the declaration and preparing to be a barrister. I got busy mobilizing a boycott of the 1990 International AIDS Conference in San Francisco, the big gathering where the declaration was to be launched. We used the injustice of the US immigration law—at this point they still stopped people with HIV from entering the country—to shine a light on the human rights of people with HIV. It was an egregious law, but only one of the many immediate acts of discrimination that people with AIDS encountered. A high-profile boycott was a perfect opportunity to bang the drum about human rights.

Although we could spend hours raging at each other about what we thought the limitations were with "dry old legal arguments" or "grassroots action," we understood that there was a powerful synergy between our approaches. Without the protests—mobilizing hundreds of people to stand together, to make noise and shame the US—the well-crafted text of the declaration could have been just fine words on a page, an academic exercise fit for a journal. The declaration made it clear that it wasn't just one bad US law that we cared about. The boycott, and the broader movement that called for change, was designed to get policy makers, the public, and our colleagues to focus on that fact: AIDS was an epidemic of discrimination and human rights abuses, not only about early death and degrading illness. This may seem obvious now, but this campaign was the start of people, and the movement, understanding that AIDS was about human rights: it wasn't "just another illness."

Jonny's group was busy digging around the international treaties and declarations. Meanwhile, I was working the phones. If his job was to present an ideal version of how the world should be, mine was to tell anyone who would listen how the world actually *was*: recounting actual stories of discrimination to the organizations planning to attend the conference and asking them to take the big hit of boycotting it. It wasn't an easy ask. This was only the sixth time that the global AIDS community had gathered. Being there changed lives and perspectives, as I knew from attending my first conference in 1989. In the pre-internet era the best way to drive change was to sit together with comrades from other countries and share war stories. Refusing to attend sent a strong message. It also hit the US financially—these massive gatherings of several thousand delegates are big earners for the host city.

The declaration was launched—long distance, from the UK—and many organizations held firm to the boycott. The noise we made was a rallying cry for all AIDS activists, irrespective of whether they actually wanted to travel to the conference. It took two more decades for the US to drop its discriminatory immigration law, but we made bigger change: the idea that HIV was about human rights and discrimination became a given. The UN convened working groups on AIDS and human rights, released their own declarations, and always made reference to the original UK one.

*

Returning from a trip to New York in 1992 I excitedly updated Jonny about developments with ACT UP, the AIDS Coalition to Unleash Power—the edgy, rapidly expanding movement that was already forcing change in America. The core of ACT UP was people with HIV, and their lovers, friends, and doctors. It worked in part because they united with "insider allies": people from government, media, and research working alongside artists, filmmakers, musicians, and other cultural disrupters. In 1992, ACT UP was five years old. It wasn't forced or overstructured, instead deploying an innovative, gritty—and at times chaotic—democracy. The movement—like all good movements, I would come to understand—was a heady mix of different types of people, all united by shared hopes, goals, passions, and personal experiences.

To me, ACT UP was a perfect example of something I was coming to understand as central to movements: the way effective action comes out of the forging of connections, the expression of common desires, values, and expectations. And friendship, of course—often the friendships forged in youth. ACT UP organised dramatic "direct actions," such as "die ins" on Wall Street; ACT UP also drafted Treatment Manifestos for backroom negotiations with researchers. There was room for all sorts of different types of people using their different sets of skills toward the same goal, for the Robins *and* the Jonnys, the creatives and the policy wonks and many more besides. They met together on Monday evenings at the Lesbian and Gay Community Services Center on West Thirteenth Street. These meetings were raucous, bonding, hugely effective—and very long. I told Jonny I had never seen anything like it.

"Oh please, Robin," Jonny responded. "Of course we love our ACT UP friends. Yes, 'Silence = Death' stickers, Keith Haring paintings, it's all fabulous. But stop being so naive. Just because a bunch of like-minded people get together and focus on a shared issue, why would that bring about change? We need to pull in genuine expertise, find smart incentives that will force change."

"Of course movements must be more than just connections between great people," I conceded, reflecting that self-help groups also connect people of a shared identity, and are often full of personal meaning, but are more static. Still, I wasn't giving up the fight. "Movements are connection with purpose," I told him. "Magical places to search for personal identity, to clarify the values that will motivate us for a lifetime; a place to find people who we want to connect with—especially when we're young, exploring. Movements are grounded in emotion, identity, culture—that's why the stickers and the art matters. When we feel, we act. We go after the treatments, the compassionate services, needle and syringe exchanges, and other prevention programs that actually work. And sure, we go after the bad laws too." Movements were about the long run, I told him: "Who knows what we'll need in ten years? Get the magic ingredients right and, together, we'll figure it out: now, and in a decade. That way the big changes will happen, again and again!"

Jonny wasn't conceding: laws changed society. Mass movements might exert pressure on the streets and get people talking, but the real business of change depended on legal experts.

"It's not so simple, Jonny!" I said. "Of course we've got to change the rules that matter most, but obsessing about legal change might mean missing opportunities. Who cares about perfect legislation if no one at the hospital will touch you because they hate gays and are terrified of infection? We have to start with what matters most in people's lives: the immediate struggles, changing hearts, minds, social understanding, getting more money in place."

I'm pretty sure I won that round. Thirty years on, ACT UP still stands as a model for how to create space for collectives of people to respond to things that are in flux. This band of angry, creative, and often dying young people is credited with forcing a massive increase in US government funds, and then a dramatic reduction in global AIDS treatment prices so lifesaving drugs actually reached people.

I'll concede that he won too. 1992 was the year that he was called to the bar. As a barrister he combined his solid legal training with all that work on the declaration to reach a bigger stage. Within a year the Labour Party had committed to a Human Rights Act; it became law in 1998, within months of Labour winning the election. Remarkable. Many friends at his funeral—all very well positioned to ensure the act has teeth—spoke about how he used his formidable passion to persuade politicians to adopt it. He then dedicated his professional life to advocating for it to be used, including training judges and even the military to apply it. Jonny used the act to win cases on gays in the military and on transgender rights; when he died he was gearing up to use it against conversion therapy.

*

One morning in 2018, Jonny and I bumped into each other in a bright, wisteria-clad café off Oxford Street in central London. Our nomadic lives had broken the daily connection between us, and now, over several cups of coffee, we spilled stories of our adventures.

Jonny had recently moved back to Doughty Street, the progressive chambers where, as the first openly gay barrister, he was having fun setting up "Outy Street" for LGBTQ colleagues. He'd spent five years running the Human Dignity Trust, a legal NGO he'd helped establish to defend the human rights of LGBTQ people globally. He spoke of the trust's wild ambition to overturn the hideous laws on homosexuality still on the books of so many countries. I was strangely moved that, despite the breaks in our daily friendship, the focus of our work had stayed the same. But I wasn't convinced by his tactics. "Why should progressive lawyers push legal interventions from on high?" I asked, "Isn't it better to stay grounded, focus on sparking social movements that will create demand from within communities? The people who suffer under the law should decide what happens!"

With formidable legal precision he argued that, as the original architects of many of these laws, British lawyers had an obligation to advocate for legal change in the seventy-one jurisdictions that still criminalized private consensual sex between adults of the same sex. He thumped the table: "Don't you think it's our fault? Thirty-four of them are Commonwealth countries!" He reminded me of the history: Britain introduced the original anti-sodomy legislation in Australia and then in India when they were colonies, and it multiplied across our empire; all these laws trace back to Henry VIII's Buggery Act, enacted in 1533. "We have a responsibility to right the wrongs!"

I assured him I loathed the laws too; of course they were an assault on human rights. "But who has the right to take them down? My African activist friends get really angry about flying in well-meaning, elite white lawyers." I told him of recent discussions with activists in Uganda, Tanzania, Nigeria, even India. All were kicking back against this approach. They told me it would backfire: outsiders rarely understood the context of their countries. Reforms would be slammed by powerful politicians and others who had adopted anti-gay thinking as culturally normative. "The groups I work with have found ways to work around, and below, the law," I told him, "They want to start with cultural change, to bring their elders with them, not force them to change. Bluntly, they see this kind of interference as simply a new form of colonial behavior; it's the legal equivalent of regime change."

Jonny was enraged at suggestions that he was colonial: "If I have expertise, why shouldn't I share it? Change society? Sure, very nice. But all a bit fluffy. And it will take decades! How many more young lesbians will be murdered? Transgender youth kill themselves? Gay men die from AIDS? You know how this plays out, Robin. It's fantasyland to say we can wait for cultures to change." He was yelling now, embarrassing the other coffee drinkers: *"How many more have to die?"*

He was dangling the old ACT UP battle cry from the 1990s. I feared this would get nasty and aimed for safer ground. By telling him about my current work, I also hoped to score a point. The previous year, I'd been asked to take the slogan "She Decides" and see if we could turn it into a global movement. Colleagues thought that my experiences living in the middle of AIDS movements could help women's rights movements to advance with similar impact.

"She Decides" had first been used by European politicians to object to Donald Trump's very first policy action in 2017: to reinstate—and dramatically expand—the US "Global Gag Rule." this stipulated that funds couldn't be used by any NGO—even HIV groups—that provided any information about abortion care, or supported safe abortion policies. I told Jonny that I'd just left a gathering of youth groups and politicians from East and Southern Africa, and would soon be flying east to launch our first national movement, SheDecides India, in a shopping mall near Delhi.

"These sound like lovely events," he said, a bit snarkily, "but why on earth aren't you using strategic litigation to sort the Trump mess out?" he asked.

We had been debating it, I told him, "but success seems really unlikely. It will be expensive and distract us from the bigger issues." I gave him the background. The Global Gag Rule was a Republican Party thing. When President George W. Bush imposed it in 2003, his focus was to cut funding for sex worker programs. At that time, US-based organizations spent vast sums of money on legal cases to reverse the rule. Human rights lawyers were engaged; they argued well and apparently got the right changes—but on paper only—and it took eight years. Along the way relationships were badly eroded with the sex worker rights groups that were supposed to gain from change. They had been tangled up in the litigation for years, and had seen no benefit; they had also fallen out with their lawyers, who deemed their arguments to be "unstrategic." The real stinger was that their organizations suffered financially: legal action closed some of the loopholes that had kept funds flowing.

"With SheDecides we need to see quick change," I told Jonny. "Prosecuting the Global Gag Rule doesn't seem viable in terms of costs, time, or the likelihood of meaningful success. And most important, we want SheDecides to be a global movement. Getting dragged into a legal battle with the US government would send the message that the US matters most." Anyway, I added, "the new Global Gag Rule is just the spark. SheDecides is about a much bigger story. All over the world laws and policies get in the way of our sexual rights and reproductive justice. Bodily autonomy is about much more than Trump!"

Jonny understood the logic of not litigating against the Global Gag Rule—"You always have to do a cost/benefit analysis before going to court"—but wasn't fully convinced: "Nothing will ever change until the laws change. That's why we fought so hard for the Human Rights Act. Now when people with HIV face discrimination we go to court. We don't just make a noise!"

That one riled me. "We don't 'just make a noise' at SheDecides, Jonny!" Sure, the first of our goals was "Stand Up, Speak Out" but there were two more: "Unlock Resources" and "Change the Rules." "Of course we want to change the rules! We just don't think the law courts are always the best place to do that." I told him about our experience in Uganda, where two progressive policies—on comprehensive sexuality education and women's health care—had been consistently blocked by a fiercely anti-abortion "born-again" health minister, until activists, under cover of the global movement, decided to make some strategic noise. A brilliant youth activist named Patrick Mwesigye had connected a wide range of people under the banner of a local SheDecides movement: politicians, NGOs, diplomats, and youth united forces. "All these 'lovely events' that you complain about," I goaded, "That's what Patrick used to force the minister to release the guidance documents. Now the health workers and teachers breathe easy. They have official documents that confirm they have government backing when they do what is right by the women and girls they see. And it happened much faster and more effectively than if we'd gone the legal route in Uganda."

Jonny liked the example—"Okay, you win this one"—but still he wanted me to earn my morning coffee: "What are movements actually for? It all seems a bit too scattershot. Do they achieve legal change? Cultural change? Some of them seem to be just fundraisers." We agreed that solidarity, community, and the expression of shared values were all good things. "But what does it really take to catalyze, build, and sustain a movement of people and organizations creating change? Can your movements engineer and sustain success?"

"What I learned from our early work, and the movements I've been part of since," I told him, "is that it's all about responding to something that just isn't right. That might span many dimensions and alter over time. When we started out in the '80s, we could never have imagined that within three decades gay marriage would be legal and transgender rights enshrined in law." We talked about how those big changes started with the early gay movements, which in turn led to the vibrant global AIDS movement—our origin story—which then picked up new issues. There was a thread, many of the same groups of people; the demands shifted as we made progress. "As new voices and passions become entwined, the focus alters. A movement shifts course and direction to focus energy and effort on emerging challenges. There's continuity, because the values remain strong. Movements are not static. Some of the most effective ones resist structures and bureaucracies and institutional behavior."

"Robin, if that's the case how can you even call yourself a movement *builder*?" he shot back. "The very way you describe movements is in opposition to structure!"

I laughed out loud. Now we were in violent agreement. I told him that all the research I'd read, and my organic understanding of movements, had convinced me that social movements were dynamic, erratic beasts, slippery and changeable, perhaps necessarily anarchic and untamed. How could you *construct* something that is necessarily fluid? In the months ahead, as I wrapped up my work at SheDecides, Jonny's observation about the impossibility of movement building rang in my ears. I too became convinced that it was impossible to "build" a movement the way we had set out to do. Movements were an art rather than a science, but if anything, this only strengthened my belief in their power to make change by connecting people who shared values and energy. Trying to construct and shape movements just made them static and dull, the opposite of what made them so special and different from NGOs and campaigns. All I could do for movements like SheDecides was plunge in, and share ideas from my experiences that might help emerging leaders find their own magic.

*

At the 2019 conference that sparked this book, I found myself talking about Jonny with one of the other participants, the Kenyan lawyer Njeri Gateru, who had inspired us with tales of her movement to decriminalize homosexuality there. When she told me about Jonny's visit to her country to support this campaign, I braced myself, anticipating a story of pompous fly-in, fly-out British lawyers taking credit for all the hard work that she and her mates had started. But Njeri told a different story. She had been suspicious, to be sure, but was soon won over by Jonny's ebullience, passion, and joyful energy. And it was more than that personal connection. When they reached court, the proud elderly judges and lawyers for the other side— notorious for their homophobia and disregard of women—sat up and listened. It wasn't just the vision of older white men flying in from the former colonial power, she told me, although of course there will always be a bit of that. What Jonny's team brought were sharp legal perspectives, drawing on international law and agreements, as well as arguments from other countries that linked the Kenyan battle to a much wider context.

If this band of local lawyers and activists had the support of such an eminent legal team, who were not just sending messages but actually turned up to argue the law, then maybe there was something in all of this? Even if Njeri's team lost their case in 2019—they have taken it on appeal—their decriminalization case shifted public discourse in Kenya. Njeri described to me a true partnership between what we have called "the power of people" on the one hand and "the power of law" on the other.

This true partnership is where Jonny and I always landed in our arguments. Over the decades we had honed our argumentative skills, learned about the power of connections, advocacy, and agreements—legal and other. We knew that, as privileged white Brits, we had power that we should wield with care and respect for the dignity of the people whose rights were always at the center of our work. We were honest about our personal disappointments: both the legal approaches and the movements had their failings. Still, we remained passionate about the power of people, the importance of hearing their voices and supporting them to create lasting change.

A couple of months before he died, Jonny and I spoke about movements on a summer's weekend at his home in Devon. It was a post-vaccine treat to reconnect in person, and our conversations ranged across the new pandemic era. We were struck by the fact that the first mass breakouts from COVID-19 lockdowns were Black Lives Matter protests. Clicktivism could not suffice: people had a visceral need to stand together to be heard, whatever the health risks.

We agreed about lots that weekend: ACT UP, Extinction Rebellion, and Black Lives Matter all share a kind of creativity that is fundamental to successful movements. Greta Thunberg and Fridays for Future serve as brilliant examples: a fifteen-year old Swedish student strikes instead of attending school; nine months later nearly 1.5 million schoolchildren in over a hundred countries take similar action, and OPEC describes her as the biggest threat to the fossil fuel industry. Greta Thunberg would never have garnered international attention had she mobilized an online petition. She defied authority, stood outside her school, and encouraged others to get out on the streets too.

Since our summer chats I've been thinking of the way movements have heads and hearts. If Jonny were here now, I would love to wrap up that last conversation in Devon by saying to him that the best social movements connect the head—evidence, research, legal arguments—with the heart: identity, emotions, true connection. Of course movements need the law, because people need the law: to protect our dignity and support our freedom. Similarly, the law needs movements: if there is no demand for change, no stories of how the law fails, then the law just sits there. What rings in my ears are Jonny's words as we left our caffeine-fueled fight in 2018: "Law and movements, it's all about the 'and,' isn't it? It's a bit of both."

Further Reading and Viewing: More about Jonathan Cooper at "Jonathan Cooper: In Memoriam," at at https://www.doughtystreet. co.uk/Jonathan-Cooper. See also coverage of the Jonathan Cooper Chair of the Histories of Sexualities, established by Oxford University in 2022 https://www.ox.ac.uk/news/2022-02-08-oxford-university-establish-es-jonathan-cooper-professor-history-sexualities#; Jonathan Cooper, "The Human Rights Act: Repeal at Our Peril," *Huffpost*, October 6, 2014. For the UK Declaration of rights for people with HIV and AIDS, and related documents: hivhumanrights.org. On ACT UP: Larry Kramer, *The Normal Heart* (play, Samuel French, 1985, and film, directed by Ryan Murphy, 2014); David France, *How to Survive a Plague* (documentary film, 2012, and book, Penguin, 2017); Sarah Schulman, *Let the Record Show* (Farrar, Strauss & Giroux, 2022). On social movements: Greg Martin, *Understanding Social Movements* (Routledge, 2015); Donatella della Porta, *The Oxford Handbook of Social Movements* (Oxford University Press, 2017). See also www.robingorna.com for more related articles and links.

South Africa's AIDS Treatment Action Campaign: Rethinking Law's Relationship with Social Justice Movements

MARK HEYWOOD

In April 2019 I left my office at SECTION27 for the last time. I had a heavy heart.

Nine years earlier, together with my colleague Adila Hassim, I had set up the organization with the objective of using the law to fight for people's rights as guaranteed by the South African Constitution. In a relatively short time it had become respected and effective, leading many successful campaigns based on human rights law and litigation. Its name came from Section 27 of South Africa's Bill of Rights, which recognizes "access to health care services" as a basic human right, and most of the cases it fought were around access to health care and basic education.

By the time I resigned, after working for twenty-five years in public interest law NGOs, I had a growing sense of disquiet about whether the law could still be used to fight for social justice in the way we had done in the past. Yesterday's certainties had become today's uncertainties: democratic (or civic) space was contracting in many parts of the world, and after what seemed to be a short golden era for the recognition of human rights, these were now under attack from powerful forces, sometimes from within the heart of the very democracies that birthed and nurtured them, such as in the United Kingdom and the United States. I have also had a rising sense of panic about the climate crisis. Do we have *time* for the kind of incremental rights realization that happens through legal advocacy, as cases move like treacle through overburdened or inefficient judicial systems?

In this context I can't help but question whether law-centered human rights activism is "working." I do not doubt that law can be a potent instrument in the struggle for human rights and social justice. But we need new thinking about its relationships with social movements; in particular with poor people fighting to protect or fulfill their rights.

Certainly, in localized petri dishes of struggle, activists have proved that human rights law can be used in multiple ways to protect dignity and save lives. The best example in South Africa is access to AIDS treatment, which has saved at least five million lives. This is the work I did before I set up SECTION27, through South Africa's AIDS Law Project (ALP) and Treatment Action Campaign (TAC). But even while we were winning the war on HIV, inequalities in access to health services were widening. The same person could live with HIV but die of breast cancer that might have been cured with access to oncological services; the same child could be protected from HIV infection at birth but be suffering acute malnutrition. Is that not a contradiction?

I worried that, in this unprecedented era for the constitutional recognition of civil and political rights, we have been unable to bring about a sustained improvement in socioeconomic rights both in South Africa and globally. Is that, too, not a contradiction?

These questions need urgent attention and new strategies if law and human rights are to remain part of the solution to struggles for equality, and indeed the survival of the human species. The stakes are very high.

In this essay, I try to probe what I think combining law and movement building achieved in South Africa. And what it didn't. My starting point is that pro-equality, pro-poor social change is best achieved by mobilized people organized in political movements. Law offers a vital system and instrument to aid and abet the power of movements—when it is wielded effectively.

Throughout my years at TAC and SECTION27, I worked hard to try to join legal activism and movement building together. We did this extremely successfully with TAC, but I'm less sure about SECTION27, an organization I hoped would take human rights lawyering to scale and make an impact in new fields for rights. Reasons that explain our more limited success with SECTION27 may be applicable to other rights movements in South Africa and elsewhere.

*

In more than two centuries of struggles for freedom, social justice and human rights—law and social movements—have often been bedfellows. Law has been a useful means toward a just end, press-ganged into service from as early as the campaign against slavery in England in the eighteenth century.

But law is not a natural ally of the downtrodden. It is clipped, clinical, and precise, logical and formulaic. When utilized in political systems it can be vital as a check on power as well as a means for resolving disputes. Societies with no rule of law are inevitably harsher than societies with it, particularly for political activists. The law can be catalytic and even cathartic. Yet on its own, it cares nothing for democracy or rights. On the other hand, people's movements, like people themselves, are hot-blooded, noisy, and messy. They are diverse. They don't often take easily to rules. They can be intemperate. Movements rise and fall. They breathe. They can die.

For 350 years, the law in South Africa was used to oppress people because of their skin color, gender, class, sexual orientation, and a range of other factors. In 1994, with the advent of democracy, it was suddenly enlisted as an instrument intended to deepen freedom and advance social justice. This switch added legitimacy to the claims of human rights activists; with hindsight, we were probably too starry-eyed about our newfound friend. We were excited because it could now, at a national level, be the basis for making claims to socioeconomic rights. It also provided an architecture for international adjudication—through UN covenants, for example. Here, as in other places, the possibility of human rights lawfare did away with the need for warfare.

But, we have learned, it's important not to romanticize law. Its ability to guarantee rights such as adequate housing or quality basic education does not mean it has the ability to deliver these rights. Poor people have experienced this, and so, even where human rights law has began to sink its roots—be it in Columbia, India, Kenya, or South Africa—a trust deficit has often remained.

Law is deeply schizophrenic, even opportunistic. It has no intrinsic loyalties. In South Africa, the law could be used to delay justice and truth concerning the shooting dead of thirty-four protesting mine workers by police, at the behest of mine bosses, as it did in the Marikana massacre in

2012. It could also deliver antiretroviral medicines to millions of people under pressure from activists.

Bearing all this in mind, I believe the potency of human rights law ultimately depends on two interrelated factors.

The first is the extent to which people can be persuaded to see in law an ally and incorporate it into their struggles for rights to things such as health care, food, land; dignity, in other words. The second is the degree to which governments and other actors are willing to surrender some of their power to "rule of law," and to abide by court judgements. The first often depends on the second—and both depend on how human rights lawyers work. These factors are important because, even though a rights-based constitution like South Africa's might offer enormous power to people, it can be easily neutered, ignored, and eventually discarded altogether—particularly if there is not popular knowledge of and support for it.

In South Africa, colonialism and then apartheid were built on the foundations of law. Over centuries, attempts were made by Black people to invoke law and ally it to claims against land dispossession and disenfranchisement. But for the most part they were rebuffed. Law had been appropriated by the enemy. Sometimes its form could be commandeered to highlight oppression and mobilize opposition, such as in 1963–1964 during the famous Rivonia political trial of African National Congress (ANC) leaders including Nelson Mandela. But it was rarely used proactively as an underpinning for movement building.

It is therefore not surprising that, for a long time, the liberation movements did not consider legal activism as a significant weapon in their armory. In fact, they were largely built outside of the law, opting for civil disobedience in the 1950s and armed struggle and underground organization from the 1960s right until the demise of apartheid in 1994. "Make South Africa ungovernable," was the cry. Only in the 1980s did trade unions and civic organizations, who were using extralegal strategies that confronted the apartheid state through "stay-aways," consumer boycotts, and strikes, start to see advantages in using law and lawyers. This was not only through political trials to defend activists accused of treason but also as an instrument to poke holes in apartheid such as the Pass Laws, which prevented Black people from residing in white areas.

On the surface, it therefore seems a great irony that the settlement that ended apartheid took the form of an agreement to make the rule of law supreme. In recent years the 1996 Constitution has been heavily criticized, especially by young people, because it gave democracy but not freedom: the legal form but not fungible substance of rights; civil and political equality, including the right to vote, as a cover for rising socioeconomic disenfranchisement and inequality. But in one very profound sense, South Africa's 1996 Constitution did mark a revolution: *for the first time in history the supreme law ordered all of government to serve the vision of social justice and human rights.* It was a launchpad, not a docking station; a departure point, not a place of arrival.

Whilst the political negotiations that led to the Constitution were taking place, an HIV/AIDS epidemic was beginning to gather out of sight, using the very fault lines of race and gender inequality and discrimination to assist its spread. The response to AIDS would be one of the first tests of whether the law was now really on the side of the poor, and of whether the state and private companies accepted the injunction upon them to always ensure the protection and fulfillment of rights: in this case of millions of people living with HIV.

This is where my story begins.

*

I joined the AIDS Law Project (ALP) in 1994, two months after the first democratic election. It had been founded in 1992 as a new unit at the Centre for Applied Legal Studies (CALS) at Wits University in Johannesburg. It was led by Zackie Achmat, a former comrade of mine from the liberation struggle, and Edwin Cameron, a human rights lawyer.

The two came from very different traditions of law.

Cameron was one of a small number of white lawyers who in the 1980s played a pioneering role by subverting the letter of the law to support liberation movements fighting to undermine apartheid. Later, he spotted the overlap between HIV and democratic movement building: one of the first HIV discrimination issues Cameron took up was challenging the dismissal of migrant mine workers who had tested positive for HIV. He also had a personal reason: he was a gay man who had been diagnosed with HIV in 1986. He knew both stigma and fear of illness firsthand.

Zackie Achmat was a Black political activist who in his youth had mobilized communities against the law. When I first met him, he was a leader of the Marxist Workers Tendency (MWT), an organization committed to organizing a socialist revolution and the destruction of "bourgeois" legal systems. Like Cameron, he was gay.

Individual relationships sometimes play a very important role in seeding social movements. I was also a member of the MWT and got to know Achmat through "the struggle." Achmat had come to know Cameron in an intersecting struggle for gay and lesbian rights, particularly the successful campaign to include nondiscrimination on the grounds of sexual orientation in an "equality clause" in the new constitution. I think these campaigns alerted him to the radical and transformative potential of constitutional law.

In the early 1990s, after he was diagnosed with HIV, Achmat too turned his attention to the fight against AIDS. For both men, legal activism to advance the rights of people living with HIV did not start in response to a preexisting campaign or mass mobilization by people affected by or living with HIV: stigma and denial meant there was no such movement. Rather, it was because they anticipated the devastating path of HIV and attempted to cut it off by using human rights law. This was very different from the role lawyers had played in the dying days of apartheid, when law had been enlisted by political activists to serve a bold, united, and rising movement.

In the beginning our focus at ALP was on building a protective legal framework for the response to the HIV epidemic. The ALP had no aspirations to become a mass movement. It was a university-based law clinic that worked on a case-by-case basis with an eye to achieving a wider public impact through legal precedent. But Achmat and I knew that this work was never going to change the course of the HIV epidemic. Although unfair discrimination was often driven by individual prejudice, the real drivers of South Africa's HIV epidemic were deep-rooted and societal. In fact, the fault lines along which HIV began to run riot were created by the very same apartheid laws that served to subordinate Black women, disrupt rural livelihoods, and dispossess Black men so as to channel their labor to the gold mines.

Because Achmat and I had grown up in liberation movements that sought revolution rather than merely trying to ameliorate the symptoms of oppressive systems, we understood that law *alone* could never command sufficient power to protect the rights of millions of people with HIV. We knew that legal advocacy and litigation could play an important role. But it had to be in the service of a movement. We faced a problem: because HIV has always been clouded in stigma, fear, denial, and silence, it did not lend itself easily to spontaneous organization or movement building. HIV begins by isolating and dividing people, rather than uniting them. A life-threatening virus is a threat to people's bodies from within—very different from the external threats that galvanize and unite many communities. If there was going to be a movement, the law—and the lawyers at ALP—were going to have play a role in making it happen.

In 1998, the death of Simon Nkoli, the legendary freedom fighter and Black gay activist who was also a pioneering AIDS activist, became a catalyst to this process. Before his death Nkoli had called for "a fighting campaign" against AIDS, much as there had been against apartheid. At his funeral Achmat spoke angrily about discrimination and inequality in access to antiretrovirals. Several days later, on international Human Rights Day, he organized a small demonstration in Cape Town. That date marks the birth of what became the Treatment Action Campaign.

The kind of conditions that crystallize social movements may have been ripening, but that was not enough. The first stage of movement building requires activism to consolidate a community. People with HIV might have been angry, but many were also immobilized by fear and felt powerless. Invoking the new South African Constitution, we hoped, would help give people a sense of legitimacy and self-confidence, and the conviction to demand equality and access to lifesaving treatment. From that moment onward the constitution became a primary weapon in our campaigns: it was pulled out and thrust at officials in meetings; it was used to educate people about their own rights; it became a prop to build self-belief in battered bodies.

But what really built support for TAC and increased its membership was the way we used law to advance the demand for access to lifesaving treatment. By turning to the courts, and other statutory bodies such as the

Competition Commission, we transformed private yearnings for life and health into public demands for medicines; moral convictions about equality into legal claims against inequality. Without seeking permission from our donors, I directed all ALP's financial and human resources into building another organization, TAC. I persuaded ALP's employees that our job now was primarily to service this rising movement. ALP lawyers were expected to attend TAC meetings, to run workshops educating activists on the cases we were involved in, and to be there to support TAC branches.

This approach took off in the early 2000s when TAC became involved in a succession of court cases. First it was admitted as amicus curiae to support legislation passed by the Nelson Mandela government to make all medicines more affordable. This campaign taught us how to use a court case to build a movement—and how to use a movement to advance a legal battle. A year later, we built on this when we went to court once more to challenge the government's refusal to provide the antiretroviral medicine Nevirapine to pregnant mothers with HIV, which would reduce the risk of transmitting the virus to their babies. This tense campaign lasted for nearly two years until, on July 5, 2002, the Constitutional Court ordered the government to roll out a program to all health facilities in South Africa. In the years ahead this judgment saved at least a million lives. It also became the touchstone for jurisprudence internationally around the right to health, referred to in legal textbooks worldwide.

From these campaigns we learned some key lessons about how to organize a mass movement through legal work. The TAC drew the attention of the media; it was able to ventilate its arguments in courts and thereby force the state to "justify" its policies publicly, and it used its branches to educate members on the constitution and the law, giving it purpose and internal coherence. Court hearings and legal deadlines gave us a potent reason for organizing demonstrations and the alliance building that went into them.

The flip side, of course, was the impact TAC's mass mobilization had on the legal process by influencing public opinion outside the court. By the time the case reached the Constitutional Court every judge on the court was well aware of its importance, its urgency, and the lives at stake. They would have witnessed our demonstrations, heard the voices of HIV positive mothers, and seen Nelson Mandela don TAC's iconic "HIV

Positive" T-shirt when he went to visit Zackie Achmat to plead with him to go onto antiretrovirals: Achmat had said he would not do so until every HIV-positive person had the right. In the court of public opinion, we had already won.

As a result of such strategies the law did, in the end, play exactly the catalytic role we had hoped for. TAC's membership grew rapidly as the campaign blooded a new post-1994 generation of activists. A handful of activists had started it with nothing but energy, anger, and the resources of the ALP. But by 2003 the TAC had its own constitution, infrastructure, staff, and funding and tens of thousands of active volunteers. It was ready to change the world's response to AIDS.

*

In the early years of TAC we had learned another big lesson. You can win big court cases and achieve a great judgment on paper, but if there isn't a movement to pick up the pieces of paper that the judgment is written on and translate it into real life then very little may happen. In 2000, lawyers won a very important judgment on the right to housing, known as *Grootboom* (after the homeless woman in whose name the case was brought). But there was no mass movement behind that judgment; apart from lawyers and activists few people were aware of its importance, especially homeless people. Consequently, homelessness is as prevalent in South Africa today as it was twenty years ago. The HIV movement was different: there have been many rights battles, but this is the only socioeconomic right where a sustained innovative campaign has led to real equality of access to medicines—and that is solely because of the combination of legal activism and political pressure to enforce it that the TAC brought together.

When we set up SECTION27 in 2010 our intention had been to replicate and scale up the TAC experience. We envisioned that SECTION27 would play a catalytic role in seeding and supporting movements around other socioeconomic rights: health more broadly, basic education, and sufficient food. Certainly, in the twelve years I was there, SECTION27 developed into a highly effective organization: it has won important cases on the rights of schoolchildren to textbooks, for example, and led on the right to safe and dignified school toilets. Still, I learned many lessons from it about the limits to our approach. Context dictates the way law and people's movements interact, and strategies and tactics have to take this into account. How much effort goes into movement building? How much into litigation? Are there times when law is ineffective and so shouldn't be used? 2022 is not 2002: the times have changed dramatically, and the methods of one era do not automatically yield the same results in another.

In the early 2000s the South African Constitution was new and its promises of human rights and equality relatively untested by activists—as were the justiciable human rights frameworks that were being introduced into constitutions in many other countries of the world. TAC's membership was electrified by working with lawyers and using the courts, by turning the fight for lifesaving medicines into a claim for legally recognized rights. This gave disempowered people a sense of power and of dignity. It made TAC a righteous movement. Back then, the still-new popular democratic ANC government had not yet been on the receiving end of constitutional claims wielded by a popular pro-poor movement. It resisted it fiercely, but it was also conflicted: it too wanted to be seen as pro-poor and righteous. At the time, the ANC was still a global brand associated with non-racism and human rights: it was therefore uncomfortable with being on the wrong side of justice. For the first decade after the ANC came to power it had a moral and political hegemony: it was confronted on very few issues. Poor people still trusted that the ANC would use its power as a democratically elected government to address the multiple legacies of apartheid, including housing, health more broadly, electricity, and education. It didn't. But such seems to be the fate of liberation movements that become governments.

Despite this discomfort, even after TAC won in the Constitutional Court, it took several more years to break through the fortress of AIDS denialism that Mandela's successor, Thabo Mbeki, had constructed through his hold over the ANC. Litigating AIDS helped us learn that there is an afterlife to a court victory (and defeat, for that matter), and social movements built around using law have to ensure they have the capacity and appetite for the post-judgment phase of litigation. Otherwise, as we have seen in relation to other rights, judgments can come to nothing.

By the time I resigned from SECTION27 in 2019 a different politics had come to be. By this point—very much due to attempts to emulate the power created by TAC—constitutional litigation has been wielded against the ANC government numerous times. The government has almost always lost. It is no longer embarrassed; it has no moral high ground to uphold and is therefore less anxious to try to defend its actions. Familiarity with legal action breeds complacency. Litigation against the government has become the norm, and, paradoxically, this means it has lost some of its symbolic power. The result, we found at SECTION27, was that it was more difficult to employ litigation in the service of movement building. We might have declared our organization a "catalyst for social justice," but we were unable to use litigation as a galvanizing force in the manner of the cases brought by TAC against the pharmaceutical companies or the government in the early 2000s. Even highly emotive cases, like that of Michael Komape, the five-year old schoolboy who drowned at the bottom of a school pit toilet, were successful in law, but did not catalyze they type of organization building that we witnessed a decade before.

Perhaps we too easily romanticize constitutional law. Certainly, the wave of rights-centered constitutions adopted throughout the world in the 1990s was a great leap forward for humankind. But constitutions are only as strong as people's power to enforce them and, correspondingly, a government's will to respect the judiciary and the rule of law. Linked to this, a realization is dawning on activists across the world: enforcing rights in an era of austerity, pandemics, and war requires a different approach to human rights litigation than when economies are growing. Austerity itself can be a great demobilizer.

South Africa, like much of the rest of the world, experienced a period of economic growth up until 2008. This meant that when the Constitutional Court ruled against it on the Nevirapine case in 2002, it had the resources to comply. But in response to the 2008 global financial crisis, many governments introduced austerity economics, cutting social spending and arguing they could no longer afford human rights and social justice. This was as evident in parts of Europe, which saw increases in homelessness and child poverty, as it was in reversals to social spending that had taken place in countries like Brazil under Lula da Silva. In South Africa, we found that the government would go through the motions of a legal process knowing that even if it lost it was incapable, financially, of obeying the courts' rulings.

One minister ironically termed this "malicious compliance" with the rule of law. We experienced this in the TAC too when, in the 2010s, we turned our focus to campaigns to fix health systems more broadly—and made little progress.

In SECTION27, we sought to replicate the TAC experience in the legal campaigns we fought to advance the right to basic education, such as on toilets, textbooks, and equal access to education for children with learning disabilities. But, even in Limpopo (one of SA's poorest provinces) we were unable to seed a new movement around basic education. This was partly because we were mounting the campaign in an age of austerity, as described above. But it was also because the political and media environment had changed so much. In the early 2000s TAC's campaign faced little competition for public or media attention. As a result, we punched above our weight and galvanized the whole of society. Now, after a decade of austerity, there has been an explosion of social crises, many resulting in protest, some in litigation, yet all demanding the resources of the state. Add to this the climate crisis, the COVID-19 pandemic, and now the ramifications of the war in the Ukraine (such as rising food and energy prices), all of which operate in an unholy alliance exacerbating the negative effects of austerity, eroding rights and redirecting resources.

The result? Activists face the greater complexity of waging intersectional struggles, and need to find greater cohesion to work together across issues. Yes, the crisis in health, or education, or of hunger and violence against women, each requires a *different* campaign. Each involves a different government department or set of public officials. Yet if these campaigns continue to be fought in isolation, ignoring the underlying economic determinants of injustice, they will tie government and civil society in eternal combat but yield little lasting change. Therefore the focal point in the next period of combining law and social mobilization must be based on an understanding that the fulfillment of any *one* right is intimately connected to the realization of *all* rights. This means tackling economic governance, challenging priorities for resource allocation, and demanding far-reaching structural economic reform.

The connection between the power of law and the power of people is this: In this new age, rights cannot be protected or fulfilled on a lasting basis without cementing an effective people's power outside of government and business. While activists use the courts, we must simultaneously challenge legal systems that create and perpetuate inequality, transforming them into ones that actually advance social justice.

Three years after I closed the door on SECTION27 I remain committed to building the power of people. On an almost daily basis I see the law's contributions to this in "small" victories notched up, especially around climate and the environment. Today, working as a writer and editor of an online social justice publication, *Maverick Citizen*, I am trying to build a digital platform that reports on people's power; a space for sharing and learning that will help forge a more capable civil society, one able to work beyond its silos; one that can evolve into a force for change that is much more than the sum of its parts.

I admit that I am more terrified of the threats we face. But I also see how across the world, under very different political conditions, new social movements are rising: around the climate crisis, against inequality, for democracy, and against fascism and war. Activists are rethinking economics, engaging with data science and new technologies, and building local alternatives.

Once more law and lawyers could have a catalytic and empowering part to play in this battle. But it won't be easy. Authoritarianism, rule *by* law, is on the rise. Many of the new generation of movements have yet to see value in the international human rights framework, and of proactively using human rights law. That is why, in a situation made more difficult by populism and the repudiation of human rights law by powerful governments, lawyers will have to dig deep to prove, once more, the progressive and transformative power of the weapon they wield. I trust they will.

Further Reading and Viewing: ALP's work is documented by Didi Moyle in her book *Speaking Truth to Power: The Story of the AIDS Law Project* (Jacana, 2015). The first decade of TAC's campaigns is captured in *TAC: Taking HAART*, a "fly on the wall" film directed by Jack Lewis, available on YouTube. I have written extensively on TAC, SECTION27, and social movements, some of my articles can be found at www.markheywood.com. See also my article "South Africa's Journey from Socialism to Human Rights: The True Confessions of an Errant Socialist," *Journal of Human Rights Practice*, vol. 11, no. 2, July 2019.

Repeal the Eighth!: The Fight for Reproductive Rights in Ireland and Globally

EIMEAR SPARKS

On the morning of May 25, 2018, my brother and I left London early in the morning for the port at Holyhead to get the ferry back home. We broke every speed limit on the way and I remember asking him between tears and laughter whether we would die on a Welsh motorway and become martyrs for the cause—but we made it. We arrived in Dublin port under exaggerated sunshine and made our way into the city. People standing at crossroads with banners were cheering and drivers beeped friendly acknowledgments of the "yes" we'd stuck to our bonnet. We rolled down the window to greet the city and, in what now seems like an excessively indulgent move, we put on "Pride" by U2. We were proud to be home, for this: a referendum to repeal the Eighth Amendment to the Irish Constitution, which had banned abortion in the country for over thirty years.

And then there were the results—the sheer elation upon hearing those first polls come in. I was with family and friends at my sister's house and we had been taking time to explore the worst possible outcome as though readying ourselves for it, but there was no need. Published by the *Irish Times* at 10 p.m., the poll showed a landslide victory for repeal, and although recent history pleads caution around polling results, we all leapt to our feet and spent the rest of the night dancing. Later that night, my one-year-old niece woke bewildered to our cheers and I remember lifting her up and holding her close, telling her as I wept that she had nothing to worry about, that it was done: Ireland's prolonged chapter of reproductive coercion and cruelty was over. She would have reproductive rights.

Thirty-five years earlier, the Eighth Amendment had been approved by Irish citizens as a preemptive strike against the wave of abortion reform sweeping across Europe in the early 1980s, in the wake of *Roe v. Wade*. The context was one of economic decline, political instability, and the aftermath of Republican hunger strikes in Northern Ireland. Since then, the amendment had had a devastating impact on women's well-being, burdening those who sought abortion care with the threat of fourteen years in jail, and forcing an average of twelve people to seek abortion abroad every day that it was in effect. But now, the ban on abortion was over—nullified by a majority, it turned out, of 64.6 percent! Amendments to the Irish Constitution are only possible by referendum, which means that "the power of people" is, in theory at least, directly behind any change to our constitutional law. In 1983, as a country still dominated by Catholic doctrine, public engagement with the issue of abortion was low, and the odds were stacked against a vote that would oppose the teachings of the Church. Conversely, in 2018, the "people" were informed and more free to speak their minds. "The power of people" banished the Eighth Amendment from our constitution, but does it ensure reproductive rights, and for how long? And what lessons can be learned, from the Irish experience for other countries, such as Poland, that are heading in the opposite direction?

*

The movement to repeal the Eighth was enormous and diverse. I saw this through the various small ways I was involved, which took in everything from the arts scene in Dublin to campaign groups at my university and involvement with the Abortion Rights Campaign.

By being part of the movement I learned valuable lessons about what reproductive rights are, and how they can best be achieved.

I founded a pro-choice arts initiative called ChoiceBox and hosted workshops and events with Irish artists whose work addressed themes of bodily autonomy while also raising money for the wider campaign. Meanwhile, I lent a hand to several actions which ranged from the headline grabbing to the mundane. There was an evening spent with activists turning traffic cones into handheld projectors to beam words and phrases like "Trust women" and "Repeal" onto buildings around Dublin. There was an afternoon spent looking for locations for a short movie, and being told everywhere that the venue owners didn't want to get involved in "political issues." There was a night spent hosting an event of poetry and music for two hundred people in Ireland's Liberty Hall, once the headquarters of the Irish Citizen Army and base for many acts of social resistance. And there was leafleting, marching, and emailing: contacting performers, businesses, photographers, and designers and asking them to do things for free.

The "do what you can" atmosphere was contagious. It was like a switch had tripped and suddenly everyone was launching their own initiatives—knit for repeal, dance for repeal, flea market for choice. All over, I heard the same conversation: a tentative proposal from somebody who wanted to launch their own initiative for repeal, and a wave of encouragement from everybody else. These were pivotal moments because they shaped the inclusivity of the moment and the idea that everyone's contribution was important, no matter how big or small. It was messy and there wasn't always a clear strategy to these actions, but the numbers of activists grew: when I joined the Action & Strategy working group of the Abortion Rights Campaign, a small number of us would meet for tea and ideas in the tiny attic-cum-kitchenette of the Outhouse, a center for LGBTQ people and their families. Months later, having missed a few meetings, I arrived to a much bigger room jammed full of people without enough seats to go around.

Of course, any perception that a movement had suddenly been sparked was false. It wasn't even sparked in my lifetime, as its origins dated back to the bravery of activists in the twentieth century operating in much more unforgiving times. Still, things accelerated. The reenergized movement around "Repeal" tapped into a white-hot vein of anger at institutional cruelty that had been bubbling under the surface for years. It came at a time when the Catholic Church had been discredited and reviled as a result of the sex scandals brought to light by the Ryan Report in 2009. This report detailed the sexual abuse visited upon Irish people by nuns and priests of the Catholic Church, giving shape to the narratives of cruelty that had for a long time hovered at the fringes of the national psyche. Stories of Magdalene Laundries and Catholic care homes were made tangible by the horrifying discovery of a mass grave for infants on the site of a Church-run Mother and Baby Home in Tuam. All of this served as compelling proof that Ireland could not—should not—look to the church to guide its moral compass.

It was, and it wasn't, about religion. In fact, the anti-choice movement had long realized that the battle wouldn't be won on religious grounds, or via a moralizing tug-of-war. In spite of funding from religious groups, connections to the Catholic Church, and belief in Catholicism, anti-choice activists hardly mentioned the church at all. Instead, the "No" campaigners said, it was about protecting the vulnerable, it was about "love." They did their best to brush over the fact that the Eighth Amendment was the product of religious conservatism, and that this same institutional thinking had never cared about women nor even the innocent lives it purported to protect. This was crystallized by the tragic story of Savita Halappanavar, who died in 2012 from sepsis when medical staff in Galway hospital refused to terminate her pregnancy, as it was not deemed a threat to her life. She was asked to wait. Savita was proof that people could die from the Eighth Amendment—needlessly, preventably.

What was previously unspoken was starting to be discussed openly. We talked and talked and talked, and this is what ultimately made the difference. But new ideas require new forms of expression, and these must have conviction, must resonate with something personal. The beginning of the campaign, for me, was a process of testing out the language. I remember grasping at the words, trying to find my own vocabulary of injustice for an issue that had always been hushed and stigmatized, and trying to understand what it meant for me personally. When I became more emboldened, I would volunteer at street stalls, hand out leaflets, and try to chat with strangers.

Irish women recognized the importance of telling their abortion stories, and hundreds put themselves in the firing line of hateful and misogynistic abuse to further the campaign. Theirs were the narratives that emerged in the government's Citizens' Assembly that gathered a random selection of Irish citizens to listen to opposing sides of the campaign and deliberate on action. Theirs were the narratives that pushed prominent politicians such as Simon Harris, the minister for health, to change his stance on abortion.

Still, it was drawn out and painful. Since changes to the Irish constitution can only be made by a national referendum, the fate of the Eighth Amendment would be decided by national majority. Everyone therefore had a say on a woman's right to health and autonomy. Everybody had to be included in the national conversation. This was often infuriating. Once, while canvassing for a yes vote in a neighborhood near my family home, I was upset when a girl answered the door to tell me that she was pro-repeal but too young to vote. She summoned her father who told me he would be voting no. It was harder to deal with this kind of situation than with the raw anger we were sometimes met with. When somebody answers the door to yell at you, there is less of an obligation to stay and talk. But an indecisive delivery of "No," or a case like this, is harder to walk away from. When I asked the man if he had discussed the issue with his daughter, he repeated his position. The truth is that many women were old enough to get pregnant but too young to vote, and many men would never face an unintended pregnancy but were allowed to cast their ballot just the same. It felt like a great injustice. I was glad at these times that we canvassed in pairs.

On the other hand, the fact that women's reproductive freedom had to be won by national majority forced alliances with unlikely groups. To get a yes we needed popular support, and so activists did heroic work rallying people you might not associate with the fight for reproductive rights. "Farmers for Yes," "Grandparents for Yes," "Doctors for Yes"— these groups tested perceptions around activism for reproductive rights and shaped the compelling narrative that we, as a nation, were learning to believe in compassion.

We are also a scattered nation with nests all over the globe. By the end of the campaign, I was a member of the #HomeToVote contingent: the designated name for those of us who had made good on the Irish legacy of migration and would have to travel back to vote (of whom there were thousands). I had first left Ireland to work on a campaign for abortion rights in Mexico with the organization Women on Waves, so I was still involved in the global movement for abortion rights. Then after that, I came back from the United Kingdom when I could—to march, organize, and canvass. But it felt wrong to not be permanently present. I felt I had abandoned the fight.

Luckily, the campaign was very much online: political updates, personal stories, actions, art, comfort, outrage, trolling, tears, fundraisers, articles, solidarity. I can't say it was a virtual movement—the most important work was done on the ground—but migration didn't spell exclusion, which was fundamental for a diaspora as large as ours. When the referendum date was called, people began sharing flight itineraries home from places as far as Sydney or Buenos Aires, which added to the feeling of momentum in the final weeks. But everyone was reluctant to trust news from the echo chamber—I remembered the uncertainty and outright rejection of many people I had spoken with on doorsteps while canvassing, and I remember multiplying this to capture what I imagined it would be like outside of the city. This was city-dweller prejudice, but at the time it only felt like fear. In the week before the vote I didn't hear a single activist say that it wouldn't be close, and many were sure that it wouldn't pass at all.

It did. So what now?

*

"Breakthroughs in legal reform are invariably not the end of the struggle," writes Marge Berer, the global activist and coordinator of the International Campaign for Women's Right to Safe Abortion. In Ireland, abortion is still criminalized under certain circumstances. If a doctor provides abortion care without first obliging the person who has requested it to reflect for three days, they are breaking the law. If somebody helps their friend to order abortion pills online, they are breaking the law. If a person needs an abortion after twelve weeks of pregnancy, doctors must find risk of serious harm to this person's health, and there is no medical definition for this. During the coronavirus pandemic, this posed significant challenges to people who discovered they were pregnant at twelve weeks or later but were unable to travel due to lockdowns.

And then there is the gap between policy and practice. Exclusion from abortion care crystallizes broader trends of social exclusion, where financial means, language, stigma, and ability to travel dictate who can and cannot obtain the care they need. This is especially true for people with disabilities and people living under Direct Provision: Ireland's inhumane detention system for asylum seekers. It is notable that two of the most pivotal moments for Ireland's advancement for human rights have focused on banishing the legacy of the Catholic Church from our constitution—first to allow for equal marriage, then for reproductive freedom. But some of Ireland's most serious human rights issues now fall outside the realm of religious dogma, belonging instead to social and economic inequalities that have been sown by the secular state. At the same time as we have celebrated wins for sexual and reproductive health and rights, we have also seen the acceleration of brutal social and economic policies—with the perverse effect that much-lauded gains in reproductive rights remain a distant reality for many people.

In spite of this, Ireland has become a poster child, on the international stage, for reproductive rights movements. As I write this essay four years after the Eighth was repealed, I work as program advisor at the European branch of the International Planned Parenthood Federation, supporting social movements for reproductive rights. In this role, I hear Ireland held up as an example of what can be achieved and I have spoken to activists from Malta, Argentina, and the Philippines who look to the Irish experience for guidance. It makes me proud that people from across the world take inspiration from Repeal, but it saddens me deeply that this is sought by activists from countries that had progressive abortion laws back when the Eighth Amendment was introduced in the 1980s, such as Poland. Or by those whose countries' laws have been changed over the decades to make it just that bit harder for women to access care—by enforcing mandatory waiting periods or canceling social indications for abortion, like Armenia, Belarus, and Georgia. Or by those whose countries' laws are not upheld by health care providers or enforced by the government, places where entire hospitals, cities, and regions refuse to provide abortion care to women, like Croatia and Italy. Or by those battling the regular introduction of bills to limit abortion care, like Slovakia. Or by the majority of women in the United States, who find themselves enraged, and astonished, by *Dobbs vs. Jackson Women's Health Organization,* which has removed the constitutional right to abortion in that country. The list goes on.

The lesson I take from this is that progress for reproductive rights is not linear, or irreversible. If the moral arc of the universe bends toward justice, it certainly suffers setbacks along the way. Laws that enshrine reproductive rights for women can find themselves at the mercy of sharp political shifts to the right; the darker parts of history have the opportunity to repeat themselves. This has become glaringly obvious now that right-wing populism has breathed life into old forms of anti-rights mobilization in assuming the fight against "gender ideology." The term was originally created as part of a counterstrategy by Catholic thinkers and the Vatican following wins for sexual and reproductive health and rights and gender equality at various UN conferences in the 1990s. They saw a more critical and nuanced understanding of "gender" as an affront to the "traditional" family (read: Christian, heterosexual, and married) and a threat to the very fabric of society. Their aim was to secularize anti-rights discourse, to make it more palatable and popular, and they have been hugely successful. Since then, the concept has taken on a life of its own: "gender ideology" is now invoked as an umbrella term for the right to oppose everything from abortion rights and equal marriage to "gender mainstreaming" policies and directives of the European Union.

In this context, the phrase "the people" is used skilfully by right-wing populists to distract the people from the socioeconomic inequality or exclusion they experience. It is a hollowed-out version of people power, which uses bogeymen—gender ideology, immigration, race—as easy symbolic distractions to blame for a broader economic and spiritual malaise to which their solution is the path toward fascism. This contrasts with true people power—the kind that was built over years in the campaign to repeal the Eighth and has the ideals of systemic change at its core. Reproductive justice for everyone: no ifs, no buts, no matter what the Catholic church or its patriarchal allies elsewhere desired.

The co-option of people power is harmful not only for women and queer people, whose rights have been repackaged as part of a nefarious, elitist agenda, but for people power itself. The disparate groups now rallying against gender ideology—powerful figures in the Church, in populist states, in the US Christian right—construct themselves as ordinary citizens rising up against corrupt, international elites seeking to impose their destructive worldview on others. They convert opposition to sexual and reproductive health and rights into something that is socially acceptable and supported by "the silent majority." And, because the powerful interests and significant financial backing behind these civic campaigns are often hidden, it becomes ever harder to distinguish who "the people" calling for these laws really are.

But the people do make their feelings known, as we have seen in Poland. In 2016, a draft law that would have imposed a near-total ban on abortion was scrapped after mass protests rocked the country. Four years later, in October 2020, a similar law was introduced, this time by way of a Constitutional Tribunal the ruling party had illegally packed with allies: such was the abuse of the "power of law" against the "power of people." The judgement of the tribunal was met with an unprecedented wave of protests across the country. Hundreds of thousands of people, led by women, turned out to defy a ruling they simply could not accept. This was the logical endpoint of years of rule by the Law and Justice (PiS) party, which has used its majority to rig the political and judicial system in its favor, enabling the party to pass brutal laws with notional popular support. PiS had been voted back into government in 2019 following an adept political campaign and in recognition of its popular social-spending programs, which secured its support among many women, in spite of the party's opposition to reproductive rights. Yet the abortion ruling was clearly not a popular decision: polls taken in its aftermath showed that between 59 percent and 71 percent of Poles disagreed with it. Four hundred thousand Poles came to the streets in some of the largest demonstrations the country has seen since the fall of communism. They braved violence and intimidation from the police and far-right, and demonization in the government-controlled public media. Nevertheless, the law was published in January 2021. It's hard to imagine a more stark representation of the chasm between law and the will of the people than that of Polish people standing together in their thousands to resist the abortion ban, only to have it made law before their very eyes. Here, the law becomes a weapon used to silence, suffocate, and harm the people.

In my work at Planned Parenthood, I have been particularly focused on Poland, given the above. How the pendulum has swung there. One activist told me that, in the 1970s and 1980s, communist Poland provided abortion care to women from France, Germany, and Sweden whose countries had denied them this right; she hoped that these countries would show similar solidarity with the Polish women who have been calling her in panic since the ruling, some of whom were in hospital awaiting a procedure when the ban became law. This is not to rose-tint women's experiences of communism, where gender equality was an official ideology that was not necessarily respected on the ground, and contraceptives were almost nonexistent. Still, today, that legacy is being ominously recalled by the radical right in Eastern Europe, where leaders like Hungary's Viktor Orbán describe women's reproductive rights (and LGBTQ rights) as a new form of totalitarian dogma.

A Hungarian activist recently sent me a Facebook post from the Hungarian minister for justice, who, in expressing concern over "gender ideology and the creation of a grey uniform society in which everyone must be liberal," warned: "history has proven several times that the pendulum can swing-out. Each action is followed by a counteraction." These are menacing words when you consider the program of bigotry embarked upon by Orbán's Hungary, but it shows quite plainly the counter-hegemonic strategy of anti-rights actors. The ruling parties in these countries and their allies elsewhere have adroitly manipulated fears about the new world order and cultivated a "Golden Age" attachment to the "traditional" values perceived to have been destroyed by former regimes. Bearing the brunt of these pendulum-like swings are queer couples, trans people, men and boys, women and girls, families, activists: the people.

Such swings also sow doubt on the unimpeachability of people power. For all the talk of mobilization, I am compelled to recognize that I would not be able to accept it if, living in a balanced media environment and free from populist tactics of manipulation, the people rose up to demand reproductive coercion. If, in 2018, the people of Ireland had voted to uphold the violence of the constitution and deny women agency, I would not have acquiesced. Parliamentary supermajorities and massive mobilization cannot be used as justification to dismantle democracy or violate human rights, to force women into pregnancy or make them risk their lives to access health care. The power of people isn't always a force for good and we should not fetishize it. The tragedies of twentieth-century fascism taught us that.

*

The activists I know are exhausted, but strong. I hear Polish women looking to Argentina, where the people pushed for abortion rights in nine parliamentary bills over a period of fifteen years, for hope. "We will get there," one says, in spite of the violence, arrests, and death threats she faces. I don't doubt it. One day, Poland will be held up as another example of how the people can rise up to win reproductive freedom. For now though, I remain sickened and dizzied by the sheer abundance of legal regimes that have been designed to answer one question: Should women have agency? The answer given is never a simple yes; it is always followed with another question: To what extent? Across the world, proscriptions of women's freedom have been interpreted, accepted, and inscribed in law—here she can access abortion until twelve weeks of pregnancy, there she is allowed abortion when suicidal, here she can get an abortion without giving an explanation, there she can attain it when she has been raped. In most cases, these limitations stem from ideology, not science, or what women need or want. Nowhere is this clearer, as I write these words, than in the United States where access to safe abortion has become a postcode lottery since the overturning of *Roe v Wade*. Abortion care is now almost totally banned in thirteen states. Clinics in these states are closing while providers in safe haven states are struggling to meet the needs of those travelling to them for care. Meanwhile, Texas is spearheading the race to the bottom with the introduction of a bounty-style system, which allows private citizens to sue anyone who helps facilitate an abortion.

I find myself returning to that moment of elation when we heard the results of the repeal referendum and I held my niece in my arms and told her, with certainty, that she had nothing to worry about: she would have reproductive rights. My certainty is shaken but I still believe this to be true. I know that soon there will be a review of Ireland's abortion law where we can mobilize against harmful provisions such as the three-day waiting period and the criminal penalties attached to abortion care. I also know that my niece is able-bodied, she will be educated and comfortable, she is an Irish citizen—she is less likely to experience the hardship of those who at present are excluded from Ireland's reproductive health care system. But what about those who are? And what about the people of Poland—how soon before health care providers can prioritize women's well-being above ideology?

"Should women have agency?" The question is unrelenting. When will we receive the simple answer—yes?

Further Reading: On a global perspective: Marge Berer and Lesley Hoggart, *Progress toward Decriminalization of Abortion and Universal Access to Safe Abortions: National Trends and Strategies.* (Health and Human Rights Journal, 2019). On the anti-gender movement: Esther Kováts and Maari Põim, *Gender as Symbolic Glue: The Position and Role of Conservative and Far-Right Parties in the Anti-Gender Mobilizations in Europe,* (Foundation for European Progressive Studies and Frierich Ebert Stiftung, 2015); Robert Kuhar and David Paternotte, *Anti-Gender Campaigns in Europe: Mobilizing Against Equality* (Rowman & Littlefield, 2020); Neil Datta, *Tip of the Iceberg: Religious Extremist Funders against Human Rights for Sexuality & Reproductive Health in Europe 2008–2019* (European Parliamentary Forum for Sexual and Reproductive Rights, 2021). Inspiring images: "Poland's abortion protests in pictures," *Notes from Poland,* October 26, 2020; Amanda Cotrim's photos in Valentina Di Liscia, "Photos Capture Historic Celebrations in Argentina After Abortion Legalized", *Hyperallergic,* December 31, 2020.

The Rule of Law vs. Poland's Repressive "Law and Justice" Regime

KLEMENTYNA SUCHANOW in conversation with EIMEAR SPARKS, with an afterword on the Ukraine crisis

Since 1993, after the end of Soviet communism in Poland, abortion has only been allowed in specific cases: if a pregnancy is a result of rape, if it endangers the life of the mother or baby, or in the case of fetal abnormality. Since it came back to power in 2015, the ruling Law and Justice (PiS) party has attempted to restrict women's reproductive rights even further as a signal measure of its conservative agenda by banning abortion in the case of fetal abnormality. When a law was introduced in 2016 banning all abortions, there were massive protests in the streets, led by the women's movement in the country. This was the birth of the movement Polish Women's Strike. Faced with this resistance, the government chose to bypass the democratically elected parliament and use the Constitutional Tribunal, the highest court in the land, which it had packed with political appointments. This was a tipping point: after the tribunal's verdict on October 22, 2020 at least 350,000 Poles took to the streets in the largest demonstration the country has seen since the fall of communism. A few weeks later, Eimear Sparks spoke to Klementyna Suchanow, one of the leaders of the movement. In July 2022, Klementyna spoke to Mark Gevisser about the effects of the Russian invasion of Ukraine, on the Polish movement.

JANUARY 2021

Eimear Sparks: How is the law being used against those who protest, and what effect has this had on how people understand the law?

Klementyna Suchanow: Since 2017, legal charges started to be leveled against people who protested abortion laws and judiciary system reforms, as a form of repression. This led citizens to try and understand the judicial system better. Before, the judicial system was an abstract concept for most citizens, but today it's a physical reality you have to confront on the street. The law has become a very tangible thing on your body. We have dozens of court trials and fines for standing on sidewalks or blocking the streets. Together with other leaders of the Polish Women's Strike, I was charged with causing an epidemiological threat, because we organized protests during the coronavirus pandemic. Marta Lempart was also charged with insulting a police officer. We could face eight years in prison for this. However over 90 percent of our cases are rejected by the independent judges who stress that people have rights to protest.

One consequence is that there is now a strong coalition between lawyers and activists today. There are fine lawyers, judges, and organizations that work with our movement: they protect us in the courts, they go to the police stations where we are detained or arrested even deep in night, and they are always ready to look for us. This is a very specific situation in Poland, given that both women's rights and the independence of the judiciary are under attack by the government, and that makes us work together. Very soon after the government started threatening the independence of the judiciary in 2017, our feminist movement started protesting in support of the judges and democracy, understanding that one day they would be important for us when our cases came to court. In the beginning, it was not well understood why a women's movement was engaging in this issue, but now it's never questioned. It's obvious and natural. It was an act of solidarity rather than strategic, but it was a good move nonetheless: we had been fighting for our own rights and now we saw another social group attacked by the same government, by the same enemy. Someone else would be next. We have to protect each other.

ES: How have you gone about dealing with legal issues?

KS: Today's strikes are happening through the women's movement, which is very interesting, given the way our voices, as women, were never previously listened to. So now, as the women's movement, we have had accept this role of leading the national process. But it's imposing a certain responsibility on us too, and we don't feel like we are professionally prepared for establishing governments in the future. That's going to be very much about the law, the reconstruction of the law, the reconstruction of the institutions. It's huge legal work. And we are happy that there are people who are ready to do it. We can count on them and we can also learn from them.

In our movement coordinating the strikes, we have formed a Consultative Council with different teams working on different issues. One of them was working on the rule of law, and what should be done once the Law and Justice party is gone. It's important to begin the discussion now, so that people understand that several institutions need to be reestablished, that certain orders might have to be reversed, that certain judges were illegally chosen, that new elections will need to happen. This is a topic of everyday conversation, a topic that has become very popular *because* of the abortion issue, far more popular than it was in 2015 when Law and Justice came to power. Ironically, the losses we have suffered in terms of our abortion rights have actually become the best way to popularize the knowledge about legal institutions in Poland.

We have an organization that's called Free Courts (Wolne Sądy), coordinated by four lawyer-activists who have become very popular in the movement, known for their appearances at events and discussions in the media. They also organized many of the protests in the last years. There were about five hundred to eight hundred people who regularly took part in the activities of our Consultative Council. The Rule of Law was one of fourteen teams. Each team presented the results of their work, and this was live-streamed by us and *Gazeta Wyborcza*, the biggest newspaper. It's become huge. There were lots of viewers, comments, and media interviews. We became the point of reference. And so the government feared we are taking over the power, that we were overturning them.

ES: And this means they become more repressive, right? How do you respond to that?

KS: Protest! Say out loud that this is not how it should be. And people do it. People feel it. And it's growing. We really have no option, because there's no platform to talk with the government. We are not listened to, there is no conversation with the people, no consultation, no commissions that consult. And those of us who have been active in the movement are blacklisted; we're not even allowed into parliament. How can we have a conversation when we are totally excluded in this way? Of course this results in frustration, and frustration brings people onto the streets. What else can we do? It's actually very simple. The history of humanity is full of such cases. We just repeat it. It's like we've moved back in time. I feel like

I'm experiencing what my father did in the 1980s [when Polish peoples' mass action brought down the communist dictatorship]. Now it's me, just one generation later. Something's wrong in this country. My father was in prison, back then, for things similar to what I'm doing now. Will my daughter see me in prison too, just like I saw my dad? It's shocking that this is happening in the twenty-first century at the center of Europe, long after communism has fallen.

It's not only tragic, it's also ridiculous, because so much of what they are trying to do is actually not working. Many times, the way they do it is actually totally comedic. For example, I had to report to the police station each week because after the tribunal's judgment, I hammered a poster on the court's doors: "Today Argentina, tomorrow Poland"—referring to the legalization of abortion law in Argentina in December 2020. I was arrested for twenty-four hours and sent to the prosecutor's office. It's a kind of control imposed on me, but actually, it gives me an opportunity to talk to those policemen every week, and it helps me see so clearly that they are with us, even these guys who have to process me. It's like we're just going through this bureaucratic act that nobody believes in. On this level government repression is not working because people, simple people, regular people on different levels, refuse to use it as a repression against you. Of course you also meet bad guys sometimes.

ES: How important are legal arguments and strategies to building your movement?

KS: It's important, but protests are much more based on emotions. It's good to know about the law, but it's better to know the emotions of the people and what frustrates them, to listen to them. When people go to the streets, they don't talk about legal issues. Usually they are upset, talk about emotions, why they are here, and they have a special reason to be there. And as to the actual legality of protest, as the government tries to restrict a right to public gathering by regulations about the pandemic, nobody cares about whether it's legal or not to do it, anymore. They just do it.

ES: What do you see as the limitations of people power?

KS: The power of the people is there, but there are no institutional platforms to take an advantage of it. What do you do when almost 70 percent of the people are for free abortion, but a government makes a law banning all abortion? What's our access to the state, to do something about this new law? You can exercise it on the street, in your NGOs, in your places of work, in educational settings, but without an institutionalized way to use this power, how can you change things?

ES: You prefer to have a situation where there were these platforms and opportunities for consultation, so that each time to get something done, you didn't have to storm the streets . . .

KS: Exactly! Because we have better things to do in life, then to take to the frozen streets in January! If there were another way to ensure that the government listened to the people, of course I would prefer that than standing on the street for several hours in the cold.

ES: What advice would you give to movement lawyers in times such as the one you are facing in Poland, when there is such large-scale mobilization against human rights?

KS: I could say, you have a chance to become heroes of your nation if you stay together with the people. You will be the persons who saved the nations together with the people. This is the case in Poland. Some of the judges have become heroes here. Because of their resistance they're given criminal charges, they suffer, removed from their positions, lose their salaries, or moved to other posts, five hundred kilometers away from their homes. It's quite a strong form of repression, but still, they do the right thing. It's an interesting situation. Democracy is built on law, and so it needs lawyers to be the people's mouth, if you like—to translate what people say in the legal language needed to reestablish the democracy. This makes lawyers crucial as defenders of the democracy because we, the people, we can do many things, but only up to a certain level. And then there is a place, there is space for the experts, for the lawyers, professionals. And we cannot do it. They have to do it. So if we are not together, all of the power of the people vanishes into nothing.

JULY 2022

Mark Gevisser: How has the war in Ukraine affected your life, and activism, in Poland?

Klementyna Suchanow: The current war in Ukraine is turning our Polish reality upside down. The very people now trying to present themselves as the saviors of the Ukranian people are those who provoked severe judgments in the international courts, for having trampled on the rule of law before, following the Kremlin pattern. I am thinking in particular of the justice minister, Zbigniew Ziobro, who is also general prosecutor, and the prime minister, Mateusz Morawiecki.

In truth, the help being provided to Ukrainian refugees is through the initiatives of ordinary people, especially those who have had organizing experience in recent years, such as in the Women's Strike movement, the climate movement, and those helping Afghan and other refugees stuck at the Belorussian border. These are the people who have efficiently practiced humanitarian aid by opening their homes to the Ukrainians; the state institutions didn't provide it until they noticed the people's solidarity and they were forced to do it. But while the state is still not efficiently providing help to Ukrainians, the government is using the refugee crisis in an attempt to cheat the EU into handing over funds from the Recovery Plan for Europe that were denied to Poland due to the breaches in the rule of law. Of course the government does not consider reversing its policy of dismantling the rule of law. Rather it takes cover behind the best humanitarians: we, the people, the movements. The same people who are repressed in other areas.

MG: What does Women's Strike movement look like today?

KS: I have a feeling that people don't want to protest now. They got burned out by the wave of protests in 2021/2022, which didn't change the abortion situation, although it did shake the power of the government, from which it still finds it hard to recover. On top of that, the war in Ukraine is working against us. In 2023 parliamentary elections are to be held. Economic problems are mounting, inflation is rising in line with the incompetence of those who are supposed to reduce it, so next year could be a hectic one. For now it is seemingly calm, but when something erupts due to economic problems, I can't imagine that the Strike won't be involved. If nothing changes, Russia, or at least Hungary, awaits us.

Ending Female Genital Cutting: What About the Law?

JULIA LALLA-MAHARAJH, OBE

It's October 2008 and I'm in Lalibela, Ethiopia. I'm walking with two small girls, Megdes and Tinebab, who are trying to sell me "knucklebones of saints—yes, really, thousand-year-old knucklebones!" for only a dollar each. As we spend the day together, I find myself captured by one thought: what could be done to spare them from genital cutting? Could I talk to their parents, talk to the elders, pay for their education? Any sort of Faustian bargain so that they do not have to go through this practice.

I was a volunteer at the time, based in Addis Ababa, and in spite of knowing about female genital cutting (FGC) for decades, I had only recently discovered that, in Ethiopia, 74 percent of all girls underwent this, usually before their fifth birthday. I knew about it, but I didn't know what right I had to do anything. I began reading more.

It ranges from a nick in the hood of the clitoris, through to the labia and clitoris being cut out; for some girls, all their external genitals are scraped away, the wound that is left is sewn closed and as the body heals, it seals the vaginal orifice. This means that when a girl is "old enough" to have sex, she is cut open—often only enough for penetrative sex. Each time she gives birth she has to be opened and, afterward, these new wounds are resewn.

Given the severity of the issue, what could be done? I sought out Ethiopian advocates and gender specialists: one question was about legitimacy and appropriation of an issue that did not "belong" to me. Bogaletch, an Ethiopian activist in her sixties said: "Julia, this is a basic human rights violation. I ask you to defend the rights of everyone and use your privilege to support us." She placed a *netela*, an Ethiopian woven shawl around my neck: "Remember this when people doubt you—you are wrapped with our thoughts."

It was a few weeks later that I went to Lalibela and was confronted with the reality of doing nothing because I didn't feel able to intervene. My thoughts spiraled out from the two girls in front of me: How was systemic change possible to help secure a better future for the four million girls due to be cut each year, a number only set to increase due to population growth? As I walked away from Megdes and Tinebab I made a personal vow: to do everything I could to support an end to female genital cutting.

Back in London the following year, I'm volunteering with an African women's charity. I'm learning that FGC is global and is carried out in twenty-seven African countries, and thirty-three more globally, including Indonesia, Malaysia, and India. The deeper I delve into the issues, the more my head reels. A girl's body is at the center of the interaction, yet she is not spoken with or consulted, only upheld as a cipher for chastity, virginity, cleanliness, and purity. The cutter is usually a female traditional birth attendant or another woman in the community. Women are at the heart of this practice, and this seemed to be the genius of patriarchy: that women have appropriated it and championed its continuation.

Think about this: every mother who has gone through FGC will in turn pass on this experience to her daughters. What did the mothers themselves think? Why did they cut their girls, knowing what they themselves had gone through? I needed to understand how communities were responding to the practice, given their innate ownership of the issue, and the wisdom they have about their own lives. When I met Megdes and Tinebab, I did not know what could work to protect the bodies, minds, and spirits of tiny girls. What, then, was possible?

I found an answer when I journeyed to the Gambia.

*

I am in Sare Ngai in the Gambia in 2011. I can scarcely believe what I am seeing. Around me dancers whirl. Drums provide the background, faster and louder than a heartbeat. The colors are bright, and in the fierce sun the whole scene seems overexposed. The cutters are dressed in red and are center stage in a village square, surrounded by hundreds of people. The cutters hold small gourds full of hooked knives and sharp blades, which they hold in front of them as they dance.

Five women come to the front, tip their knives on the ground, and place their empty gourds before them. Another woman approaches them, holding a lit torch. They take off their red gowns and, in a gesture magnificent in its finality, they catch their gowns on the torch so that each goes up in flame. They turn to the crowd and raise their voices, shouting clearly and firmly, through the noise of the drums. Doussou, my host, is next to me: "They are saying that from this day on, they vow never to cut a girl again." Each cutter breaks the gourd underfoot. Their robes are gone into ashes. Change is upon us.

The theory is simple: what unites us is a common purpose to uphold peace, unity, and safety. These moral norms are shared by people all around the world. In communities like that of Sare Ngai, the spark of change is provided by an African empowerment group named Tostan, which begins the process with a question: To what do you aspire? Invariably, the answer is peace. The next questions are around issues that might threaten such peace, and in the skilful hands of a facilitator this leads on to an exploration of the concept of human rights and dignity, and what this means in reality.

These questions open out a three-year program that covers democracy, human rights, problem-solving, hygiene, health, literacy, numeracy, and management. Ending FGC was not, in fact, a topic that was identified initially, but now, as an unintended consequence of the program, over nine thousand communities in eight African countries have abandoned it.

This is what happened. Once people learnt about basic rights to health and freedom from harm, they started to question their own behaviors. They spoke with one another and discovered the stronger links between, for example, FGC and tetanus: if you don't know your daughter has died from tetanus, because you've never understood that there are invisible germs that lead to an infection, would you necessarily relate the two?

Fundamental to change is that women find their voices and have a safe space to explore their human rights and their responsibilities; equally important is that they learn how to put these sometimes intangible concepts into practice. In the Tostan model, communities themselves identify what no longer serves them. In this way, the changes made are sustainable and owned.

What I witnessed at Sare Ngai made tangible the theories of change I had been exploring. There are entire unwritten codes of practice that wind their way through all of our lives and are upheld in every society. We belong by conforming to these codes. We might call these codes "social norms," one of which is female genital cutting. Often a norm is not discussed or made visible, but its power is extremely strong. A social norm such as FGC can exist unquestioned for centuries, because it might uphold a stronger, more visible community-wide moral norm: for example, wishing to have a form of social protection for daughters, to keep them safe. In this instance, the form of perceived social protection might be marriage (in itself another social norm). Thus the reasoning behind upholding the social norm remains hidden because the moral norm takes primacy. There is a profound and simple beauty, though: a social norm can shift.

While I was at the Sare Ngai ending-cutting ceremony, I met a pharmacist named Saikou Jallow. He told me that previous NGOs working on the FGC issue had lectured people about how wrong they had been, which had only made people more intransigent. He spoke with dignity about his decision not to cut his youngest daughter, which had "allowed me to reach for my own higher good." I realized that what had been offered to him was an ability to exercise his own agency in his decision-making, rather than have it imposed on him.

Saikou Jallow exemplified the power of Tostan's approach. Once a community is allowed to question the social norm, to understand how it is often overshadowed by the moral norm, and grasps the reality that cutting is harmful to a girl, people move quickly toward its abandonment and are able to declare an intention to stop the practice. The declaration is vital because it is public and witnessed by other nearby communities. Thus everyone knows that a girl will be uncut: both their families and their future social network. This "declaration" is a moment like no other: when the social norm actually visibly shifts from "all girls are cut," to "all girls are uncut."

Laws against FGC exist in twenty-six of the twenty-eight African countries that practice it, but this doesn't correlate to any trends of a reduction in its practice. If the social norm is one where all girls are cut, then everyone within that community is meshed together in a web of decision-making, which makes them complicit with the perpetrator—and hence part of the prosecution process, if the practice is outlawed. How then would a legal, enforceable framework operate at that scale? When communities believe that the social shame and stigma of being uncut is, in fact, a social death for a girl, they will do all they can to ensure that their practice is maintained, even if it means breaking the law. But if the entire community has been educated, informed, and told about the law and its repercussions—if people have gone through a values shift that upholds the rights of a girl and then the law enforces that—then real change can happen.

The sequencing here is important: the social norm shifts and then the law upholds that shift. I have learned, from my work as an advocate for the end to FGC that if a legal norm does not mirror a social norm, then there is an inherent tension that can remain unresolved. The law should not be avoided, but nor is it a panacea; we need to work with people and with social norms.

*

When I returned to London from the Gambia in 2011 I set up Orchid Project. My vision was a world free from FGC. Because the practice affected a girl and the decision-making was generally at the household level, I wanted to support work that intensively led to fewer girls being cut, then to show others how this can happen. I also wanted to ensure that those who were mandated with structural, systemic change actually did more at a global level to create the right environment. It was a two-pronged approach: honing action to support communities, and holding to account those who wield the levers of power.

Early on in this journey, I found myself confronted by how to work with the law. I was constantly questioned: "Why haven't we ended this practice by making it illegal? Why aren't more people prosecuted?" It was tempting to follow this line of inquiry myself, but I was worried about pursuing it, given the evident ineffectiveness of the laws in countries where they had been passed.

The questions also felt like they were a way for people who don't practice FGC to make sense of something that was "other" to them. When confronted with the unspeakable, people navigate toward the law because it is a construction that is an easy moral indicator of what is right and what is wrong. It is a conversation that is built around discomfort that can then be sanitized by placing it in reference to the law, a patriarchal system that defines and upholds what is known. The unsafe becomes the safe.

My worry that a legal approach might be too blunt an instrument came from what I knew about laws. I had been a campaigner for public transport infrastructure in London and had worked in the previous decade to get parliamentary legislation for a new railway beneath the city. This meant creating the right climate so that a law could be introduced. I spent a decade meeting with politicians and stakeholders, writing policy papers, negotiating finance packages, talking to detractors, building coalitions—all of this in advance of turning toward the law.

Unless I wanted to visit every country, work with civil society in each one, and begin the glacial advocacy around law enforcement at the national level, this path was going to be too slow, too inefficient, and actively targeted at the wrong audience. It wasn't lawmakers who needed to adopt the change—it was the communities and households that believe cutting is the right thing to do.

As I did this work, I hugged a family secret close; once which I came to see influenced my approach to legal advocacy. After years of striving to be the "good immigrant," my Trinidadian father had realized his dream and started studying to be a barrister. One evening walking home from a work dinner at the Inner Temple in London of the 1960s, he was attacked and knocked unconscious. He recovered to find he was in jail and in front of the magistrate the next morning, denied his basic rights to representation. He realized, as the trial progressed, that he was being convicted of attempting to steal a car and of resisting arrest. His attackers were the two policemen giving evidence against him and he was found guilty. His law class came to his aid and his tutor mounted his defense, successfully acquitting him. But his tuition fees were wasted, eighteen months had passed with him living the shamed, alienated life of the wrongfully accused. His beloved law had betrayed him. I asked my mother about it later; she told me that he lost his faith in humanity after that time. In fact, he lost more. He had his first major heart attack that year, just before I was born, then his second fatal one in 1978, when I was eight years old and he forty-nine. Our secret? In my family, the law was the death of my father.

So legislation had served me when it was about the dry arcane world of infrastructure and process. But when it wove its tendrils into the fabric of lives, then it was about humans on humans, mano a mano. I felt there was too much at stake to use so inflexible an instrument, so separate from communities. I realized that I shared something with the pharmacist Saikou Jallow, a feeling about the law as an intimidating and rarefied part of our lives: something to fear, or to be invoked or accessed only when one is in deep trouble or when, in some way, life has become so risky that it doesn't allow for any other options to be explored. Life closes down.

*

"Do you want me to lock up everyone involved in cutting a girl?"

It was a challenging question, and it demanded an answer. I was face to face with the minister of justice for Puntland, in Somalia, in March 2012. The prevalence of FGC here was 98 percent. "How am I going to lock up 98 percent of the population for breaking the law? If I make FGC illegal, then I have a duty to enforce that. Surely you can see it isn't possible?" I stumbled in my answer. If something contravenes so many rights, then there must be a way to have an enforceable law against it. Surely?

There is such a law in Kenya, and a Kenyan lawyer named Sofia Rajab-Leteipan explains to me its unintended consequences as we sit together in a café on a road out to Nairobi, in February 2019. Sofia is a human rights lawyer who specializes in violence against women. She works with Orchid's Kenyan partners, and we are traveling, together, to the Loita Hills, to witness a ceremony in which a whole Maasai group will commit itself to end cutting.

"But, Julia," Sofia says to me, "the law is being used in the wrong way, with the wrong people, and is actually upholding injustice. Women's bodies are always the battleground that the law seems to clash on."

I ask her to explain more and she takes a deep breath. "I have been trying to defend three women recently. One was just a teenager, the others were older. They have been arrested and prosecuted for 'aiding and abetting' their own cutting, and also for 'failure to report' their cutting to the authorities."

This takes a while to sink in. "You mean they went through cutting and now they are being prosecuted for being party to the crime?"

I can scarcely believe what I'm hearing. Sofia tells me that the girls were arrested the same day they were cut and were taken, bleeding, into the cells. They were sentenced to three years in prison, of which they served two. "This takes criminalizing victims to a whole new level," she says. Later we are able to ensure Sofia is one of the expert witnesses to give evidence at the UN's Office of the High Commissioner for Human Rights in Addis Ababa, talking about community law and sanctions, and options that allow the discourse around law and FGC to work more closely with the community.

Sofia's example is one extreme of the unintended consequences of the use of law; there will be many other examples of successful litigation across Kenya, where cutters and others are prosecuted and convicted. Case by case, we are locking up cutters, or parents, making an example of them and punishing them for undertaking what has long held value within their kinship system. Unless we work to allow communities to understand why this practice will no longer serve them or their daughters, they will be at odds with the law.

It led me back to what I had witnessed in the Gambia, Senegal, and more widely—that the community-level work had to come first. This became the focus of what Orchid Project has concentrated on. First we support grassroots organizations working actively at the community level to shift the social norm. Then we share and amplify that change so that others can adopt similar models. Finally, we mandate those who should be doing more, to do more. This has seemed to create a virtuous cycle of change.

*

Sofia and I continue our journey, in February 2019, on to the Loita Hills, where our host, Amos Leuka, awaits us.

Amos is an elder in his Maasai community. The previous year, he had met me in London, to speak to the Canadian and UK governments about his long involvement in work to end cutting in his community in Kenya. We sat upstairs at Canada House, overlooking Trafalgar Square, waiting to meet with ministers. In spite of the freezing weather, Amos was in his Maasai robes, and he perched on the side of the armchair where I sat so we could have a snatched conversation about how his work was coming along.

He reminded me that in the law, there are a number of people who can be prosecuted along the chain or web of intent to cut a girl—her parents, her family, the cutter—and this applied across borders. Most recently, Kenya, Tanzania, and Uganda have tried to strengthen these border laws, so that the loophole of girls being taken over borders to be cut was closed. In response, FGC was going underground, and in this region, girls were being cut at a younger and younger age, sometimes before they were verbal, to avoid detection and hence prosecution.

This was terrible news. But Amos had a solution. With a fierce smile on his face, he told me that he and other community leaders had gone to the elders and guardians of tradition. They said that once the practice had gone underground, it could no longer be associated with a ritual or an upholding of positive tradition, as had been seen before. "We asked the question— since cutting will no longer be linked to positive traditional practices, how was it possible that it was still allowed to continue? I am waiting to hear their answer when I go home . . ."

Now, a year later, in Loita Hills, the answer to Amos's question is gloriously before us. We watch thousands of Maasai, wrapped in their *shugas* and carrying their staffs, stream toward a gathering place on a hilltop, the Tanzanian border visible just beyond. They form into a square, hundreds on each side, most standing, children sitting, babies playing in the dust. The middle of the square becomes a stage for the ritual, on which the elders offer an alternative rite of passage, whereby a girl is no longer cut: instead, each girl has agreed to a ritual moment where milk is poured across her legs, to mark her transition into womanhood. The Moran warriors, the defenders of the group, have embraced this new ritual: they perform their traditional dance, a strong throat hum supporting their song, while the audience watches. entranced. Everywhere I look there are people, hundreds of them witnessing this moment, the very air tremulous with the whispers they share.

We had been working with Amos and his organization, SAFE Maa, since 2013. We had even been able to send him and his colleague Sarah Tenoi to Senegal to study the Tostan model. Now I watch as Amos stands at the head of the procession of the elders, center of the square, center of the plain. He catches my eye as he begins the speech that will herald this historic moment. Mine are flooded with tears.

*

As I write this, eleven years since meeting Megdes and Tinebab in Lalibela and choosing to walk away from them toward a systemic constellation of change, I wonder about the urge to not punish, to not use the law in a way that can break communities, parents, hearts, but instead to use dialogue, empathy, trust, respect. I think I hear a rustle of learning, echoing through time. I realize that the very month in which I am writing these words, as I edge toward my fiftieth birthday, I have just outlived my father. Who knows what the path of a daughter is in expiating or reframing or relinquishing, but as I continue this journey, is it possible that I feel his hand on my shoulder?

In the last decade there has been much more awareness about FGC, and some progress. The movements that catch the headlines and the dollars have a commanding "top down" approach—and often a legal mindset in their DNA. For them, there is a teleological march toward change, mainly linear, that extends out from the introduction of legislation. There is often a moment, with much fanfare, that shows the adoption of such legislation.

In contrast, small community-led organizations are often not financed. Such organizations do not look to legislation—and often don't even know it exists. And yet, in my experience, they are the ones that will actually bring about sustainable, long-term change, village by village, fostered in dialogue, brought together by the individuals Malcolm Gladwell calls the "mavens" in his book *The Tipping Point*. A maven, says Gladwell, "is an information broker, sharing and trading what they know." Amos is a classic maven and he pursued his work until he brought people to, and then beyond, the tipping point.

In thinking about this, I draw inspiration from nature: the murmuration of starlings. A glance at YouTube would envelop you in the magical experience of watching thousands of small black birds swooping into an impromptu dance that has no choreographer. The movement is there but there is no single leader: whichever bird is in the lead in one moment passes on that imperceptible lead in the next and the flock turns and follows and twists and reconfigures. It transpires that there's a magic number of seven birds that are in constant contact with each other.

The movement to end FGC needs to be starling-fluid as it interacts in each moment with, say, a new religious leader, the encroachment of urbanization, the learning of new languages, the intermarriage of different ethnic groups, the rise of technology and data, a growth in access to education, or the changes in health care and knowledge at the community level—a tide, an ebb and flow of humanity. How will each cell of seven people, the ones who might be seen to be part of the constellation of decision makers for cutting a girl, respond to each moment?

For each new ripple of intervention, the swarm changes and reacts. A legal approach would need to be fluid too, and to be conceived in ripples. This suggests a form of restorative justice, enforced by the community. If we are overreliant on the law, it could very quickly overwhelm the complex nuances of community-level movement work that I know to be the lifeblood of what needs to be supported. Conversely, imagine if we can start weaving more together with the grassroots change, with the law as a living, breathing tool that has relevance and accessibility for communities.

The time is now, the opportunity is now, and before millions more girls are cut, we need ourselves, with greater legal literacy, to take flight and join the flock of change.

Further Reading: For further reading on ending female genital cutting, see: *Changing a Harmful Social Convention: Ending Female Genital Mutilation/ Cutting* (UNICEF Innocenti, 2008); and the novel *Cutting for Stone* by Abraham Verghese (Vintage, 2009).

Law and Stones:
Sex Workers' Rights in Kenya

PHELISTER ABDALLA

My name is Phelister Abdalla. I'm a feminist, a mother with four children, a lover, a patriotic Kenyan, and I live positively. I work as a sex worker, and I am the national coordinator of the Kenya Sex Workers' Alliance (KESWA). This puts me at the front line of creating awareness and advocating for the rights of sex workers at national, regional, and global levels. My work includes lobbying, public awareness, and doing advocacy for policy reform—and, most recently, leading the process of decriminalizing sex work in Kenya through public interest litigation.

I have frequently spoken publicly about the importance of decriminalization as a way of giving sex workers a human face, and of normalizing our work. But the real power of this process was brought home to me personally when I spoke about it on national television in 2019. I had been estranged from my mother for many years, as she disapproved of my work. But she happened to see the broadcast, and she phoned me afterwards. She told me that when she watched me, she remembered me as a little girl, saying that I wanted to become a lawyer: "Now when I hear you talking about going to court, I can see how, by being a sex worker and an activist, you have accomplished your vision. You are so passionate and articulate, and you speak out in a way I was not able to."

We have become friends again: despite whatever else I am, firstly I am a daughter, and she is my mother. Now I can take my kids home to her, and she can enjoy the pleasures of being a grandmother; now she can accept my help too, from the proceeds of my work. Some words my mother said in that conversation have really stayed with me: "You are picking up the same stones people are throwing at you." By that my mother means I speak back when people call me names.

In Kenya, the "stones" are real too: we as sex workers suffer terrible physical violence, and even get murdered. But the "stones" my mother was referring to are not just violent words or actions; they are the laws that legitimate such violence by making our work illegal. In this context, "picking up stones" means using the law itself to fight back. We maintain that the Kenyan laws prohibiting us from earning a living through sex work are unconstitutional. They stigmatize sex work: make us seem evil and dispensable, and make it impossible for us to look after our families. They encourage violence against us, putting us outside of society, in effect. However, through public interest litigation, we hope to change this.

*

Before the COVID-19 pandemic, I was preparing to tell my story along with five others petitioning the Kenyan high court to make it legal to earn a living from sex work.

Our plans were disrupted by the lockdowns of 2020, but these showed us more than ever the urgency of our goal. KESWA has a toll-free hotline in several of Kenya's counties, and we usually receive over five calls fortnightly reporting physical violence. During the months of lockdown in 2020 these calls more than doubled to between thirty and forty per month, per hotline. Kenya implemented a nighttime curfew: this made it difficult for sex workers to do their job under the cover of night, and working during the day made them more visible and vulnerable. Curfew also meant that clients tended to stay over with them, thereby exposing them to more violence. It also made it difficult for them to call for help, as others feared breaking the law by leaving their homes. On top of all that, there was the arbitrary violence of police officers themselves, using the emergency regulations to harass sex workers. Because of the way the pandemic slowed down the court processes, and most of all because we needed to redirect our resources toward the emergency relief of our members, we put our litigation plans on hold.

But in early 2021, our membership told us that they felt a decriminalization case was an absolute priority, and mandated us to begin preparing for it again. If the litigation is successful, it will produce positive changes in laws, policies, and practices that affect sex workers in Kenya. It will create the potential for safer working conditions and healthier living environments. In addition, other key communities could use such a judgment to address violations affecting them. But the truth is that the odds are against us actually winning in court, given the conservatism of Kenyan society. Because of this we see any strategic litigation as part of a broader, long-term advocacy strategy, which is primarily about giving sex workers a human face.

We have already had some success doing this in previous campaigns. There was a time from about 2015 when sex workers were being murdered in significant numbers, and we ran a short video with a very moving song. We included a few pictures of the women who had been slain, and for those who consented, also pictures of their children holding their mother's coffins during the burial, with the message underneath: "Is it really right to kill people for choosing a different career? This was a mother, and her children have now become orphans." The video moved a lot of people, and gave us an indication of how powerful a public advocacy campaign can be in giving people a different understanding of who we are and what we do.

Seen within this context, we are certain that if we continue to use a public advocacy approach, we will "win" anyway by filing the case, despite the outcome in court. People are going to be reading about us, hearing us, thinking about who we are and what value we add to society. We will be changing the narrative, and this alone is a "win" enough for us. The fact that we will have gone to court, that we will have shown our faces, that we have attracted so much media, that would be the win for the Kenyan sex workers. Not only will we be making our case to the judges in court, but to the politicians in government, and the people who elect them.

There are other potential benefits to the litigation too. We believe it will help strengthen the existing sex workers' movement, especially at a grassroots level, by mobilizing and involving members at every stage of the litigation process. And it will help the movement to strengthen existing relationships with likeminded allies and form new coalitions. By highlighting gender-based violence, in particular, it will address a common issue that cuts across different sections of the Kenyan society.

In preparing for the litigation, we have consulted other movements, and in particular the LGBTQ organizations that litigated for the decriminalization of homosexual acts in the Supreme Court, in 2018.* They lost the case, and have taken it on appeal; they have been able to share with us both the risks and the benefits of such litigation. We shadowed them every step of the way, and for me the most valuable lesson I learned was to conquer my own fear. I explain it like this: "You cannot be criminalized twice." What I mean by this is that, given that we are already viewed by the law as criminal, we have nothing to lose: they can't make it worse than it is already.

Practically, one of the key lessons we have learned from the LGBTQ case is the importance of developing a clear communication strategy together, so that everyone understands, in simple language, and can go back to brief their regional groups. This way, you keep everyone on board, but also build your movement. Another lesson is the importance of research and networking: We have not only been talking to sex workers but also to their supporters and their opponents, to public officers, to parliamentarians. We want to get the opinions of a broad sweep of people and find out how sex workers' cases have been treated. This leads on to the third lesson: the importance of evidence. It is vital to have good raw data from sex workers about what happened to them. This means selecting the litigants who will give our case the best possible human face, whose stories will move the court and the public. But it also means doing your research properly. We want to make sure we have good reporting, with statistics, showing the violence the community is facing.

We made sure to get our research methodology and ethics approved by the Kenya Medical Research Institute (KEMRI), a government body, and we made sure we had a good technical team. One of the questions put to us by KEMRI was about how we could assure that this research would not push child prostitution. We responded by investigating underage sex workers as well. We asked the children, "What is your biggest fear?" Their answer: "Adult sex workers." The reason they gave was fascinating: they said that the adults were always chasing the children away from their areas, and reminding them that they are kids. This is essential data, for it corrects the misconception that adult sex workers push children into prostitution, and proves that we wish to protect children, not exploit them. According

---

* See Njeri Gateru, "The Decriminalization of Homosexuality in Kenya," on page 160 of this book.

to our research, minors tend to become sex workers because of the pressure of their peers. Another thing that came out very clearly was that police arrest kids without even knowing they are kids, and that the whole criminal justice system treats them, incorrectly, as adults: judging and jailing them on that basis. That is very sad from our side, because it shows that children are not being protected by the law.

*

Deciding to use the law as a strategy is not simple for me, personally, or for many of my fellow sex workers, given the way the law has always been used against us. But given our experiences at the hands of the law, we are even doubly committed to work toward the decriminalization of our profession.

I think my own life experiences make this point. Once, when I was being chased by street children in Mombasa, I saw a police car and I thought I was going to be rescued. Instead, five policemen carried me into the car and started harassing me about what I was wearing, and whether or not I was a sex worker. They took me to where they lived and they all raped me. For three days they locked me up and just kept coming back. I had no food or water. I had heard them speaking about how they were going to kill me and dump me. When I heard someone at the door, I thought they were back again, and my life would end. But it was the older woman who did the washing. She told me that other girls like me had been killed, and she let me out of that place. I could hardly walk but she helped me. She risked her life by choosing to save me.

What made it worse is that I had nobody to talk to about it. Other older sex workers said, "Oh, this happens all the time." This was something really painful because the more I kept on feeling it, the more it felt like a wound inside my heart that could only heal if I did something about it. I kept on pressuring people, asking what we could do, or if we could just even talk about it. At that time counseling was not available: all you could do was go to the hospital and access health services. There was nothing else to move forward with, or look forward to.

So I think the pain I felt at that time really pushed me to act. I was already a trained HIV/AIDS peer educator, but that was limited: we could only talk about our health, we couldn't talk about the law or about being violated. But I felt like I needed to talk about the violations I faced as a sex worker, I needed to tell people and report cases and see people arrested. I then started doing my own research, finding out online what could be done, and I realized that I could be trained as a paralegal. I decided to get that training because I wanted to be able to defend my community. The organization that had trained me as a peer educator trained twenty of us as paralegals in Mombasa, and that's where I began. When I started going to meetings outside Mombasa, in places like Nairobi, I met different people who were passionate, talking about the rights of gay people, for example, and I thought, it is high time I started talking about the rights of sex workers; it's high time we fight for our rights, it's high time we do things differently, it's high time we break the barriers, because we had barriers within us. Somebody had to speak about something.

My mother is right. I have always wanted to speak out, but my own life experiences made it impossible for me to realize that childhood dream of being a lawyer. I was born out of wedlock, in a very conservative Muslim community in Mombasa, and so my mother was ostracized and stigmatized from the start. She had three children, whom she raised singlehandedly through selling *chapatis* at the Mombasa port. She struggled day and night to put food on the table for us. I think that the combination of that pressure, and the stigma and discrimination she endured, sent her into depression and madness, and she was unable to look after us anymore. I was sent to live with my aunt and uncle in Malindi, up the coast, as they were childless.

My uncle would sexually abuse me when my aunt went to work. I never smiled, ever.

Around this time a young woman—beautifully dressed and made up—noticed me, and asked me why I never smiled. No one had ever asked me what was wrong before, and I opened up to her: I told her my uncle was raping me. She helped me run away, and I found shelter in a brothel. This was when I began doing sex work. It was not an easy beginning: it turned out that I was pregnant, from my uncle. The woman running the brothel looked after me: I was very skinny, and she said I was in no condition to have an abortion. She said I could stay—some men liked pregnant women—and that my baby would be given up for adoption. This is what happened.

Reading this, you might think I was forced into sex work, but I don't believe this was the case. For someone like me in the coast region of Kenya, a woman on her own unable to depend on her family, the other option would have been working as a house-help in other peoples' houses. I knew I would hate that. The truth is that when that beautifully dressed woman helped me escape, I had been noticing her, and others like her, for a while already. I really admired them—how they came home smartly dressed, wearing makeup, with fancy phones. They clearly had money, and style! But it wasn't just that. Particularly given my own family experience, I loved the way they seemed so independent and open-minded. They would speak about *anything,* and seemed in control of their lives. I admired it so much. I knew I wanted my own power, and this seemed to be the way to get it.

And indeed, it was. It paid for my schooling, it paid for my rent, and it continues to provide for my family.

*

It has been complicated to find people to be petitioners, not just because it is risky, but also because we need to have people whose cases are well documented. They need to have documents showing: I was arrested, somebody tried to kill me, I reported it to the police, these are the police officers handling my case, the person was arrested, we went to court, this is what my file looks like. We need to have all the evidence in place, and not everybody has that. Getting it is difficult but not impossible, because we have already been preparing our people and telling them that they need to start documenting the violence they are facing. Two or three years ago when we were asking the government why they were not making health more accessible to sex workers, they kept on saying there was no data. That was the moment we realized that, as a community, we were failing. We need to tell each other about documenting. So we started educating people about what documents they needed to collect when they were violated. People will listen when you have evidence; even the Ministry of Health listened. That is why we have emphasised that sensitization is vital at KESWA, and why we have connected and trained sex workers as paralegals to help fellow sex workers all over the country with filing and following up on their cases.

Sex work is secret work, because of the stigma attached to it, because of the violence it attracts, and because—of course—it is illegal. Given this context, you can imagine how complicated public interest litigation is for sex workers. It is going to open our lives up to the public, especially those who are the litigants. We need to be really prepared, physically, mentally, and also financially, because some people will have to travel to Nairobi. We need to put together a committed team of people who know what to expect so we don't break when the process gets hotter. Because it will get hotter. It will attract many opposing parties. The petitioners' faces will be out there on public media, in communities; people will be discussing them and the environment might no longer be safe for them and their children.

As you might imagine, we have had really tough discussions about how to prepare our kids around seeing our names in public—and about what we do for a living. Instead of them seeing us on the TV, how can we have a conversation with them at the dinner table? KESWA has actually held family days in different counties to we prepare kids for what might happen, and let them meet children who might be facing the same challenge, as children of sex workers. It's very intense. But we think it's worth it to tell people our stories.

Talking to fellow activists and potential litigants, I share my own story about "coming out" to my kids. When Alex, my oldest, was eight, I told him about my HIV status: I wanted him to know what the medication was that I was always taking, and how taking it allowed me to be alive, to look after him. This meant, of course, talking about transmission, and I was very open and genuine with him about that too.

We call my son "Pastor Alex" because he loves going to church so much. One day, I took him to church and the pastor told a story about a certain kind of woman. He was clearly talking about me, and everyone was turning around and looking at me. When we got home, Alex asked me, "Who was that woman the pastor was talking about?"

"Go get a glass of water, my son, and come and sit down," I told him. "I am that woman."

"Does that mean you're a prostitute?" he asked.

I explained to him why we use the phrase "sex worker" rather than "prostitute"—because of the derogatory connotations of that word—and what it actually meant: someone who earns a living using a part of their body, so they can look after their families. It's a conversation I have with him, and his sister, at least a couple of times a year, checking in with them, answering all their questions, and making sure they're okay. My main message is this: "Sex is my work, and activism is my work, but when I come home, I'm your mother."

It's not always easy for them. Alex, who is fourteen now, was bullied at school after I was on television once. But he knows how to defend himself, and he was very proud of himself for standing up to the bullies: "She's not a prostitute," he told them. "She's a sex worker. Sex workers are human beings with blood running through their veins, like anyone else. Stop attacking me about my mom. I don't attack your parents."

And then there's Angel, my eight-year-old. She is like me. She loves speaking out. One day in class, she gave a talk: "My mother is a sex worker. She is beautiful, I love her. People attack her. I want to be a lawyer because I want to protect people like my mom."

I got good feedback from other parents. The school said they wanted to talk to me. I was a little concerned. But they didn't seem to mind terribly. They just said, "Won't you talk to Angel, Phelister, so she doesn't keep on mentioning your job in the classroom?"

I had to laugh. Angel will be a lawyer, if she wants to be.

*

My name is Phelister Abdalla. I'm an active female sex worker living positively with HIV, a feminist, a lover, a patriotic Kenyan, and a mother. And one of the things about being a mother is that it automatically gives you a different feeling. When I gave birth to my firstborn, the moment I heard him crying, I just got a feeling I'd never felt before. I still feel it today, when I look at him, and with time I came to realize the feeling was love. Despite us sex workers facing a lot of hurt, when we look into our children's lives and see who they are becoming, they bring that feeling back to us again. They remind us that love is a very special thing, and everybody deserves to feel it. The woman who saved me when I was facing violence acted out of love. I've learned, from my life and my work, it was love, not luck, that made her act. That person had the option of walking away and saying, "Let me leave this woman alone here to die." But she decided to save my life. I believe love exists, and people with good hearts make it powerful. People who make us smile all the time, our children, our partners, people who support our work, people who stand with sex workers, those are the people doing it out of love and understanding. That's how I see it all the time. When we go to court, we will be going for the love of our community, and the understanding of how a change in law could change our lives.

Further reading: For more on the Kenya Sex Workers' Alliance, go to keswa-kenya.org. See also Phelister Abdalla, "Kenya Must Legalise Sex Work for the Sake of Human Rights and Public Health," *The Guardian*, December 17, 2015; and Chi Adanna Mgbako, *To Live Freely in this World: Sex Worker Activism in Africa* (NYU Press, 2016).

A Community, Its Abusive Chief, and the Role of the Law: The Story of Nwoase in Ghana

NANA AMA NKETIA-QUAIDOO

Every year, between May and June, the community of Nwoase in Nkoranza South gets flooded with about six hundred trucks from all over the country, coming to buy watermelons to carry to markets all over Ghana. The people of Nwoase are the second-best watermelon farmers in the district, and it is a delight to see them, men and women alike, wiping the sweat off their faces as they count out their watermelons for buyers, and pocket their hard-earned money. In 2017, when I was working there, there were 137 households in the community, each with an average of eight people: the total population was 1,100.

The village has two boreholes and electricity—and its greatest pride, a school. But the deplorable eighteen-kilometer road to Nkoranza is all but impassable during the rainy season, and because there was no accommodation for teachers in the village, the teachers often simply did not show up during these months. And so, when my organization, Advocates for Community Alternatives (ACA), made a microgrant to the community in 2018, they decided to build teachers' quarters with it. This was in order to accommodate the teachers in the village during the rainy season, curb their absenteeism, and improve the children's education.

But as we worked with the people of Nwoase, we discovered a major impediment to their progress: their very own chief, Atekoanohene. Some of them are Indigenous families and some are descendants of migrants from the north, but they have lived on the land for generations and treated Atekoanohene and his predecessors as their chiefs. They have contributed money for the construction of his palace and the funerals of his family members, and (in the case of the tenant farmers) shared the profits from the land according to traditional arrangements for many years. In return,

Atekoanohene is required to manage the land on their behalf. But it turned out he had done the opposite: he had stolen it, and sold it without their knowledge or permission, to a private buyer.

What had begun for me and my colleagues as a quite straightforward community empowerment project thus became a major lesson for us all: you cannot address community development if there are underlying human rights violations, and community development needs to go hand in hand with a legal challenge to human rights abuse. The gap that exists between communities and development is power. When communities lack power, they lack self-identity. When they have power, they can decide, and demand changes to policies to things that are inconsistent with their development vision. They become more resilient: they fight to see results and are less likely to be discouraged by the inevitable delays and setbacks.

Working with the people of Nwoase, I realized that I needed to use my skills as a community mobilizer toward a different end than the one I had originally intended: to find a solution to the community's legal problems. This became clear in our meetings with the community. They had all these ideas for progress—to improve sanitation, or education, or such like—but how could they even embark on such progress if they could not be sure their land tenure was safe?

We had initially become involved with the people, along with three neighboring communities, because the huge gold deposits in the district meant that they were threatened in 2011 by a mining plan developed by the American corporation Newmont. In an unprecedented response, these four communities had stood their ground against Newmont because they saw it as threatening their farmlands, livelihoods, and water supplies: the community mobilized itself and staged a demonstration after visiting another Newmont mine and seeing the results—how deprived and devastated the communities at that site were, and how they suffered from extreme hunger due to loss of crops and a suddenly high cost of living. The resistance of the Nkoranza South communities was inspiring: they dressed in red and chanted war songs and dirges, with inscriptions on cardboard, on the day the Newmont officials visited in 2011, accompanied by government officials and the district's paramount chief.

When we met the communities five years later, many residents expressed the concern that either Newmont or another company would be back, and that poverty and internal divisions might sap their strength to resist them again. It therefore became very necessary for the communities to have a well-streamlined mechanism that would unite the them around a positive development initiative. In other words, as we put it at ACA, "a future to fight for, rather than just an enemy to fight against."

Little did we expect that the most immediate "enemy" was not a multinational corporation, but the local chief. This became clear to us in the first phase of the three-year-long Facilitated Community Action Process (FCAP). The FCAP is designed to give communities control of the development process, resources, and decision-making authority, and assumes that communities are the best judges of how their lives and livelihoods can be improved. In the first phase, which takes a year, the community identifies its vision and goals, and plans how to use the microgrant. A key part of this process is the building of a cohesive community structure, and it was in this process that the negative role of the chief became clear.

It turned out that in the years before we became involved with Nwoase, Atekoanohene had continually destabilized their lives, terrorizing them with the possibility of eviction and using this threat to extort ever-increasing, arbitrary payments. At least twice in the previous seven years he had announced that he had sold some or all of their farmland, and informed members of the community that they would have to leave. It became clear that this was a form of extortion: in both cases, he backtracked when community members agreed to pay higher rent in order to remain. Later, he told the community that the gods did not approve of their practice of rearing goats, dogs, and pigs in the village; when they protested that they had always done so without falling foul of any spiritual obligation, he once more changed course and decreed they would henceforth be required to contribute sheep to him to appease the gods. On top of this, the chief had prohibited any of the residents of Nwoase from dying in their homes: an ill person had to be carried out to the bush to die and was charged the price of a sheep for burial in the village. He threatened the community constantly with charms and sorcery; everyone was perpetually engulfed in fear.

Then, in July 2017, while the community was planning the school teachers' quarters with us, Atekoanohene suddenly sold 245 acres of land—the livelihoods of about fifty families—to a total stranger, and destroyed all the crops on their land, with no compensation. Six months later, he did the same again with another 145 acres, sold to four soldiers to grow cashew nuts. In effect this was a form of eviction, because the community's sole means of livelihood had been removed from them: they were no longer able to live and work on the land they had occupied for generations. This really affected our work with the community and for weeks our organization had no option other than to pause our Facilitated Community Action Process, and redirect our focus to helping the community overcome their predicament.

The community was paralyzed: these people, who had so valiantly resisted a major American corporation, literally feared death if they stood up to their chief. We found out that there were many legends about Atekoanohene: how he made his cousin blind for challenging him, how he turned someone into a cow and shot him dead. He carried guns in his car, and was given to shooting them in the air—at funerals, for example, to demonstrate his power. For these reasons, the people of Nwoase had failed to get anyone in their community, such as Atekoanohene's sub-chiefs, or even neighboring communities' chiefs, to speak to him on their behalf: everyone was terrified.

Our approach was to work with them on a mapping activity, in which they brainstormed, analyzed, and identified key stakeholders who could be involved in settling their dispute with the chief. They were presented with the possibility of litigation, but rejected it, given how long it takes and expensive it is. In our organization's other work across West Africa, we had come to see how communities lost interest in legal processes due to their cumbersome nature and the idea that court processes take almost forever to complete. It is so difficult for a community to stay focused, given these factors, and what really helps moderate the "legal fatigue" is the use of the organizing tools that keep the community alive and engaged. This approach recognizes the power of community, and therefore allows people to deliberate and offer suggestions in every decision they take as community. They become solely responsible for the outcomes.

It was fascinating to note the way the Facilitated Community Action Process itself—which is all about community cohesion and civic engagement—helped the community members overcome their fears and divisions. When we first started holding meetings in Nwoase, the crowds that would normally attend public meetings would melt away as soon as anyone mentioned Atekoanohene and the land issue, because no one trusted one another and everyone was afraid of the chief's spies. But as they became accustomed to the idea of planning for the future together (into which process we successfully co-opted the spies themselves!), people became bolder, and found that their common interests were more important than their divisions.

In Nwoase, there was also the problem of documentation: most people did not have proof of their rights to the land. So, we all decided that mediation and negotiation was the best option, despite its challenges, and the community petitioned the Commission on Human Rights and Administrative Justice (CHRAJ), an independent statutory body that safeguards human rights against state abuse in Ghana. We knew we could do this because, according to Ghanaian law, traditional chiefs are actually state agents: they get their authority from the government. Had the aggressor been a private company, we would had to have used other tools, and our decision to go to CHRAJ is an example of how important it is to know your opponent and the context, and to pick your tools accordingly.

Mediation and negotiation would be faster, and less procedural, than litigation. ACA supported the community with lawyers to provide them expertise and information needed to write the petition, which 109 people boldly signed. Within the community, two teachers played the lead, calling on the others to be bold and step up, and to empower themselves with the land and human rights training being offered.

The CHRAJ responded by calling for a meeting with the community, which Atekoanohene was legally bound to attend. He failed to turn up: perhaps because he did not understand the communication (he is illiterate), but more likely because he did not believe that the community had the capacity to challenge him, and so he ignored it. Even when the CHRAJ called him by phone, he exerted his usual fierceness. And as before, he used the "divide and rule" tactic, calling individual villagers to his house, threatening them with instant eviction if they did not rat on those who had signed the petition. If they collaborated, on the other hand, they would be given additional land, confiscated from others. These "spies" did their job well in one instance, when they informed the chief of a demonstration planned during a proposed visit to the community in October 2017: he stayed away. We knew that these "spies" were keeping the chief informed, and so we had to work strategically to win them over. We did this by assigning them roles during the meetings, which made them highly involved in the decision-making. In the end they signed the petition themselves, and even became the community representatives during the mediation!

The CHRAJ asked for the community to limit its representatives to twenty people and, after dodging the first meeting, the chief attended the second in March 2018, accompanied by two friends. His behavior at this meeting—a series of verbal attacks—led to such a heated argument that the CHRAJ had to adjourn it, and it took eleven months to mobilize both parties and reconvene. Finally, in February 2019, the chief attended a meeting in which he said the late paramount chief of the district had told him to sell off the 245 acres to pay for medical bills, and that this was irrevocable. He claimed, too, that he sold the additional 145 acres because those members of the community were not paying their rents regularly. The villagers disputed this and added that the chief also prevented them from growing staple subsistence crops and yet demanded these crops from the community as a contribution to his annual festivals. Finally, the CHRAJ mediator told Atekoanohene that, because of the community's right to food, he had no right to sell land that denied them their livelihood.

The sale of the land was thus an infringement on the community's fundamental rights, as enshrined in the Ghanaian constitution. It has also long been recognized that forced eviction and compulsory acquisition of land are inextricably linked to the right to food, enshrined in the Universal Declaration of Human Rights and the International Covenant on Economic, Social and Cultural Rights. According to the Ghanaian constitution, traditional leaders are given the responsibility over "stool lands" (lands belonging to the tribe under customary law), but may not dispose of them unless it is part of a government-approved regional development plan. The chief was thus acting illegally by selling them. Again, the Ghanaian constitution vests stool lands with traditional leaders "on behalf of and in trust of the subjects of stool in accordance with customary law and usage." No stool land can be disposed of unless the regional Lands Commission has determined that the disposition or development is consistent with approved regional development plan. The bottom line was this: the chief was not free to dispose of stool land. He did it for pure and personal economic gains.

The CHRAJ mediation resulted in a commitment from Atekoanohene that he would give alternative lands to the affected people: an hour and a half's walk away from the village. The community compiled data on all affected families for this new allocation, and documents were signed by both parties, to reduce the chief's unpredictability. At first the chief appeared to be cooperative. The Nwoase community believed that this is because he got a fright: he did not expect its members to stand up for themselves and, like so many bullies, he backed down quickly when confronted with "authority," in the form of the CHRAJ. Previously, he had been using sorcery, spirits, and curses to instill fear in the community, but when he saw that people were able to appeal to a higher authority, this brought his spirits down to such an extent that it seems he realized he had to cooperate.

Everybody understood the risks. Even if the chief was chastened, it was in his nature to intimidate, and he would resume this practice. And so we at ACA provided advocacy training, to enable them to forecast and preempt potential threats in the future. We also facilitated a Citizens Committee Network in the area, made up of representatives from all four of the communities we have been working in. It was launched by the mayor of the district, Nkoranza South, to function as a civic organization to lead communities in addressing challenges they may face at present and in the future. I wish I could report that women were playing a major role in these processes, but in a traditional setting they remain largely confined to the domestic sphere. Still, through this process we have seen marginally more women coming out strongly, to make their voices heard.

The community's worst fears about the chief have, alas, proven to be correct. In March 2021, almost two years after he made his promise during the CHRAJ meetings, he flouted his commitments, and invited five hundred of his cows to graze on and destroy the few crops the community had managed to grow to sustain their families. He even made a public statement that he planned to replace the community with cows!

But how different the community was now, from the paralysis we had initially encountered. They made no secret of their irritation, and decided to broadcast to the world about their wicked chief, through a press conference that was carried on two TV and four radio stations across the country. They appealed publicly to the government through the Ministry of Chieftaincy and Culture of Ghana as a matter of urgency to intervene before the matter could get worse. There was a result: a few weeks later, the ministry placed a hold on all activities on the lands the chief had sold to strangers, and began vigorous investigations into the situation at Nwoase together with the paramount chiefs in the area. Finally, there is the hope that there will be a lasting solution to the problems in the community. And even if there is not, I can be certain of one thing: the community will take action again, with clarity and purpose.

I have learned several lessons from the experience. First and fundamentally: to be a good listener and pay attention to communities' beliefs and systems. And, in such an unpredictable environment, to be flexible, and always have backup plans to avoid discouragement when a plan fails. I have also come to realize how little communities in Ghana know about their land rights and human rights. Most of all, I have come to understand that communities have capacity, but what they mostly lack is confidence, direction—and of course power. I saw in Nwoase how both our interventions and the presence of the CHRAJ process provided the community with these. I believe that the fundamental goal in respecting people's rights is to empower them, give them the knowledge and skills to take control of their own lives and decisions that affect them.

It is clear, listening to the stories of the people of Nwoase, that in the past they were kept in such darkness they could not cough in peace without fear of their throats being cut, because of the way their chief set spies among them. Now there is a sense not only of empowerment but of community cohesion too, and a belief, among community members, in their own capacity to lead. Everyone is ready to take up roles and responsibilities, mobilize and empower each other to keep fighting and resisting the oppressor's rule. I see a new Nwoase that has the strength to carry on.

Further Reading. On the Nwaose case, see www.advocateforalternatives. org. See also: Constitution of the Republic of Ghana, art. 218(a) (1992); International Covenant on Civil and Political Rights, December 16, 1966, 999 U.N.T.S. 171, 176; International Covenant on Economic, Social and Cultural Rights, December 16, 1966, 993 U.N.T.S. 3; and African Charter of People's and Human Rights, June 27, 1981, OAU Doc. CAB/LEG/67/3 rev. 5; 1520 U.N.T.S. 217; 21 I.L.M. 58 (1982).

Standing Up at Standing Rock:
An Indigenous Warrior's Experience

KRYSTAL TWO BULLS in conversation with MARK GEVISSER and KATIE REDFORD

Mark Gevisser: Krystal, you served in the military, doing active service in Operation Iraqi Freedom. On return you led the Drop the MIC (military-industrial complex) campaign in the About Face veterans' organization. Could you talk about your transition from "soldier" to "warrior"?

Krystal Two Bulls: I come from a long history of organizing. My parents organized around the Otter Creek coal mine here on Northern Cheyenne territory. And I have grandparents in Pine Ridge, South Dakota, who organized against uranium mining and for the hemp industry, dealing with the Feds burning their crops down and all that.

Growing up in an Indigenous community, it was drilled into me that warriors do what is necessary for the benefit of our people and for the benefit of those not yet born. But then I went into the army, and learned how to be a "soldier." What I don't think they accounted for is that I learned skill sets, and I learned things from them about how they operate.

It was a huge learning curve, making the transition from soldier to warrior once I came back from active service in the Middle East, a rite of passage both physically and metaphorically, going from child to adult, recognizing I had been used as a tool for imperialism. The transition was from being a soldier following orders to being a warrior who will do whatever is necessary to protect and preserve our way of life—using skills from military and putting it into practice in my activism.

I had been in logistics, based out of Kuwait, responsible for the inventory of every piece of equipment, personnel, supplies under control of central command in Iraq, Kuwait, Qatar, Egypt. When I got back in July 2010, my parents were organizing against coal mining in our territory, and they had been invited to Black Mesa in Arizona, for a big gathering of the Climate Justice Alliance. They couldn't go, so I went down in their place. Sharon Lungo of the Ruckus Society noticed me, and started asking me questions. I was already translating what I'd learned in the army to movement organizing: planning an action, scouting, identifying roles, safety, security, personnel, land navigation. For me that all made sense—in the military we get an operational order, and we are tasked with making that happen, to complete the mission. All these things translated directly to direct action and organizing. The military gave me language, it gave me curriculum, and I could start translating my military skills over to nonviolent direct action.

MG: How did you put these skills to use specifically, as an activist at Standing Rock, once you answered the call to attend the Red Warrior Camp to stop the Dakota Access Pipeline [DAPL] encroaching on Lakota land?

KTB: I was logistics coordinator. I also helped hold some nonviolent direct action trainings, and eventually left the camp to start the DAPL global solidarity campaign, whose focus primarily was on uniting all the other movements also being impacted not only by the fossil fuel industry, but by private security firms. It birthed the divestment campaign that came out of Standing Rock. My role shifted from on-the-ground logistics to global campaign organizing.

MG: At Standing Rock, you were part of the debate on civil disobedience. What guided your thinking, and what were the consequences?

KTB: There were two parts to my thinking. The first was based on my understanding of the Doctrine of Discovery, which gave settlers the right to rule Turtle Island [North America]. I challenge that, and still feel strongly that—like my traditional government, which we've had since time immemorial—the natural law supersedes the Doctrine of Discovery. And so I answer to natural law, which requires me to defend our land, right?

Specifically, at Standing Rock, the Lakota nation did work through the court system to stop the pipeline. There was a long legal battle being fought before anyone even hit the ground. But then when we started to see the excavators unearth human remains and forcibly prevent the Standing Rock tribal chairman, David Archambault, from stopping this, it became clear to us that this corporation has no respect for human life and for our customs as a people. We were going to need to begin nonviolent direct action.

MG: Despite your limited time at the camp and the fact that you have been largely involved in solidarity work rather than in nonviolent protest at the camp yourself, you have been targeted for prosecution. You were charged under the Racketeer Influenced and Corrupt Organizations (RICO) Act, and listed as one of the leaders of the Red Warrior Camp, as part of a sprawling conspiracy to spread falsehoods about the DAPL corporation, Energy Transfer. Could you talk about that?

KTB: The pushback did not come until like a year later. In fact, the camp had been dismantled, and I had moved forward into other organizing spaces. Then all of a sudden I got a call from the Greenpeace legal counsel, to say, "Hey, did you know that your name has been added to a suit?" I went into a kind of in shock. I didn't know how to respond because I didn't think that that was even a possibility. I wasn't on the front lines, I wasn't getting arrested.

I went numb. It was only when you called, Katie, and told me that they dismissed charges and we won, that the emotional impact of this case hit me. I realized how drained of energy I had been by the case.

My biggest worry had been about how it would impact my family. The mail was going directly to my mom and my family's address, and so every time there was something from the courts and my mom saw it, I know they had anxiety about what would happen to me. If I were found guilty, what would happen? Would I be on probation? Would there be jail time? Would we have to pay money? Would my family lose me? I put my family first and show up for them no matter what. I'm an everyday part of their life.

I've always lived my life in a way to be a role model to my younger sisters and to the young people I work with. I don't feel guilt about what I did at Standing Rock. I would do it again. But I felt uncomfortable about role-modeling breaking the law in general, even though I felt what I did was right. I don't want the young people in my life to mess with the police. I don't want them to get into a battle with the legal system because, as we all know, it's not fair for Brown people.

And then of course, I worried about being a liability to movement spaces—that, just by being in certain spaces and having that over my head,

I might negatively impact any other space. And so it did hit on all of those levels.

Katie Redford: As a lawyer, I can say that all of this—what Krystal felt—is absolutely intentional and a goal of what is known as a SLAPP (Strategic Litigation against Public Participation) suit. The companies bringing these cases know they are unlikely to win. They have no intention of winning. What they want to do is disable activists—just as they disabled you—getting you to question yourself in relation to your family, other activists, alleging conspiracy—which makes you worry about being a liability to the movement. Having a sense of shared purpose, and collective power, is what movements are all about, right? But when companies like Energy Transfer start alleging that by having a shared vision to oppose their pipeline you are somehow participating in an illegal conspiracy, then they are trying to hit at the heart of what makes movements work.

KTB: Katie, I didn't even pick up, until this conversation right now, about how they were making me question myself with the SLAPP suit. I'm really blown away by that, because we all think we're these really strong people and I consider myself strong and well-educated and knowledgeable, and I have life experience, but I see how they conditioned me through this lawsuit to question myself and then to also, like, question my ability to show up in spaces as well. And I had no clue this was happening. It makes me realize how we have to continue organizing on all fronts, and how we do have to look at law as one of the primary strategies that we use to fight back. If we don't, we would just be shooting ourselves in the foot and we would lose automatically.

MG: How *did* you use the law to fight back, in this case?

KTB: When the Greenpeace lawyer told me I had been charged, I was already thinking: Who am I going to get in as an attorney? I was mapping out a fundraiser in my brain to pay for all of this. Then he got back to me and said, "We're part of this coalition called Protect the Protest, with EarthRights and the Center for Constitutional Rights," and they took it from there. It was such a blessing. Had I not had that relationship, the burden would have been immense. Like, I'm in rural Montana, it's an hour and a half drive to the nearest airport, and flights in and out of Montana are super expensive no matter where you're going. It would have devastated me financially.

KR: We went at them super hard, to make the point about the danger of these SLAPP suits, alleging conspiracy. And particularly since the suit was striking at the heart of what movements are—meetings of the mind and collective power—we set out to *form* a movement to protect the movement. That's what Protect the Protest was. In February 2019, a federal judge ruled swiftly in our favor, with some really strong statements, slamming the charges and scorning the idea that this movement could be sued. So Krystal is okay, but other people are obviously still vulnerable to having the law used against them, cynically, in this way. And the scary thing is that corporations and other elites can do this endlessly, because they have way more money and resources. Still, the RICO suits are interesting, because they are a clear recognition that protest works and movements work. And that's what they're afraid of. If they weren't, they wouldn't be targeting people like Krystal, who are movement leaders.

MG: Looking back at Standing Rock, do you think you "won" or "lost"?

KTB: Both. I think that we could have prevented equipment from being moved had we been more strategic. But Standing Rock brought in thousands of people from across the world, not just in this country, but across the world. And every single one of those people were politicized and they gained experience. They gained skill sets and seeds were planted, and they all went back to their own communities and are now organizing in their communities. On that front, it planted seeds all over this world about what is possible organizing in our own communities. Even though we may have lost as far as the pipeline actually being built, what we built was so much more. As organizers, we are often organizing for a future that we may not see in our lifetimes. And I think that, because of that, we have to be oriented to acknowledge and celebrate the small victories and the small wins. And I think those are the things that are going to sustain us as we move forward. It's often a very Western and very American way that we define success, through "wins," as in a courtroom. And I, obviously, reject that. I don't think that we always need these big massive wins, although they are very appreciated and keep us moving.

MG: At one point in our conversation, you mentioned that one of your reasons for considering civil disobedience was your allegiance to a deeper Indigenous law. But you've also spoken about the power of using the law to fight back against the SLAPP suit. How do you, as an Indigenous warrior, deal with the law of the United States?

KTB: This country, the "United States," is founded on the Catholic Church's Doctrine of Discovery. We're not unique in that, of course. Being an original person from this land, I'm conscious of how we are founded on this cracked foundation. No matter how many houses we build, paint jobs, renovations, it's not going to matter. Until we address the issues, what we are doing by working with the law is a form of harm reduction. Which is very valid and very necessary given it can save life.

If we are going to move toward the change we hunger for, needed for the survival of planet, we have to redo our foundation. But I do believe in harm reduction. We have to infiltrate these systems and bring them into these spaces to prevent further harm done.

The Western form of law was imposed on us. Indigenous peoples had teachings of how to govern themselves, and I believe in reconnecting to those. I'm not saying, "Let's go back to the 1800s"; I'm saying, "What do those models look like?" My bottom line is that I just want to live here, on my land; to be able to hunt my own food, harvest my own food, drink my clean water, free of oppression. I want that for my children, nephews, siblings, the kids I work with in our community. This led me into spaces I want to fight for, for people to consider.

CASE STUDY

Climate Emergency

Why Climate Lawyers Need to Break the Law: The Lawyer's Perspective

FARHANA YAMIN

On April 16, 2019, I superglued my hands to the pavement outside the headquarters of the oil company Shell in London. I tried to get to the main door but fell short as I was surrounded by dozens of neon-jacketed policemen. I had been a legal advisor in the United Nations climate negotiations for nearly thirty years—but that Tuesday I decided it was time to join those who had decided to break the law. How else could we get people to pay attention to the climate crisis already upon us? I wanted to draw attention to Shell's prior knowledge and cover-up of the devastating impacts of climate pollution and their continued funding of oil exploration. But I also wanted to show how ridiculous it was that a law-abiding mother of four should walk away in handcuffs while one of the world's major corporate polluters remained unaccountable for its role in causing irreversible planetary destruction.

"This old way of doing things isn't working. The oil barons are flouting laws and committing ecocide. We need to alert the world to this injustice." This was the message I wished to convey. And this is why I had joined Extinction Rebellion (XR), which uses nonviolent civil disobedience to highlight the global climate emergency. It might have seemed like an unusual thing for a lawyer with my profile to do—but it was precisely because of my profile that I made the decision to become involved with XR, coordinating the movement's political strategy team, and deciding to break the law.

For over a decade, I have been using my legal training to help governments (primarily of small island states) negotiate and implement commitments under treaties, such as the 2015 Paris Agreement, and through national laws that have created carbon markets. Such treaties and laws provide a crucial framework for action, and alongside my activism, I have continued this kind of professional work. Given the urgency of the crisis, we need all kinds of legal strategies to build a global movement powerful enough to challenge business as usual: while some lawyers work in the UN and the Paris Agreement, others help Pacific Island students demand an advisory opinion from the International Court of Justice about the crime of ecocide, or bring class actions against big oil companies like Exxon on behalf of small-scale Indigenous farmers. And some, like me, must balance making laws with breaking them.

I would not, under any circumstances, want to abandon international diplomatic and legal wins like the 2015 Paris Agreement. It took a mammoth international effort, lasting ten years, to get two hundred countries to agree to limit the global temperature increase to 1.5°C, and to agree to ratchet up their national climate actions every five years. Paris isn't perfect but it has already had a significant impact on the real economy, as over 90 percent of the global economy, covering thousands of businesses, has started to incorporate its stipulated 2050 phase-out of deadly gases into their plans. That is why climate deniers, like the Trump administration and its authoritarian allies like Saudi Arabia and Brazil's Bolsonaro government, tried so hard to undermine the Paris Agreement. It is also a lifeline for some because it contains legally significant provisions on providing finance for the loss and damages being sustained by vulnerable countries already facing climate devastation.

My work with such countries, the frontline small island states, has shown me that nothing is won without a fight, and that progress is always possible if vulnerable people speak up for their rights. It was a consortium of these states that put forward the idea of a legally binding phase-out of toxic greenhouse gas emissions back in 1994, and that again took the lead at Paris in 2015 by insisting on the 1.5°C global goal. We cannot give up on them when they are asking us to fight with them in solidarity for their survival, to keep global temperatures below 1.5°C. This is still possible even if, sadly, it may now include abandonment of certain islands that have been peoples' homes for thousands of years.

But while these processes are necessary, they have taken too long and have been stuck in an incremental mindset. And while climate litigation ratchets up the pressure, such cases tend to ask governments to control air pollution, or do a little more mitigation of greenhouse gases, rather than asking for systemic, radical change. They also shy away from seeking reparations for loss and damage already running into billions of dollars, the burden of which is on the poor. The successful 2019 Urgenda Foundation suit against the Dutch government will help to phase out coal use in the country, for example, but it deliberately shied away from raising legal issues about who bears the cost of climate damages. In 2015, a case in Germany tried, and failed, to set a precedent around this, when the indigenous Peruvian farmer Saúl Luciano Lliuya sued the energy giant RWE in a rare attempt to seek damages: the farmer failed to convince the court that the company, one of the world's worst polluters, could be proven to have contributed to the glacial melt that had destroyed his house.

Litigation too takes more time than we have, given the urgency of the climate crisis—especially when companies with deep pockets drag out cases every step of the way. And litigation can also leave plaintiff communities feeling disempowered when the lawyers involved are not connected to the social movements and political demands of the communities they seek to champion. I have come to the conclusion that any solutions the courts can deliver right now will not be fast enough or sweeping enough to deliver the transformational changes we need in the next few years—unless and until they are accompanied by people rising up in a global movement that is powerful enough to take on polluters and complacent politicians. This movement cannot rely on petitions, marches, and elections every five years to do the job. It has to embrace *breaking the law* and be based on peaceful civil disobedience. It may have many different components, a movement of movements, representing the realities that climate injustice takes many forms. The fight for clean water, land rights, sanitation, healthy food systems, workers' rights, and ending tax havens and corruption are as much of the climate struggle as fighting for clean air and net-zero greenhouse gas emissions.

It's critical that some of those forging new movements are lawyers themselves. Lawyers are often rightly seen as part of the establishment. But lawyers also have a special part to play in mobilizing mass movements.

Look, for example, at two of the greatest movement-builders of the twentieth century: Mahatma Gandhi and Nelson Mandela. It is no coincidence that both were *lawyers* who first worked within the law launching campaigns based on petitions, marches, and litigation. But both ultimately chose law breaking as the key, decisive tool in their successful opposition to imperialism and apartheid. They understood that no court could overturn the complex mix of social norms, rules, and systemic political abuses of power that entrenched discrimination across so many levels of Indian and South African society. And they understood that the necessary change would not happen if they kept advocating incremental change and staying within the rules.

Gandhi and Mandela teach me that lawyers who apply themselves to the social good must become adept at knowing how far, and how fast, you can get changes within the established rules that constitute the present legal and political order. And they must also judge when it becomes impossible to adapt those foundational rules any further. Given this, few people are better placed to speak some fundamental truths: to say, as I now do, that the present form of capitalism, defined as the maximization of private profit, cannot be fixed with a tweak to a law here and there, because it's the whole system of relentless nature destruction, based on overconsumption, that generates wealth for faraway shareholders, which is creating a planetary emergency.

*

When I think about my thirty years as a lawyer in the climate field I am filled with sadness and rage. In these very years the crisis has accelerated. Governments, egged on by corporate lobbyists, found ways to water down or simply evade their legal obligations under the 1992 UN Framework Convention on Climate Change and its 1997 Kyoto Protocol. Long before the 2015 Paris Agreement, weak legislation and tweaks to "business as usual" practices had become the norm, contributing to the environmental devastation we now face.

The turning point came, for me, in October 2018, when the Intergovernmental Panel on Climate Change (IPCC) released its Special Report on Global Warming of 1.5°C. Even though it was hopeful in some ways—it showed we still had some chance of stopping complete eco-cide—it was also terrifying, because it showed how little time we had to change things. I knew I had to do something dramatically different from my previous diplomatic and legal work. My disillusion with diplomatic negotiations had set in the previous year, and when I attended the annual UN meeting on climate change in Bonn at the end of 2017, it made me furious to see apparent climate leaders—like Norway, the UK and Germany—backsliding, and not doing enough to implement their existing climate commitments. Finally, it became clear to me that polite diplomacy wasn't going to result in delinking the global economy from fossil fuels: we needed new political movements filled with outrage, and new ideas to topple the toxic form of nature-debasing capitalism. I thought these movements needed establishment-friendly people like me to bless and support their right to use peaceful civil disobedience as countless other movements had done.

If, indeed, the old way of doing things were not working any more, I had to contend with the realization that I had been part of this "old way" since the very beginning of my legal career: when I went to the Earth Summit in Rio de Janeiro in 1992, fresh out of law school. I learned then that there is always space for creative thinking in lawmaking, and that wordsmiths can birth new norms and rules to limit polluters and protect natural resources.

But when I think back to that time, I realize that I did not appreciate the scale of destruction being unleashed by neoliberal capitalism on nature and the frontline communities defending it. Nor how richer countries would export their dirtiest industries such as textiles and manufacturing to China, India, Bangladesh, and my home country, Pakistan, because these countries had even weaker environmental, social, and welfare laws and thus generated more private profits for global elites and faraway shareholders. Like many in the climate movement, I worried about how I would look talking about elites and saying something as radical as "the system is broken." I chose to play within the rules. Looking back, I feel that I focused too much on the "inside" political negotiations, trying to exorcise the bad parts of capitalism, drafting words that papered over cracks and "greenwashed" uglier realities, and not enough on the "outside" movement-building dynamics challenging these realities.

Too many of us saw climate change as a scientific and economic argument to be won by research and advocacy rather than a power struggle that required mass mobilizations. Consequently, for decades, we helped define climate change as a technical-managerial problem that would be solved by getting the best scientific and economic minds to write reports that would persuade governments to act in the long-term interests of their citizens. But we left three critical elements out of the equation: mobilizing people, respecting their human rights, and restoring nature. In hindsight, I understand that you can't do it all alone through elite advocacy, based on reports from experts, particularly not on issues that require such fundamental and structural change.

Of course, there were people in social justice movements present at the 1992 Rio Summit: the following year they would form La Vía Campesina, and talk more radically about system change. Then there were those thousands who took to the streets of Seattle in 1999 to reject both globalization and the climate negotiations, which they saw, with its incrementalism, as a sellout. Because I believed in multilateralism based on fairer rules, I worried they were making "the perfect" the enemy of "the good." I believed you needed some wins to build confidence, and an evidence base for more radical steps. Surely some agreed action was better than nothing at all? There was no point throwing the multilateral baby out with the bathwater.

There was a deeper reason for my attachment to the insider game. I so wanted to believe that our democracy—our governments elected on existing political processes—could provide transformational change that was fair and pro-poor. I believed you could not have system change without some basic rules, intuitions, and processes in place to make the new system work. And that the 1990s was the era for building some basic global rules and global institutions to protect people and nature. But now, looking back, I see that we failed to make those rules and institutions fair from the outset, something we might have done if we had also focused on building movements to challenge the corruption and power of incumbents, and on centering our vision on protecting human beings and restoring nature. I regret that I didn't see those calling for system change as closer allies. Their points were totally valid, and they were right to be skeptical of the government negotiations going on that were resulting, year in and year our, in diminished chances for planetary safety.

Looking back at my career, I realize I was mesmerized by the appeal of using traditional forms power that I felt I could "use" to change the system itself. I was an immigrant who wanted to succeed, to fit in, to make it to the "top" and be seen as a leader. This was not only because I wanted to make my parents proud of their sacrifices, but because I was a feminist: I wanted to smash the many glass ceilings that held back women, working mothers, and women of color of like myself. Like Melanie Griffith in *Working Girl*, I enjoyed wearing power suits and designer clothes. Tired and exhausted by working long hours, I felt entitled to a couple of nice holidays abroad a year as a reward. I didn't connect my personal lifestyle choices, income, and long-term security with my climate politics. I didn't think I needed to be a different kind of person and have a different lifestyle and aspirations, because I didn't associate my own lifestyle—and career, and strategy for changing things—with a *system* that was wrong.

Now I've basically done a complete personal 180 degrees, and that's what the environment movement is waking up to: it's not system change or personal change, it's both. Now I realize that what I aspired to as a young lawyer, a feminist wanting equality in a toxic system, is part of the problem.

*

It took something of a breakdown—personal and political—to come to this realization. In the two years before the October 2018 IPPC report that shook me into action, I had been somewhat paralyzed, burnt out by the UN negotiations, and suffering from a deep depression triggered by the untimely deaths of my mother, father, and brother in close succession. All the hopes and hard work I had put into Paris seemed to be unravelling, particularly with the inauguration of President Trump in January 2017. This went hand in hand with the rise of climate deniers and extremism, especially virulent right-wing movements in the EU targeting migrants and refugees: those people fleeing from regions badly affected by ecological devastation like Syria. Innocent people were being blamed and attacked, in mainstream media and on the streets, for the problems created by dysfunctional economic systems benefitting fossil fuel elites and other incumbents.

Instead of uniting against the threat of ecological extinction, the far right was pushing theories of the extinction of white people to the fore. From 2016 onward, nationalist climate-denying anti-immigration politicians won electoral victories in countries ranging from the UK and Australia to Turkey, India, and Brazil. Racism and fearmongering were deliberately being fomented in classic divide-and-rule strategies to weaken social movements by, for example, pitting black, brown and migrants' workers as the "problem" as exemplified by the Brexit campaign in the UK and the MAGA movement in the US.

I felt powerless and angry: I withdrew from work because I felt we had failed, and that it was too late to do anything useful. But I was surrounded by a loving family and had the good fortune to take several courses and spent time in wilderness. I read *Coming Back to Life* by Joanna Macy and Molly Brown, which is addressed to activists and focuses on how they can keep going in tough times. I allowed myself to grieve. I read the histories of social movements that had overthrown slavery and colonialism; tackled disenfranchisement and violence against women, gay, and transgender people; and got legislation passed to protects workers' rights, including access to health care and social welfare. When I reacquainted myself with the courage and sacrifices of environmental activists, especially people of color, like Kenya's Wangari Maathai and Nigeria's Ken Saro-Wiwa, I found myself able to find solace in the midst of sadness, and to accept grief, anger, and fear not as signs of personal failure but as healthy responses to the harsh realities of our time. Alongside many colleagues in a similar space, I learned to reconnect my feelings of rage and sadness to that innate sense of injustice that had prompted me to become a lawyer in the first place, when I was in my twenties. I started to figure out there were others like me, who felt isolated by their feelings of failure, who wanted to try something very different, and were also keen to work more collaboratively in order to seize legal opportunities arising from the social, political, and ecological turmoil of our age—but to do so in ways that allowed self-care and regeneration at a personal level. Acknowledging and honoring my frustrations and grief allowed me to see with new eyes and to channel my anger creatively in the collective resistance that I would find in XR.

Finally, at the age of fifty-five, I found my voice and the courage to speak my truth as a mother, as a migrant, as a lawyer, and as an activist. We are not born greedy, apathetic, and selfish. We are taught to fight each other to get to the "top" of a system that is based on divide-and-rule and the destruction of nature. We are taught that borders and walls are necessary to keep out "others," and to value our comfort more than their rights. Our economy equates well-being and happiness with buying more and more stuff. I am trying to find other ways of measuring well-being and happiness, by measuring my own against that of the planet, and all its people.

If I had to give advice to young people and activists today who wanted to use the law to fight patriarchy, white supremacy, and other injustices, I'd say: that's great, but law alone isn't going to work to tackle systemic injustices, so don't forget to be an activist in your community even as you dream big. I'd also say: Prepare for the tough times ahead. Building non-nationalistic, regenerative political communities—where people and nature coexist—will need committed, courageous people to fight many different battles *for a long time to come*. So, learn about self-care and how not to burn out. And surround yourself with friends and family who will share both your inner journey and your professional one. It took twenty minutes for the police to unglue me from Shell's office, but it will take much longer to do the work our planet so desperately needs to build new forms of cultural and political communities that respect each other and nature.

Time is not on our side. We need to use it well.

Postscript, March 2022: I waited a year to see if I would be prosecuted for trespassing at Shell, but the police did not press charges. Those who were charged were found not guilty by a jury, an astounding legal victory that showed how the public understood the need for XR's disruptive tactics—although by late 2020 these had alienated parts of public opinion and proved divisive within the movement. I stepped back from XR in 2020 because of these differences but also to focus on working with donors to make the UN Climate Summit in Glasgow—COP26—a success.

The COVID pandemic meant Glasgow was delayed to November 2021, and that civil society protests could not happen in the build-up, due to lockdown restrictions. COP26 was a test of the five-year "ratcheting mechanism" agreed on in Paris in 2015, for all countries to increase the ambitions of their climate policies and to deliver $100 billion to vulnerable countries. The new Biden administration created a better atmosphere but in the end the US and other rich countries failed to deliver. Only a handful of countries improved on their emissions targets even while affirming the 1.5 target! Developing countries made a last ditch effort to secure a Glasgow 'facility' to provide funding for climate related loss and damage. They failed.

This led to a deeper resolve at COP27, held in Egypt in November 2022. Due to unprecedented political pressure from civil society and a rare show of unity by developing countries, the US and richer countries were finally forced to concede the establishment of a fund for loss and damage. Pakistan's leadership of the G77—the negotiating bloc that unified the developing world—was key to this, as were the Pakistan floods that took place immediately before COP27. The floods left one third of Pakistan underwater, over 1500 dead and thirty-three million people displaced.

We cannot be certain of a future based on respect for human rights, solidarity and ecological balance. Russia's war against Ukraine has accentuated structural inequalities among and between nations, with record energy prices in Europe and African countries already experiencing famine. There will be more conflict, migration, and displacement. We must shift away from fossil fuels very fast. This is not just to reduce dependence on the global coal, oil, and gas industry. It is because this industry threatens life on earth and everyone's peace and security.

Further Reading: By Farhana Yamin: "A Manifesto for Justice for COP26 and beyond," *The World Today*, Chatham House, October 2021; "The High Ambition Coalition," in Hedrik Jepsen et al. (eds.), *Reaching the Paris Agreement: Insider Stories from the Negotiations* (Cambridge University Press, 2021); "Die, Survive or Thrive?" in *This Is Not A Drill: An Extinction Rebellion Handbook* (Penguin, 2020). Also: Vanessa Nakate, *A Bigger Picture: My Fight to Bring a New African Voice to the Climate Crisis* (Pan MacMillan, 2021).

From Racial Apartheid to Climate Apartheid: The Veteran Activist's Perspective

KUMI NAIDOO in discussion with MARK GEVISSER

Mark Gevisser: Kumi, you have been working as an activist and campaigner for justice since you were a teenager, when you were expelled from high school in Durban, South Africa, for your anti-apartheid activism in the 1980s. More recently you have led major global organizations, Greenpeace and Amnesty International. What lessons have you learned about the relationship between "the power of law" and "the power of people"?

Kumi Naidoo: The first time I was engaged by the question of how the law could be used for the struggle was in 1983, when there was a drought in Durban, and the council imposed water restrictions and then fines if you exceeded them. In the area where I lived there were six- or eight-unit blocks, with only one water meter, and the excess amount was divided by the council equally amongst all tenants. If you were a single, elderly person you would be fined as much as a large family. As community activists we fought this using all the normal means of resistance, like marches, but I was in my first year studying law at university and I thought, *Surely we can find a legal loophole to prove our case?* I'm eighteen at the time and I take this idea to senior comrades, and one of them, Shoots Naidoo, says, "There is a good chance we'll win in court. But we will lose a really big opportunity."

"Isn't the objective to win the case and justice for the people?" I asked.

"The objective is to make sure that the people feel they have won justice for themselves," he replied. "A law firm will make clever arguments and the community will feel, 'Oh, some people from the outside came and won the struggle for us.' They'll lose their motivation. So let's keep the legal option in our back pocket, and use the opportunity of this injustice about water fines to mobilize people." Just as people today say recycling is a good place to start your activism but a bad place to end it, we were very consciously using bread-and-butter issues to mobilize people for the bigger struggle: against the apartheid state.

I came to appreciate this wisdom. Winning a campaign is important, but winning it in a way that you are able to fight your next struggle with confidence and boldness is even more critical—even better if the next campaign goes to the heart of the unjust political system rather than simply its symptoms. Even if you win in court, it might not help you with building your movement and your bigger strategic objectives.

MG: What happened in the water fines case?

KN: We won in court, and all the fines were written off! But we only went to court after many, many resistance activities, including the Bayview Residents Association taking three busloads full of really old grannies and grandfathers to occupy the city council when it was in session. For many of these people, it was the first time in their lives they stood up for themselves, and challenged authority and the injustice that was part of their daily lives as Black South Africans. The council responded brutally, trickling the water or cutting it off entirely. Only then did we go to court, but only after ensuring that the people we had mobilized felt a sense of ownership of the lawsuit, and understood it as part of the bigger struggle. At least forty people who emerged from that water struggle became the most active members of the association—a few actually ended up in the armed wing of the African National Congress, Umkhonto we Sizwe! One of my best friends, Lenny Naidu, was killed by a government hit squad; another, Jude Francis, was convicted of terrorism and served six years on Robben Island.

MG: Do you think the mobilization outside court affected what happened inside court?

KN: It's a myth to think courts are completely cocooned from the reality of public opinion. Still, I couldn't claim a direct causal link between what we did in the streets and at the council, and the fact that the court ruled in our favor. Rather, our legal argument was accepted: council policy was a public health violation. It's an interesting lesson in using the law, even when it's the law of the oppressor. Because even under apartheid, the South African state insisted it abided by the rule of law. If you had a good case, and a rational judge who was not bound by apartheid ideology, you actually could win against the state. Particularly in the 1980s, anti-apartheid activists were doing this more and more, and lawyers had a particular status in the movement.

MG: Is that why you were studying law in the first place?

KN: I'm currently writing a memoir in the form of a letter to my mother, who committed suicide when I was fifteen. That was the year I got involved in school boycotts and was expelled, so I write to tell her what happened after she died, and how I eventually found myself a Rhodes scholar at Oxford. It so happens that I've just written these words, today: "Remember you did not want me to study law because you believed that many lawyers were involved in politics—and politics to you and many in your generation meant daily police harassment, banning orders, detention without trial, and much worse. The reality is that the values you instilled in us would have made it impossible not to stand up to the horrible injustices of the apartheid government, irrespective of what we chose to study."

Actually my first two choices were physical education and social work. I thought phys-ed would allow me to take young people away legitimately for weekend activities and give me the space to mobilize them into the struggle, and social work would give me community access. There were actually my favored choices. But I couldn't quite take them up—for physical education I needed to be a better swimmer (I could barely swim at all!) and social work required a lot of practical work, which would have impacted my evening activism. So I landed up in law, but by the time I had to choose graduate study, the program just seemed too heavy, given my activism. And, even though my father did not complain, he was struggling to pay my university fees. So when I got a bursary to study political science, I grabbed it.

MG: What did these early experiences teach you, and how do you apply these lessons to the climate movement?

KN: There is a question I learned to ask in the South African struggle, that I have always tried to apply: How do you use the law to advance justice? It's more than legal advocacy. It's about using the law to defend the rights of people who want to speak freely; act freely; associate freely—ultimately to be able to do all those things and not be at the risk of death, as many activists around the world are today.

In South Africa we used the legal system to try to get activists out of jail. We weren't always successful, but that wasn't the only objective. We mainstreamed the debate by using the publicity that comes with a trial. We presented an argument not just to the judge but to the people of South Africa. To those who were oppressed we said, "This is really bad, we must stand up and act against it." And to those who were the oppressors we said: "This system is unjust, unfair, and untenable, and so it is not sustainable— the sooner you recognize the need to change, the better."

A society moves forward when enough people understand what the truth is, and are moved to defend it or to oppose their adversaries. The biggest challenge is not how good we are at organizing a march, how good we are at writing a policy, how good we are at climbing an oil rig, or how good we are at going to court. We can be very, very good at all of that, and not make a significant enough impact. The climate emergency shows this. What we have to be *really* good at is communicating what we stand for to the largest number of people directly impacted.

Jürgen Habermas of the Frankfurt School had a theory of "communicative action," which influenced my early thinking. When I became involved in the environmental and climate movements, I began to think of the communicative power of law cases, as I had seen happen in South Africa during the struggle. There are so many communication jewels that come out of a litigation that might ultimately lose in the court of law, but win in the court of public opinion.

Let me give you an example from South Africa. The former president Jacob Zuma was pushing a huge nuclear deal with the Russian company Rosatom and two amazing women, Makoma Lekalakala (Earthlife Africa) and Liz McDaid (Southern African Faith Communities' Environment Institute) decided to litigate—on the basis that the deal was being done in secret and proper procedure had not been followed. At a time when there was increasing national outrage about Zuma's corruption, there was much evidence of corruption in the Rosatom deal too. So in 2016 I joined Liz and Makoma in setting up the Campaign for a Just Energy Future in South Africa, mobilizing support for the court case by building a coalition of civil society and trying to win over support of business leaders who were also concerned about the damage to the economy by the nuclear deal.

We also mobilized those parts of the ANC that were beginning to stand up to Zuma's corruption, and generally provided alternative perspectives about the nuclear energy question. In court, the best we could hope for was to slow the deal down on procedural grounds: we weren't going to stop the deal using the law. But that's all we wanted from the courts, and that's what we got in February 2017: a directive that the government had to go back and start the procurement process from the beginning, this time with due consultation. The court judgement bought us time to lobby the government, through politicians and the business sector, and to exert popular pressure on the government too, by showing them how unpopular this deal was. We managed to shift public opinion decisively to our side—and the deal was dropped . . . for now.

MG: How did you become involved in the environmental movement?

KN: In apartheid South Africa, Black people thought of environmentalism as something rich white people did—after all, most white people treated their animals better than they did Black people. And so I am somewhat ashamed to admit that I came very late to the movement, in around 2005, when I was chair of the Global Call to Action Against Poverty. I was lobbied by people in the environmental movement, and as I started reading more, I became convinced by the argument that climate and the environment intersects with everything else. After all, what does it mean to have a development program in Bangladesh today if you don't plan for sea level rise and the fact that everything's going to be flooded?

I can't remember if the phrase "climate justice" was already being used, but I started thinking of the *injustice* of the climate crisis. When I realized that people in the Global South were already suffering loss of livelihood and loss of life because of the global warming caused by people in heavily industrialized countries, I, with others, started using the term "climate apartheid" to describe this injustice.

MG: What is the tactical advantage, for the climate movement, of understanding the climate emergency as an injustice, rather than a scientific or meteorological phenomenon?

KN: Even though the United Nations Framework Convention on Climate Change is written in a legalese that excludes the overwhelming majority of people from being able to be part of the conversation, its central notion of common and differentiated principles basically says that while all countries have a responsibility to do certain things, there is a differentiated responsibility based on which countries carry the historical burden for the problem. And so when we went to the Conference of the Parties meeting in Copenhagen in 2009 to argue successfully for a Green Climate Fund, we didn't argue it on the basis of charity. We argued it on the basis of justice: countries in the Global North had built their economies based on dirty energy, and this was causing impacts we were already seeing in the Global South. According to the terms of the fund, rich countries are to make available a hundred billion dollars a year to poor countries trying to mitigate climate change impacts. Needless to say, these rich countries have not stuck to their commitments—which makes it more difficult when dealing with skeptical people in African countries who say, "The rich people in the Global North messed up everything, and now they're telling us we can't do oil, coal, and gas, even while they fail to meet their own obligations!"

Even so, once the injustice of the situation is acknowledged, at least we can begin to talk about how rights have been violated and what the solutions are. I began doing this as soon as I joined Greenpeace, by talking about how "Green Rights are Human Rights." These are, of course, the "first-generation" rights to liberty and equality and freedom and expression and assembly that are essential for our very mobilization. But then there are the "second generation" of rights too, the socioeconomic rights. From a legal perspective, in the environmental and climate movement, this means broadening our focus from property-centered law ("Do you have the right to do this kind of business on this type of land?") and taking a far more intersectional approach, insisting that the struggle to avert catastrophic climate change and environmental collapse, and the struggle to address human rights and poverty and equity, *must* be seen as two sides of same coin.

For as long as we stick to property law, we discount the human dimension of it, and it's the human dimension that brings urgency to the debate. Where are the cases where we can argue that peoples' socioeconomic rights—their rights to health, to livelihood, to their traditional practices— have been violated by the continued exploitation and burning of fossil fuels? One powerful case in the Netherlands leads the way, where seven environmental groups filed a lawsuit on behalf of seventeen thousand Dutch citizens in April 2019 against Shell, on the basis that their human rights had been violated by the effects of climate change. This led the supreme court to order the Dutch government to cut its greenhouse gas emissions by 25 percent by the end of 2020 after ruling the government was putting its citizens in "unacceptable danger."

Finally there are what are known as "third-generation" rights, environmental, cultural, and developmental rights: the right to live in a clean and healthy environment, the rights of nature itself, and to one's cultural relationship with the environment. Today more than 140 constitutions include these "green rights," and the UN Declaration on the Rights of Indigenous Peoples sets out that Indigenous peoples have the right to maintain and strengthen their distinctive spiritual relationships with their traditionally owned lands. The constitutions of Bolivia and Ecuador actually give rights to nature itself. There's much potential to grow a movement using these laws and conventions.

MG: Several of the contributors to this book have said that we no longer have the time to make laws or to litigate, given how slowly these wheels turn and how urgent the crisis is. Is it time to be looking outside of the law?

KN: I'm not a defender of the rule of law under all circumstances. I take wisdom from the great American labor historian Howard Zinn, who, when asked to speak about "the problem of civil disobedience" said, "The problem is not civil disobedience. The problem is civil obedience." It was civil obedience, after all, that created Nazi Germany. Zinn looks at how Western civilization has come up with this concept of "the rule of law," and goes on to say that this so-called "rule of law" has consolidated all the injustices that existed before it was put into place. Zinn says, provocatively, that the rule of law has become "the darling of the oppressors and the tyranny of the oppressed."

With this philosophy, I was comfortable in intensifying the tradition of civil disobedience at Greenpeace. When our activists occupied a rig in the Greenlandic Arctic they were given a judgment that was fair to us, actually, but that leveled a 50,000 euro fine should we ever take an action again. I made the decision with other colleagues to break that order consciously, which is how I found myself, in 2012, very nervous about my fate as I sat in a small inflatable dinghy on rough seas in freezing temperatures.

In fact it was while we were sitting in jail in Nuuk, Greenland, that I said to colleagues, "If they can use the law against us, we can use the law against them." It was then that I began thinking about litigation as a strategy to be pursued alongside civil disobedience. At Greenpeace we had a legal department of six people, and 95 percent of what they did was create contracts to do with our ships and other matters that needed to be taken care of: getting people out of jail, of course, for civil disobedience efforts, and defending Greenpeace from court actions. I started asking questions about using more affirmative, offensive strategies to achieve our goals: "Can't we do to the fossil fuel industry what the anti-tobacco lobby did to the tobacco industry?" It wouldn't matter if we didn't win immediately; it was simply about opening up new avenues of struggle. Winning the lawsuit wasn't as important as educating people about rights they were not yet aware of, or publicizing the issue, or opening up other legal challenges that might succeed or lead to a change in legislation to address the deficit in the legal system.

When Typhoon Pablo hit the Philippines in 2012, I was at the COP that year, in Doha. One of the Philippines government negotiators took the floor and made a heart-wrenching speech about the need for action. Greenpeace's Southeast Asia head, Von Hernandez, led a process to see if we could hold fossil fuel companies accountable for the one-billion-dollar damage and loss of more than a thousand lives due to the typhoon. But litigation against fossil fuel companies is extremely difficult. They can claim to have operated within the law and that they have the license to operate. And they can claim they were not aware of the gravity of the situation, even though we aimed to counter that by showing that they had known about the impacts of carbon for several decades. Still, you cannot show direct causality, which is probably why it has not been tried in the past. In the end, we chose to lodge a complaint at the Philippines Commission on Human Rights, which in 2019 found that forty-seven major fossil fuel and carbon-polluting companies could be held accountable for violating the rights of its citizens for the damage caused by climate change. The hearings attracted much media and public attention—I was one of the many who testified—and we scored a major "communicative action" victory. But will the fossil fuel companies be held accountable, now?

I think a lot about the efficacy of law. In our last conversation, my best friend, Lenny, asked me the question, "What is the biggest contribution you can make to the cause of humanity?" I said, "Giving your life," to which he said, "No, it's not giving your life. It's giving the rest of your life." When he was murdered I had to think deeply about this distinction. How can we all give the rest of our lives, in a meaningful way, toward solving this problem that threatens us all, in the most consequential decade in the history of humanity? There is no one-size-fits-all solution. In different countries, the law and politics work in different ways. However they are combined, I'm completely convinced that, if not connected to movements, legal strategies will not deliver the kind of impact they otherwise could. We should never underestimate the impact that popular mobilization can have on public opinion, and how public opinion ultimately impacts on legal judgments, particularly in new areas of law not enjoying much precedent.

MG: Given all the above, what advice would you give a young climate activist who is thinking of going to law school?

KN: There's an amazing optimism to using the law. If you take a view that the struggle for justice has always been a marathon and not a sprint, and that the bigger the struggles that you're engaging in the better the chance those struggles will outlive you, you see the value of building precedents for lawyers who are going to come after you, and the clients they will represent—and the hope that they might win more easily. I think there's something vitally important about helping build the body of environmental law, more generally, and climate law more specifically, because if humanity does somehow get to the other side of this crisis, there will be lots to do—in contract law, in liability law and loss and damage stuff, and of course the ongoing COP negotiations.

A career in law is a meaningful, honorable, impactful career to pursue as part of your contribution to trying to make the world a more just and meaningful place. If you are passionate about law, there is certainly a need for your skills. You can use law to defend activists, you can use your legal training to pursue fossil fuel offenders, or to make sense of the language of international agreements and intervene in them, on behalf of ordinary people. The COP is, literally, a "conference of the parties," a legal contract. And given the fact that it is rooted in legal convention the climate movement will always need a bunch of smart environmental lawyers who can just help us hold our ground against the folks on the other side.

There is so much value in all of that, but it would be shortsighted to view the law in isolation, outside of other bigger processes of policy development, advocacy, mass mobilization, electoral politics, and so on.

MG: Do you think that becoming a lawyer is an important way to gain access to the corridors of power?

KN: One of the biggest mistakes I've made in my own life has been to mistake access for influence. Just because we get access to the COP or a national ministry in South Africa that's doing a consultation on a white paper for some policy, doesn't mean that we actually have influence. These exchanges are usually ritualistic and formulaic. We tick a box to say we did advocacy with the government; they tick a box to say civil society was consulted. If I reflect on my time at Greenpeace and Amnesty, I would say that 90 percent of the time I went into meetings, they knew exactly what I would say, I knew exactly what they would say, and both parties knew roughly where we would end up. What was the point of it all, beyond keeping the door open and keeping dialogue flowing? Dialogue is essential, but it alone won't save us, particularly when we don't listen to each other.

MG: Where, then, would you direct people—and specifically young people—who really want to make a difference?

KN: Into activities that are building power, building numbers, building strategic mobilization capability. I would suggest three primary areas. The first—this one might surprise you—is "artivism," the link between arts and culture and activism, as a way to communicate to a much larger audience rather than the usual suspects to whom our politics usually speak. Something I often say, in this regard, is that we need to come up with a climate equivalent, in communication terms, of what "taking the knee" was to structural racism.

Then, of course, there is peaceful civil disobedience, not only for the communication value, but also because we need to allow disciplined outlets for people's anger to be expressed. Without this, we're going to end up with anarchic violence, which will be used by our enemies to turn the struggle against itself and be used as a propaganda tool to delegitimize it.

Finally, I would suggest propositional alternatives. There are so many amazing things that mainly young people, but also older people, have come up with in terms of sustainable alternatives to the way we live. People are not stupid. They're going to look at the facts, they're going to look at the weather patterns, and they're going to get increasingly pessimistic. We have to plan for that, because the pessimism of our analysis can only be overcome by the optimism of our actions. In this regard I reflect on my own life, and the tragedy of my mother committing suicide when I was just fifteen, at a time of intense political upheaval in South Africa too. One of the choices I made—it was a survival choice—was to go and live as a housefather in a children's home for two years, even though I was only nineteen myself. Yes, of course, there's all that high-flown stuff about systemic and structural change and overcoming the system and the revolution. But today, here and now, as a human being, I want to feel I'm making a difference to what's happening around me. I come back to my experience in the ANC: some of those who became the most dedicated members of the armed struggle started off organizing cake sales. They needed to *do* something. This is first-level activity. We must never underestimate its importance.

But of course I'm not just talking about cake sales here. I'm being very specific about what I mean by propositional alternatives. I mean initiatives like those four young women from Zambia, some years ago, who designed a generator that can give you five hours of electricity run by one liter of human urine. They made it all the way to the African science and technology fair that year; they don't only offer hope, but the possibility of a low-cost solution for rural electricity—so let's see if there's something more in it.

These propositional alternatives can be very simple too. If the IPCC is saying that one trillion trees need to be grown as part of the solution then let's bloody well plant one trillion trees, immediately! If, in just twelve hours in 2019, the Ethiopian government could plant more than 353 million trees, why can't the rest of the world together not be able to plant one trillion trees? The answer is political will.

So, yes, I would prioritize artivism, civil disobedience, and propositional alternatives over legal energy, because otherwise our movement is only going to have hard-core people in it. You've got to have people who come in by just wanting to do good, people who don't know all the theory but just know that their children's future is at risk and they want to do something to help. We need to create the basis for action, for all those millions of parents who have been moved by their children, as well as young people themselves; for that energy to be channeled. It's for us, as activists and campaigners and, yes, even as lawyers, to provide people with pathways to get there. And sometimes the pathway to get there is by people starting with a recycling program in their community. It's very important that activists, especially those of us that have been around for a long time, exercise much greater humility in understanding that people conform, sometimes, because they don't have that many opportunities to resist.

Kumi Naidoo's book, Letters to My Mother: The Making of A Troublemaker *was published by Jacana Media in 2022.*

On Being a Young Brown Woman on the Frontline: The Youth Activist's Perspective

AYISHA SIDDIQA

September 20. 2019. 8 a.m.. The New York City climate strike isn't to start until noon, but all twelve of us organizers are here, at Battery Park. With us, too, are international activists: Xiye Bastida, Helena Gualinga, Vanessa Nakate. Greta Thunberg has come all the way from Sweden. It's a powerhouse on the city's streets today, ten days before the United Nations General Assembly's Biodiversity Summit: all of us talking about this one issue of the climate emergency, together.

There are helicopters in the air, and a ring of thirty adults creating a protective barrier; beyond us, the police. In the crowd, I have my megaphone and my walkie-talkie. At 10 a.m. sharp we start to move from Foley Square up to Bryant Park, and pass through New York's financial district. In commemoration of the occupation that took place in these very streets eight years ago, the words "Wall Street, Wall Street, We see your greed" echo again—this time out of the mouths of 350,000 youth. Each time I start a chant, I hear it ripple for rows and rows behind me. This is not just history in the making. This is the earth reminding the people of money and corruption that they will have to answer to their children. "Another world is not only possible, she is on her way," wrote Arundhati Roy. "On a quiet day, I can hear her breathing." In this moment, I want to tell Arundhati that not only can I hear this other world breathing. I can hear her chanting.

By the time we reach Bryant Park, my chest heaves for air. The police are frustrated: we applied for a two-thousand-person permit, and they now have to open the barricades to all 350,000 of us. I recognize old teachers and friends from elementary school. I can't believe I am a part of this. Never did I imagine that I, a nineteen-year-old Muslim Pakistani immigrant, would be leading the biggest climate protest ever on American soil. I think to myself that, years from now, if the planet is still habitable, people will look back to this era and examine how a bunch of kids walked out of their classrooms to teach world leaders a lesson. All over the world, 7.6 million of us took to the streets that day. We all, in our own ways, became guardians for our planet. Our chants reverberated against the most powerful buildings and people in the world.

When we finally get to Bryant Park the other organizers rush to the stage to handle the speeches and performers. I am left in charge of the crowd. I am so thirsty and sweaty, my chest sore from chanting, that I drop myself on the floor, crisscross my legs, and attempt to keep the crowd from getting impatient. This works for about five minutes. So I do what I know best: I get everyone to sing, clap, and dance with me. We have a concert before the official concert. It goes something like this:

We're going to strike because the waters are rising,
We're going to strike 'cause our people are dying,
We're going to strike for life and everything we love,
We're going to strike for you, we strike for us.

My role in the preparation of this strike has been to coordinate college students in New York City. Together with high school and middle school students, we met every week for three months in a basement at the New York Society for Ethical Culture, and then split into teams. I was responsible for outreach, which required me to conquer my shyness. "Outreach" wasn't just about handing out flyers on campuses or on the subway: it was approaching strangers, engaging them, and then persuading them to show up to the strike. But I was pleasantly surprised by the enthusiasm and interest people showed. I guess things change when teenagers, with their backpacks still attached to them, spend their after-school hours asking adults and their peers to care about an issue that affects us all.

By the time I am in Bryant Park on September 20, something has completely transformed inside me. I have found community in activism, a sense of purpose and belonging, for the first time since I arrived in New York City, aged six, from Pakistan. I have found the vessel of hope from which our world is made, one that I can share with others.

*

There is something profoundly significant about putting your body and immediate liberty on the line for a cause you believe in. I came to learn about civil disobedience at Hunter College while studying poetry and political science. I discovered in my political theory class that the history of resistance in the United States is largely Black and Brown. If there was a lightning-bolt moment for me it was while we were watching a documentary about the Greensboro Four: Black students who showed up every day at a diner in the Woolworth's store in Greensboro, North Carolina, to protest segregation. They would order, but instead of being served, food was thrown at them, spit shot at them, dogs set on them by police. Still, they showed up day after day. If they were injured or arrested, other students would come in and take their place. A revolutionary movement grew around them, one that played a decisive role in overturning segregation in the southern states. Studying the Greensboro Four I learned about persistence and duty and, more than anything, that most of the world's present crises are tied to white supremacy. These kids were my age, some of them in college, like me. They met power at her doorstep, knowing full well all that they were risking, but it was worth it. Freedom could not be attained by request.

I realized that it isn't enough to imagine how you might have acted if you were alive during times of extreme oppression. The litmus test is what you do when injustice occurs in your own lifetime. And in my lifetime, the crowning injustice has been the destruction of the planet—given the way it is tied, as I have learned, to racial, economic, and class injustices. This set me thinking about how all the hard work, sacrifices, and pain endured by Black and Brown people who came before me would be for naught if humanity ceased to exist. Furthermore, the job was not done. The structures of oppression were no longer as explicit as colonies, but they had morphed into things like food scarcity, pollution, environmental sacrifice zones. And if we didn't see the Black, Brown, and Indigenous people who were suffering from the climate crisis in the present time as worthy of fighting for, we would all face rising temperatures and seas, and extinction, soon.

I joined the climate movement, at first through Extinction Rebellion, and then through NYC Climate Coalition. Most of the time I was the only person of color in the room. The white middle-class kids around me were from private or well-resourced schools. I am the eldest daughter of Brown immigrants, who attained her education in under-resourced schools in one of the most educationally segregated cities in America: New York. I did not have the phrase "environmental injustice" in my repertoire then, but I witnessed it every day when I stepped out of my house into the streets of Coney Island. I lived it.

What I was learning, in my college courses and my reading, was helping me make sense of my own life and those of my family members. I could understand now how the climate emergency and capitalist greed that has caused it was responsible for the disruption of my family's agricultural life in Pakistan. I came to understand how the price of oil and the pollution of the Chenab River (our main source of water) was interconnected and responsible, in one way or another, for the deaths of my family members. I came to understand too that the systemic "War on Terror" was really a cover for a war over fossil fuels and resources. I was reminded, every day in middle school, that I was Muslim and of a people the US was waging war on. The race for oil not only displaced millions, it destroyed the middle East and South Asia. It blew children up. It stained an entire generation's memory. It made Pakistanis loathe blue skies because drones fell when there were no clouds in the air. It caused Syrian toddlers to wash up on European shores. It made me walk, talk, and present myself with a perpetual sense of caution because in any situation I was more likely to be labeled a villain than a person.

At the same time I came to see how my family's lack of wealth, and the poverty of the people around us—in both Pakistan and South Brooklyn—made us the most vulnerable to the climate emergency, physically as well as financially. Coney Island, where I live today, is a front line, because the only thing standing between a tsunami or flooding from the Atlantic Ocean is a wall of public housing projects. Public housing is reserved for people who do not make enough of an income to afford rent in NYC. The city was designed so the poorest are expendable against the rising tides.

*

I come from a tribal community in Northern Pakistan. My mother was a teacher at our village school and left me with my grandparents when she went to work. Every night, my grandmother put me to sleep with a story. In our tradition, oral tales are often tied to lessons: myths mixed with folktales and day-to-day mundanities to teach children right from wrong. I was raised with the sense of a spiritual realm that could be accessed through dreams. Meaning, there is conscious, sentient life beyond what humans can see and understand.

The responsibility to the earth has stayed with me. It has been part of my upbringing long before I knew how to say "carbon." It is the same one my grandmother, who did not know anything about climate change, could sense: the leaves are letting go. The well of nature in which we once washed, to get clean, is running dry. And the spiritual, scientific, religious prophecies are all one and the same: we are running out of time.

One day, when I was about five, I was mindlessly uprooting one of my grandmother's herbs with a stick. I think I was attempting to make a dirt, rock, and leaf concoction, mimicking the ritual of lighting wood and cooking. When my grandmother noticed she gently chastised me: "When you tread on the earth, you must walk with gentleness, because the earth feels pain, and knows when you're about to cause havoc and abuse on it. The earth records your footsteps wherever you go, from when you first learn to walk until you return back to it."

I understand this lesson to mean that when you inflict violence on a place or in a place—whether it's the killing of animals in a cruel way or hurting people or hurting the environment—that place keeps it in its memory. It's not just humans that have that memory. The earth has a memory much longer and much deeper than our own.

Because I grew up in a tribal community, most of my neighbors were immediate family. My grandparents' house didn't have a door: There was a curtain, and anyone could walk in at any moment of the day. Uncles and aunts would come in asking for spices or eggs or milk in a way that was never awkward or intrusive. I didn't know it then, but I grew up without a sense of personal property. In the memory of the village of my childhood we could take what we wanted, as we needed, and we all tended to it. This childhood sense of community and closeness to the earth was something I only experienced again much later, in the climate movement.

Economic hardship drove my parents off the land, as it did all their siblings. My father won a visa lottery in the year 2000 and came to the US to find work and to facilitate the family's immigration. My mom followed a couple of years later with me and my three siblings; by that time the American "War on Terror" had made Pakistan an increasingly difficult place to live in. Whenever we went back, we couldn't stay longer than a few months. By the time I was in fourth grade, the United States was droning Pakistan, looking for Osama bin Laden. Radical Islamism took hold, and there were constant suicide attacks in rural and urban areas. People like my grandparents put up doors and locked them, curfews were enforced, and even in daylight you stepped out with caution because mosques and schools were being blown up. Villages became recruiting targets for terrorist organizations, because of extreme poverty, lack of resources, dirty water, and dying crops; groups like the Taliban offered compensation, protection, and ideas like "eternal glory." At the same time, there was a rush to keep up with the economies of countries like China and India and so the agricultural sector declined. The military and army became the strongest industries, and oligarchy returned to Pakistan. The rich got richer, the poor got poorer.

The first few years in America were difficult. We lived in a one-bedroom apartment for a very long time, all six of us sleeping on the floor. I didn't have a bed until I was ten. In the very beginning we didn't even have paper. When my mom wanted to write a letter to my grandmother, she would ask our neighbors for a used notebook, erase the handwriting, and reuse the paper.

When you're a kid, you don't know you're poor. It's just how things are. It only starts to become clear when you go to school and you can't fit in: you're not only culturally different and physically different, but you also can't afford most of the things that the other kids can. We didn't have wealth in Pakistan, but the class difference was only exacerbated when we moved to the US: our few thousand rupees were the equivalent to a couple of dollars.

When I began high school, I started reading about what was occurring in the Southwest Asia/North Africa (SWANA) region. I read that the US Department of Defense had a larger annual carbon footprint than most countries on earth and was also the single largest polluter on earth. Its military presence in the SWANA region has cost taxpayers over eight trillion dollars since 1976. The war was not only causing pain: it was actively harming the planet. I could not understand what those people, who looked like me—whose children knew nothing of America but warplanes—could possibly have done to warrant starvation, rape, homelessness, and poverty.

The SWANA region is home to more than half of the world's crude oil and a third of its natural gas reserves. The United States waged the war on terror in order to maintain control over oil and gas, to generate profit and force parts of the region into economic subservience. The need for oil, and the lengths to which people would go to get it, was directly connected to the struggles of my family, my people, and the destruction of the environment. Western-led wars for oil have not only caused an increase in CO_2 emissions, but the use of depleted uranium by US forces in Iraq, Iran, and Libya has caused the poisoning of air and water, and led to birth defects and to cancer for thousands of people.

The US is certainly a different environment than Pakistan, but the patterns of socioeconomic inequality are very similar. My Coney Island community is mostly Black and Brown; 30 percent of it lives beneath the poverty line. As I write these words, a decade after the catastrophic Hurricane Sandy, the remedies promised to the neighborhood have not been delivered. The area still lacks a seawall, public housing has not been modified, the streets are still buckled, and pipes are still being installed to repair the water and gas damage.

*

How can we gain the kind of power that ensures we are listened to?

I have been thinking a great deal about this since the climate strike I helped organize in September 2019. It's a question that has led me to help found the youth climate organization Polluters Out, and that is also leading me to think about my future and going to law school.

It began with my disillusion, and frustration about what happened following the strike, at the UN Biodiversity Summit and after. In September 2019, our movement stopped major cities in most countries; we forced humanity to look into itself. But since then the climate crisis has only gotten worse.

I had been convinced that September 20 would be the turning point. I had been convinced that the UN was going to make the Paris Climate Agreement binding. I had been convinced that the United States would actively limit its carbon emissions and stop its fossil fuel constructions and hold up its end of Paris and domestically put in place a Green New Deal. I truly believed, as did all of us, that we were about to change history as we knew it.

Yet here we are, still headed toward extinction. Time and nature will not wait for us to get our act together. When an interviewer asks me what my hopes are for the future, it takes every wisp of hope in me to make a bet on humanity.

The disillusion began immediately, on September 20, in the way many of us were not even allowed access to the UN summit. There were some tickets given to youth, but the numbers from activist groups was limited. Of those of us who organized the New York City protests, only three were able to attend—and even these three were not granted access to the floor where the actual meetings were held. In the meetings set up specifically for the youth, we were lectured and spoken down to and applauded in the most patronizing manner. We were given lessons on how to be "influencers" and use social media, as if we hadn't just organized a 7.6 million–strong march! No one was interested in *really* talking to us, or in listening to us, let alone making the kind of changes needed to give us a chance for a safe future.

We thought it was essential, at the UN, to hear the testimonies of the people who came from all over the world, to talk about how the climate crisis was already affecting them. And then we hoped that world leaders from those countries would agree to take action against the projects and industries that were hurting those people. Had it happened, and had there been binding agreements, we would not be where we are at the time that I write this, three years later: in the same place.

What really enraged us was who actually *was* there, in our place: representatives from the fossil fuel industry, and the "green capital" sector. A similar thing happened three months later and then again in 2021, at the COP25 and COP26 summits in Madrid and Glasgow. People from the front lines, including youth and Indigenous people, had limited access and their voices were muted or even ejected. Meanwhile, bankers and industry representatives were everywhere. If you follow the money in the whole climate negotiations arena, it leads right to the door of the fossil-fuel industry. This industry actually *paid* for much of the COP25 summit. Most every policy that has come out of COP, including the Paris Climate Agreements, has had edits made by the fossil fuel industry directly contradicting the demands of civil society. Because of this influence, the most important binding agreement signed by over ninety-four nations does not call for fossil fuel de-proliferation. These edits harm Global South nations and Indigenous communities most, because protection and autonomy of land is not guaranteed.

After our success on September 20, 2019, everybody talked about the "power of youth," from Greta to Fridays for Future. We realized we needed to direct our energy to challenging the power of the fossil fuel industry to make a proper difference. My friend Isabella Fallahi, who attended COP25, reached out to me with a proposal to form a youth coalition that focused exclusively on the fossil fuel industry. With the skills I learned from organizing the climate strike, we set up the framework for this coalition: a set of bylaws, a constitution, teams, and an objective to unite the youth climate movement and get "polluters out" of the UN debate. Polluters Out was born. If no one was going to take Big Oil on, then we would.

Our primary demand is that the UN and its Framework Convention on Climate Change (UNFCC) sign a conflict-of-interest policy with fossil fuel companies, so that fossil fuel interests no longer influence the policies that come out of COP. The problem extends beyond fiscal influence, to the damage this influence does to robust climate legislation. If the fossil fuel companies fund the COP, this compromises initiatives like carbon taxing, the cessation of new pipelines, and the bans on injections of toxic waste into the Artic.

As a young activist fighting to save this planet and humanity, I am gearing up to have all the skills I need to fight the fossil fuel industry, including the law. I have also realized the limitations of mass mobilization. You can have thousands of people on the streets chanting "climate justice" at the top of their lungs only for the people with money and power to ignore you. I want to acquire the ability and faculties I need to bring about the changes I have been fighting so hard for; a law degree will allow me to do that. I want to be part of the decision-making process and I want to learn the language of those making the policy. I know there's a lack of environmental lawyers holding people accountable and making sure that there's proper reparation paid for lands that are destroyed, for water that is polluted and causes people to die. I can be part of changing that and so I am eager to pursue law.

But I also remind myself to remain focused on what's at the core of this movement: radical love and joy. For me, the fight for climate justice at its core comes from a place of deep love for humanity. Even as I become a lawyer, I tell myself, I must never forget that.

*

In late 2020, a few weeks after the climate strike and the disappointment of the UN summit, and while we were planning Polluters Out, I wrote a poem as a way of trying to figure out how I felt, about being of the last generation that can make a difference. The poem is titled "Extinction."

Vaporless and personal,
    ours is a vulnerable storyline.

There is no setting because the vegetation and river-run and trees
        and
buildings and the ordinary characters inside the itchy buildings
        have disappeared.

There is no theme but waves of empty scapes and the
        underside
bellies: all extraordinarily ruptured, and our children never meet.

No one sticks their dirty fingers into peanut-butter jars or
fights over the remote control.

Monopoly boards never fly to meet the ground.
No one spills coffee over their favorite pants.

Deep appetites do not go unfulfilled, so no one becomes victim
     to
the condition of truth and no one is lost enough to

compose music or ask:
"Oh lord, how come I born here?"
                    (And God, never gets to stand us up)

The grass never stretches upwards with the lolling cocoons and
the ants do not go marching two-by-two.

No one is there to watch the Sun seep nectar into the sapphire.
No precious chirping and shivering of feathered bodies.

Jeremiah never wails.
Elijah never sobs.
Jesus never weeps.
And no one really cares.

This is recent, these underlying beliefs;
the earth as dead matter,
the soil as commodity,
the land as property,
that the long-time horizons can be altered and

I suppose that is why compromise feels like sin.
This pale blue dot in this dark surface of skin.

These various networks of heartbeats with their various problems:
     gone?

Completely gone.

No chance to show off their resilience.

The peace deal never comes.

And no one is there to lament us, now that we are gone.

*

Against that are our words and action.

Further Reading and Viewing. On climate: Greta Thunberg (ed.), *The Climate Book* (Penguin, 2022), for which I have written a chapter; Henry Goldblatt, "Could 'Don't Look Up' Have Ended Differently?" Netflix Tudum, March 16, 2022; *Terra Nostra* a multimedia symphony about climate change composed by Christophe Chagnard with poetry by Emily Siff and a film by Charlie Spears. On the fossil fuel industry and conflict in the SWANA region: Greg Muttitt, *Fuel on the Fire: Oil and Politics in Occupied Iraq* (The New Press, 2012); Toby Craig Jones, "America, Oil, and War in the Middle East," *The Journal of American History*, vol. 99, no. 1, June 2012; Mottaghi Devarajan, "The Economic Effects of War and Peace," *MENA Quarterly Economic Brief*, January 2016.

The Youth Climate Justice Movement:
A Conversation

DAVID WICKER, EIMEAR SPARKS, KATIE REDFORD, FARHANA YAMIN, and MARK GEVISSER

When the organizers of this project convened the contributors to this book at the Rockefeller Bellagio Center in Italy, in September 2019, it was on the eve of the biggest global climate strike yet, led by students from all over the world. One of these was David Wicker, then a fourteen-year-old ninth grader from Turin, who had been in the initial group of students, along with Greta Thunberg, to set up the Fridays for Future movement and who had, together with other Italian youth organizers, brought millions of people onto the streets of Italy. David had been striking every Friday since January 2019, as well as helping lead mass protests in Turin. These are extracts from his interview with Eimear Sparks, and the responses, from others, to his question about how to use the law in the climate movement, followed by a conversation the editors had with David in 2022.

1. September 2019

On Movements and Momentum

Eimear Sparks: How did you become involved in Fridays for Future?

David Wicker: The movement in Italy was born around the beginning of January 2019. And it was all very unorganized, sudden, but incredible. Here in Italy, about twenty people formed Fridays for Future Italy, and then this snowball effect happened and now we have an assembly of over 160 local groups. A lot of young people gathered around us and slowly, every single week, week by week, more people joined us. In Turin, in the first week of January, we were four people. And then we were twenty. Honestly, on the fifteenth of March we organizers were expecting about five hundred people and we were going into school saying, oh, there could be two thousand people. But really we thought, you know, five hundred, and then on the streets we couldn't see the end of the march because there were so many people. It grew this fast and it really surprised us all. And now the movement, I really don't know how it happened, but on the fifteenth of March in Italy, we gathered over 470,000 (!), people striking and marching with us! I think it was the biggest number in the world!

ES: What caused you, personally, to act?

DW: One word: fear. I don't know what my future is going to look like. The school system in Italy asks us to select a study path to select a high school and then a university and then select the work we would like to work in, but I don't know what I would like to do. Before I learned about the climate emergency, I want to be a programmer. But now I'm really trying to understand what I can study to help me survive in this world that we don't know what will look like.

For me, it began when I saw this girl on Instagram who was holding a simple paper sign saying "school strike" in Swedish. A group of seven people on WhatsApp was formed. And at the time it was really like, "Should we have the strike on the afternoon so that we don't have to skip school?"

On Strategy

ES: How are you organizing?

DW: We are trying to get organized, but it's really difficult because we're so many and all of us come from different backgrounds. But we keep in mind that the emergency is here and if we don't act fast and organize ourselves fast enough, then it's going to all be lost time. And so we accept it and we work the best that we can as we are able. We are all teenagers and we don't have the experience of structure building, interacting with companies, lawyers, politics, or other associations.

We use a lot of social media. I think nowadays it is effective, to say the least. And before the fifteenth of March we went into schools and we held lectures along with some professors of the Politecnico di Turino. And we kind of did tours in all of the schools of Turin. And then when the teachers walked out of the class to grab a coffee or something, we just told the students, "You know, you can actually do something about this; you can put pressure on the government on the fifteenth of March, which is going to be a huge strike".

Now a new group has been born in Turin, called Parents for Future, which is also developing on an international level. It's basically parents of us strikers who understand what our fight is about and who say, "Okay, this is actually really important. I need to support my children in this because their future will be greatly, hugely affected by this." And this group of parents started coming to our strikes. They started skipping their work times. And it's really nice because now at the strikes we see ten or twenty young children aged four and five who run around and play ball during the strike. *[In 2019, the Turin parents would be instrumental in the Parents for Future Global "A Plea to Parents at the Climate Summit," which reads: "Our children are the greatest love of our lives . . . We cannot accept that this is the world we are handing over to our children."]*

ES: To what extent do you feel like you're part of a global movement and how do you maintain this energy?

DW: I feel we are 1,000 percent in a global movement. It's really, really nice. You can go to whatever city, at least in Europe, and on a Friday you can see that there is actually a group of people striking in that city. So if you travel around Europe, you can join whatever local group that's striking in a protest on a Friday.

Basically, we don't do anything alone. We do everything, almost everything, altogether as a global movement. There are working groups popping up every minute and it's really hard to keep track of what's happening. But it's really also fascinating and helpful that the movement is going so fast and with so many people involved.

On Using the Law as a Strategy

Katie Redford: David, your generation is rightfully frustrated, even outraged, with ours for not doing more to prevent this crisis—in many ways, you are left to clean up our mess, so we are certainly not the experts here! Your generation has done more to focus attention on this issue in nine months than ours has done in decades! In spite of that, do you have any questions for us?

DW: My question is about using the law. How can we push the government in a legal sense, strike them hard in a way they cannot escape?

KR: You hit them where they care, which is their political power, or if it's the corporations, it's their profit, or their reputation, or their brand. You hit them in every single place. And there are so many strategies, but you are doing the right thing, as far as the first step, in terms of building power.

In the United States, EarthRights is suing Exxon and other oil companies for the actual damages that they've caused. If we succeed, there will be money available for the harmed communities to help them be resilient in the future, and it will be clear that there is *cost*, an actual monetary cost, to burning fossil fuels. Such losses might force them see that the continual burning of fossil fuels is no longer a viable business model. Finally, by making them lose in court, we take away their social license, which is essential, because in the US—as I'm sure is the case here in Italy—the fossil fuel industries have a chokehold on government.

Farhana Yamin: Litigation is just one kind of legal tool, and there are many others—like striking, which you're already doing—that are immensely effective. There are many suits going through led by children and young people, and they have a galvanizing power, which is special, of their own. Striking has happened in many countries led by children, for example in Ghana, because their schools are inadequate. Maybe there's a way education officials themselves could be sued if they don't give permisison for striking; using the fabric and infrastructure and legal duties of school in the education sector or suing the minister for education for miseducating you and wasting your time. That would be quite nice!

But something I want to commend you on is that I can see you don't look at legal strategies in isolation. Sometimes lawyers can overplay the legal parts, and not pay enough attention to mobilization and advocacy— and you seem to be doing that part just right. The striking is particularly compelling, because it's not something you have to spend money on. You are withdrawing your labor from school, and you're choosing to use that politically.

There were other answers, about using culture and the arts, engaging with the media over language use, and occupying the offices of elected officials.

Mark Gevisser: It's fascinating to me that you asked a question about using legal tools to a roomful of people, most of whom are lawyers, and with the exception of Katie's example of Exxon, not one responded with an explicitly legal strategy! This reflects, perhaps, what we've all been talking about over the past few days, which is that using the legal tools is not a magic bullet or solution that solves the problem, and that even if you are a lawyer, you have to see the law as part of a broader strategy. More often than not, you use the law not necessarily because you expect victory, but because by doing it you shift the debate or attract attention to be more visible. Obviously it's great to think about what legal strategies you can take to change the law. But it's also great to think about what legal strategies you can use to get more attention and get more people to know about you and care about the issue. So if, for example, you sued the minister of education, you would be doing so to make your issue visible in a whole new way. It doesn't even really matter if you lose the suit, because you're going to be getting all this free publicity.

KR: And then that minister might think, "I might lose that suit. Now, what was it you wanted me to do?"

March 2022

Mark Gevisser and Katie Redford: David, it is two and a half years since we met at Bellagio. You are now seventeen, finishing high school, and an "elder" in the climate youth movement. There was a real sense of urgency that was driving you when we met. Do you still feel that in your movement, there years later? What are your reflections on what has happened since then?

David Wicker: I can assure that the urgency did not dissipate; if anything it increased with time, as we watched the clock ticking and the window of action to contrast the climate crisis in order to stay under 1.5°C getting smaller and smaller. Last year I got a sense of how uneven activism is globally when I moved to Armenia to study. I saw that the movement did not find roots here. The Armenian people are obviously more preoccupied and directly affected by the conflict in Artsakh (Nagorno-Karabakh) and with the oppression and constant intimidations by the hand of Azerbaijan.

MG and KR: When we met in 2019, you asked for advice about how to use the law. Were you at Glasgow COP in 2021, and how did you feel about that process? Is it possible to make a difference "from the inside"?

DW: I didn't go to COP but I was invited to the TED Countdown Summit in Edinburgh a couple of weeks before. Through this opportunity I was able to reflect on the possibility of creating change from the inside. The TED team thought it was a good idea to invite as a keynote speaker Shell's CEO Ben van Beurden; we climate activist invitees pushed the organizers to prevent the CEO of one of the most powerful fossil fuel companies to take the floor as part of Shell's greenwashing campaign. The eventual compromise was that a representative of the movement took the stage in a panel discussion with Ben. This allowed us to directly confront the CEO of Shell on the stage and in front of cameras. The action picked up quite a buzz in the media. Shell's stock dropped considerably!

MG and KR: You are close to finishing school. You must be thinking of next steps—both for yourself and the movement.

DW: I'm trying to find a path that allows me to join my passion and drive in climate activism with my passion in computer science and climate science. I am studying environmental systems and societies at my high school and I intend to pursue a degree in computer science at university. These plans might sound like they clash with my original drive of climate activism. I started striking when I was fourteen (crazy to think about) and in the past three years I have realized that other than keeping up the pressure on institutions, I also want to have a more direct impact on the science and on the aspect of mitigation of the consequences of the climate crisis.

MG and KR: There is of course a new generation of youth climate activists coming up behind you. What are your observations about this generation? Are they similarly driven by fear for the future? Are they more disillusioned?

DW: The more we look into the future, the more I can predict the youth will be hungry for drastic change, as their future is at stake. I don't believe the new generations are disillusioned. With time, we are starting to accept the importance and relevance of the smaller milestones that are being reached while keeping our eyes on the goal of 1.5°C. While this goal is progressively getting harder and harder to meet because of the continued delay of climate action, I think activists are also realizing the importance of fighting to make sure that other goals are met and that the broader conversation on mitigation begins, closely related to the fight of climate justice and equity.

Epilogue:
Rules for Radical Lawyers

KATIE REDFORD

*Survival is not an academic skill. It is learning how to stand alone, unpopu-
lar and sometimes reviled, and how to make common cause with those others
identified as outside the structures in order to define and seek a world in which
we can all flourish . . . For the master's tools will never dismantle the master's
house. They may allow us temporarily to beat him at his own game, but they
will never enable us to bring about genuine change.*

> —Audre Lorde, "The Master's Tools Will Never
> Dismantle the Master's House"

Law, of course, is the master's tool par excellence. And for those of us who
are lawyers, the hallowed halls of the master's house are often our playing
fields. Here, we wield our coveted tools and training; we analyze, we parse,
we debate. Here, we maintain professional distance, replace hot emotions
with cold logic; we argue any and every side. Here, we rely on past precedent rather than reimagining the future, as we ask for incremental changes.

But some of us entered law school with bigger visions of truth and
justice—of "fighting for the little guy" and "saving the world." I became a
lawyer because I'd seen the movies and was inspired by the moral force of
lady justice, with her blindfold and balanced scales. It's a lovely theory, but
in practice legal education prepares you for a legal *career*; you are trained to
play a certain role, and then perceived to be playing this role. Regardless
of who or where we were before we got there, the law is an elite field,
and we feel and absorb this status when we go to law school. Surrounded
by this sense of privilege and power in the most ivory of towers, we are
taught to cultivate the skills that will make us excel professionally. Whether

intentionally or not, we became part of the fraternity preserving the very status quo we went in to change.

This isn't what I thought I signed up for. As a high school student awakening to my activism during the anti-apartheid movement of the 1980s, I wanted not only to know what to do, but also how to do it, and why. I read all the "how to" books, devoured every "manifesto" I could find. Looking back on it, I see my pre-lawyer tendencies, wanting to understand the theory *and* practice of social change, and needing to develop a level of expertise that lawyers spend careers honing in other subjects. Back then, Saul Alinsky's *Rules for Radicals: A Practical Primer for Realistic Radicals* was the progressive activists' lodestar, and for many it still is. As many of my classmates began carrying around their mini Constitutions, I was wishing for my own pocket-sized Rules for Radical Lawyers, but it didn't exist.

I responded then, and still do, to the word "radical." Its literal meaning is "root," rather than what many today think of as "extreme," and I've always understood a "radical" agenda as one that either addresses root causes, brings us back to our roots as humans (our shared humanity and connection to the earth), or both. I also love its implication of change that is sweeping and transformational rather than incremental or ordinary—and of course its slang meaning: "cool"! But especially for a budding pre-lawyer like myself, I now realize that what also attracted me was the whole alliterative package of Saul Alinsky's book title: the pairing of "radical" with "rules" and "realism." Rules are a lawyer's home turf, and realism—a strategic assessment of what is possible—is the crux of our training.

When I got to law school, seeking to be a realistic yet radical vehicle for social justice and the rule of law, I encountered lofty legal theory, judicial opinions, and one hypothetical fact pattern after another presented by brilliant law professors. But where was my practical primer about how to make real change for real people? Certainly not in the legal textbooks filled with Supreme Court decisions. I yearned for something based on lived experience, and reflective not only of laws and precedents, but of their contexts and impacts. This was why I set out to make this book: to add to the library of any law student or lawyer—in fact, any person at all interested in how to use the law as part of their activism—something that was so painfully missing from mine when I was studying. The process of making this book has helped me clarify the ten Rules for Radical Lawyers that follow below.

All the writers in this book walk the talk of these rules, whether they are legal practitioners or activists or both. They demonstrate that survival—as Audre Lorde puts it—is not an academic pursuit. Nor is transformational change an academic pursuit driven by the sharpest analyst, the best debater, or the strongest evidence in the room. Whether they are writing about villagers in Burma who worked and died as slaves for a US oil company, about sex workers and members of the LGBTQ community murdered in Kenya, or about Black people in Ferguson and New York stopped and frisked and killed by the police, each knows that life, and death, can turn on who makes the rules and who enforces them. And each chapter of this book is equally clear that the elites who benefit from business as usual have used the tools at their disposal—in government, academia, media, finance, religion, the military—to resist change and preserve their power.

The essays in this book demonstrate that transformational change is driven by people power—and that people power runs on emotions and connections as well as ideas. The changes we need to save ourselves from the planetary collision course we are on now *must* be led by those fighting to protect what they love, and reclaim or seek redress for what they have lost. This was the stunning lesson from the youth climate movement, which did more to focus global attention and action on the climate crisis in months than the scientific and legal "experts" did in decades. From the climate movement and the Movement for Black Lives, from the resistance of Indigenous people at Standing Rock to those on the streets of Beirut and South Africa, the message of this book is clear. The law is important; more than that, it has the power to be transformational. But the revolution will not be litigated. It will be fought by those with the most at stake, with the help of the law in service of the movement.

What does that mean for those of us who are trained in the law, and who still believe in its transformational power?

Power is at the center of every movement story and legal case. Whether advocating for racial justice, sexual and gender equality, human rights, Indigenous self-determination, environmental protection, or corporate accountability—this book's contributors, and the people they work with, are exercising and demanding power. Law is one language of this power, and it is for this reason that it is one of the master's go-tos. But if law is a language of power, need it be the exclusive preserve of the powerful? Can it be invoked to strip away power from the abusive and unlock it in the abused? This is the fundamental question this book has set out to answer: not just whether, but how, law can be the servants' tool for systemic change to such an extent that they cease to be servants at all, but become masters of their own destiny. One answer is clear: to shift law from its establishment moorings cannot be done unharnessed from the power of the people.

"The arc of the moral universe is long but it bends towards justice." I still believe, passionately, in "the power of law," but—like many contributors to this book—I too have become frustrated with the glacial pace of legal advocacy. How do we grapple with this when the threats we face—to life, dignity, the very survival of the human species—make clear that we *just don't have the time to wait for that arc to bend*? Increasingly, those of us who seek radical and meaningful change understand that movements are the answer, with the sweeping, rapid change they demand and have the potential to deliver.

As lawyers try to think differently about our roles in the world—and the movements we are part of—we need to unlearn the behaviors, skills, and practices drilled into us in law school. That means we must relearn how to be humans and advocates first, and lawyers and technocrats second. Whether we call ourselves "movement lawyers," "public interest lawyers," "radical lawyers," "cause lawyers," or even "judicial activists," we must see ourselves differently and use our training in a very different way.

Rules for Radical Lawyers is a starting point for this unlearning and relearning process. It's a way to be proud of what you do as well as good at it.

*

Rule #1: "Make common cause with those others."

"Lawyer" means "advocate," and every movement leader, activist, protestor, and "radical" is an advocate for a cause. The myth of neutrality is one of the first to reject if you are seeking genuine change by dismantling the house and building back a better one. You are not neutral: you came to your life's work because it's personal to you, so take it personally! In spite of this, one of the first skills you learn in law school is to be able to argue any side of a case and your legal education trains you to do that. Legal training emphasizes intellect and professional distance; while these are critical to remember and to practice when appropriate, movement lawyers need to practice empathy and tap into emotion too.

The examples in this book show how movements are born of pain and rage, and sustained by the powerful urge to protect and fight for what we love. Lawyers disregard this at their peril: we must cultivate connection by grounding our practice in our own lived experience of trauma, injustice, and love. This does *not* mean that you make your legal work about yourself (even though, as with many in this book, you may well be part of the community you seek to help and represent). On the contrary, empathy requires that you take a step back and think deeply about what others have experienced, as if it had happened to you. Failing to do so can miss the point entirely—as when my cocounsel and I celebrated our first major victory in *Doe v. Unocal.* We rejoiced in making legal history, until we were reminded that our victory made no immediate tangible difference for our clients from Burma, who were still living in poverty, in exile, and in even more danger than before because of the heightened attention that this legal victory came with.

Planning for such disconnects and tensions between, for example, clients' immediate needs and movement goals is part of our work. We need to leverage the combined power of personal connection and empathy while also applying our traditional legal skills. This can bring about the particular win-win for which we movement lawyers search: achieving justice with our clients rather than simply winning the case.

Rule #2: Begin with a vision for genuine change.

Martin Luther King did not say, "I have a hypo to think through." Nor did he say, "I have a minor problem that needs tinkering." He articulated an audacious vision with such clarity that others could see it and work toward it, take risks or make sacrifices for it, and then ultimately feel it to be inevitable.

Lawyers and law students start with fact patterns, legal issues, and technical questions, then spend hours, even lifetimes, debating their implications on hypothetical, fictional scenarios ("hypos"). They rely on past precedents from existing case law to develop legal strategies that influence the outcomes of the situations with which they are presented. More often than not, their job is to convince a judge, jury, or other decision maker that they are not really asking for change, but instead that the outcome they seek rests on the rational order of past precedent.

Movements are similarly grounded in facts, but they focus on actual injustices of the here and now to urge and advocate for the necessity of a radically changed future. While lawyers come up with legal theory and apply the facts of their particular case to convince a judge or jury to side with their client, movements aim to mobilize the masses around a particular incident or injustice that typifies the systemic injustice they seek to dismantle. They then build and sustain momentum by connecting that initial outrage to an inspiring vision of societal change. In contrast, a lawyer's case ends with a decision or verdict—for or against a particular perpetrator who has harmed a particular person, people, or place. We may have achieved a legal victory in forcing Unocal to pay reparations for the human rights abuses our clients alleged happened on their pipeline, and deterred future harms by attaching costs to that kind of abuse for the first time. But the work of the movement for corporate accountability, human rights, and indeed democracy in Burma was certainly not done.

All the movements described in this book have demanded fundamental, transformational change—and articulated a vision for a world that addressed the root causes of the injustices they were fighting against. Movement lawyers understood and decried not only the injustices against Michael Brown in Ferguson and Jane Doe 1 in Burma, but also the police impunity, white supremacy, and unregulated corporate power that allowed for, and even encouraged, such abuse in the first place.

Rule #3: Think strategically.

It's not enough to "want" to make the world a better place, or to believe in typical lawyer ideals like truth, justice, and the rule of law. Putting that vision, and the legal theories that underpin it, into practice requires you to be able to map the connections between your work and the specific, fundamental—radical—change you seek to create. Aside from or alongside litigation, legal tactics may include legislative advocacy, developing public policy, media activities to influence the "court of public opinion," or even constitutional reform.

Law school provides ample training and exposure to various legal strategies. But it often fails to distinguish between tactics and strategies, to connect strategy to a broader vision, or to ask the basic question: Does it achieve anything outside of winning the legal argument? Like all US law students, I read the Supreme Court opinions in Ruth Bader Ginsburg's and Thurgood Marshall's famous sex discrimination and school desegregation cases; like most US law students, I studied those decisions in a vacuum. Left out was the fact that litigation was one tactic in a broad legal strategy for civil rights aligned with an even broader vision for gender and racial equality that has been entrenched and advanced by movements.

Radical lawyers must not only focus on a winning legal strategy, like a jury verdict or a judicial opinion that sets precedent. They must also be intentional about how and whether those strategies fully serve the broader outcomes, and societal changes, sought by their clients or the movements they connect to.

Rule #4: It's all about power.

Power mapping is a cornerstone movement strategy, and one that lawyers all too often either skip or are unaware of. This may be because of the myth we're taught about law being the great equalizer: the poor and rich alike can seek justice, which is blind. Even if this were true in the courtroom (it's not), lawyers must understand the context outside of the courtroom to realize the lasting benefits of any legal victory they seek. Ask yourself not only who has the power, but also who enables that power (which is often less obvious), how they have it, and how this power can be shifted and reallocated using the law and other levers. If you define yourself as a lawyer seeking social, environmental, racial, or economic justice, your role must be that of a "legal Robin Hood," disrupting the power and privilege of institutions and individuals that use such power to abuse and exploit.

The lawyers in this book teach us that our role is not just to hold power to account. We must also focus our work to help our clients realize the power that they already have; to provide access to new tools, including but not limited to legal ones, and help our clients wield them effectively; and to create opportunities for clients and movements to unleash that power on the systems and structures that seek to suppress it. This is not the work of building power, but rather acknowledging that the power is already there, and *unleashing* it in the most impactful way the law allows for. This could be by creating opportunities for people who have been silenced to raise their voices and tell their stories; or providing a forum for those who have been harmed to seek relief for themselves and create change for others; or buying time for movements to organize themselves and mobilize additional support; or using their access and training to reform unjust laws and legal systems. For a movement lawyer, justice is fundamentally about disrupting and shifting power.

I saw this in *Doe v. Unocal* when I watched Jane Doe 1 confronting the American oil corporation's lawyers in her deposition, knocking them off their game and leaving them speechless; or when John Doe 5 proudly showed us the school and community center he built with the money he received in the settlement. My clients were no longer victims, but active survivors who took charge and had a say, literally, over their own lives, their families, and their communities.

Rule #5: Listen to understand rather than to argue.

Lawyers are trained in *listening to argue,* a process of pulling out and parsing pieces of what we hear to determine whether they support our case, weaken our opponents, or both. But *listening to understand* is different; something that the contributors in this book did as an ongoing practice over visits to clients' homes, canoe trips to their villages, sharing family stories, and breaking bread, returning time and again rather than swooping in and disappearing as dictated by the rhythms of a case.

This takes both time and humility; time that lawyers trained to charge by ten-minute increments might not feel they can offer, and humility to let go of the "argue to the death" mentality drummed into us at law school. Indeed, serving your clients vigorously and with total allegiance does not mean you do whatever it takes, at whatever cost, to win the case. Rather, it means understanding not just their legal claims, but who they are, and how they align with the broader movement. It requires spending time with your clients' families and listening to their hurts and fears; or addressing a community's confusion, and remembering all their concerns as you move forward with your legal strategy. There is little room for "not my client, not my job" in movement lawyering.

The best corporate counsel know their client's business inside and out, and advise clients to drop or settle lawsuits against the corporation when it makes business sense. Movement lawyers could take a page from this playbook, centering what makes "movement sense" as integral to their clients' interest. When done right, your clients can ground you in the movement. Your legal strategy should leave them, their community and the movement stronger and more cohesive regardless of the outcome of the case.

A focus solely on winning can mean you listen to analyze instead of empathize, and to find support for your case instead of your client or the movement. And so listening to understand is a step lawyers often skip as they develop a strategy to win their case, and seek out clients and witnesses whose "facts" align with a strategy for legal victory. But this emphasis on addressing past harms, rather than working toward a vision of a better future, limits our impact as movement lawyers.

Client intake must include specific and targeted questions to ensure you have the right combination of facts and law to mount a successful legal strategy. But it should also happen over multiple conversations, in their community and environment, and include open ended questions like: "What does winning mean to you? What does success look like for you, your family, and your community? What change are you seeking and what will be different for you after this case?" The legal system might not be the right one to deliver these goals, but the lawyer can still share them, and support or help facilitate their achievement. Shared values with clients and movements, and the long-term change strategies that can serve everyone, come through personal relationships cultivated and tended over time.

Rule #6: Embrace the power of storytelling—not just as a legal strategy, but as a form of justice itself.

Over the years, I have asked clients and potential clients why they want to bring a case, and what they hope to achieve. The answers are as diverse as the people and places they come from. But there is one thing they all say: I want to tell my story. Movement lawyers serve clients and marginalized communities; having their day in court is already a profound shift. It bestows dignity on the storyteller, who is fully in control over the narrative she chooses to share and highlight; it requires the defendant—or at least their attorneys—to listen; and it bestows a level of gravitas and importance to the harms the litigant has suffered.

Storytelling is at the core of most cultures and traditions, and the legal tradition is no exception. Stories are the lifeblood of legal cases and movements, and certainly provide critical content for the media. This is particularly true when defendants have a public reputation to maintain: exposure can compel settlement talks, activate shareholders and corporate boards, or make unsympathetic judges more cautious in their rulings. However, there may be times when a storytelling priority is in tension with legal strategies. Keep all of this in mind when considering what details to put into a complaint, remembering that your audience—and the individuals and institutions that can deliver the change you need—often extends far beyond the judge(s) upon whose desk it lands. A journalist once told me that our climate change complaint against Exxon "was a page-turner that read like a John Grisham novel." I was delighted to hear this: mobilizing the court of public opinion, and government officials beholden to it, can often bring change faster than what gradual legal processes can accomplish.

For our clients, telling their stories validates their claims, their experiences, and their suffering even if the ultimate outcomes of their cases don't. Storytelling is a form of justice: whether it happens in a trial, in the media, in a deposition, during client intake, or even a settlement negotiation.

Rule #7: Words matter—know what you're talking about, to whom, and why.

Attention to detail is one of our strengths, a skill we spend years perfecting. We are so good at parsing when reading and writing briefs, and we'll spend hours on a single word or semicolon, debating its meaning with opposing counsel and judges. There is an irony here. Given that our profession rises and falls on an ability to manipulate details with the right language and rhetoric to "win the case," this strength makes us sometimes lose sight of what our work—and our words—really mean. Where is this attention to detail when thinking about our clients ?

Is a "remedy" really a remedy? Can money damages ever "compensate" someone for their dead family members, or "repair" the loss of dignity and security that survivors of rape and violence endure? And what are "damages," really? For a lawyer, it's the money we demand for our clients. But for our clients, damages are the actual and tangible harms to their bodies, their health, their family, their home, their culture. Damages are the lived experience—often unspeakably terrible—of our clients.

As lawyers, our "evidence" is our clients' lived experience, too, and details that make for a "great case" can be the absolute worst for our clients who never wanted their personal tragedies to be boiled down to a case name and a discussion of legal elements. Likewise, gathering client and witness testimony is another way of asking people to recount and relive their trauma. Storytelling can, indeed, be a form of justice, but it's a double-edged sword, for the legal system's emphasis on witness and client testimony requires people to be retraumatized by telling their stories over and over again. Understand that your function as an advocate is to navigate and translate without assuming that the language and procedures of the law serve or even make sense to your clients.

There are many reasons why people don't like lawyers, and one of them is the way we treat people and talk to them. Not every person is a judge, jury or opposing counsel, and not every communication is a legal brief. So don't try to win in every conversation. But do prepare for every interaction, and treat every person in the movement and the case with the same level of gravitas and respect as you do your judge. The information you carefully provide to your clients and families can ease their fears, increase

their agency in litigation and their confidence to keep fighting. Winning
the change you seek often turns on your ability to explain complex legal
issues to the media or the public in regular human language, not legalese.

Ultimately, the way we speak and listen to people, and actually care
about them, can deliver not only a legal win, but also the dignity required to
achieve the true justice outcomes our clients seek. Restoring this sense of
hope is perhaps the most important remedy—not in the idealistic wishful
thinking sense, but in the way it creates a fierce desire to keep fighting even
in the face of danger. This is the dignity and hope that unleashes power.

Rule #8: Celebrate wins, but learn how to lose—and celebrate that too.

Learning how to lose, and identifying the wins to the movement despite a
loss in court, is critical to the long game of a radical lawyer.

To do radical work, we have to hold two things at once. First, it is vital
to cultivate a vision of the better world you want to realize, and to feed
your belief that your work is bringing us all closer to that better reality.
Those who benefit from the status quo also benefit from the pernicious
(and pervasive) view that our current moment in time, and all the inequity
that comes with it, is an inevitability. "This is the way things are and the
way they've always been. You're dreaming, and you need to focus on how
to survive in the world we've got." By taking on entrenched power structures, we are doing something audacious: hope, confidence, and vision are
prerequisites for achieving audacious goals. As is often said: everything is
impossible until it's not.

At the same time, it is just as vital that we foster resilience, both in our
movements and in our own individual selves. Oftentimes we *are* fighting
against the odds, the money, and the ingrained power structures. Losses
along the way *are* inevitable. You will often lose and that will sting. But
doubt and despair are the master's tools too, because they lead to a paralysis
that is unhelpful to the fight for change.

Movement lawyers must identify, articulate, and celebrate the wins
even if they're small—and see the wins in losses too. Sometimes what
feels like a failure is the result of herculean and *successful* efforts to prevent
things from being worse than they would have been. It's impossible to ever

know or measure deterrence, yet we know that the threat of accountability and justice can prevent bad actors from deciding or continuing to do bad things. Losing your case may not make you want to pop a cork, but don't skip the celebration of what might have been achieved. Did your client tell her story? Was the perpetrator named, shamed, and held accountable in the court of public opinion? Did you buy time for the movement to organize, mobilize power, and get ready for the next fight? Winning is not only about the lawyers and the law.

Here we really should listen to the movement leaders in this book. Movements, and lawsuits, are born of pain and damage. But movements— and, yes, movement lawyers—are necessarily sustained by celebration and joy.

Rule #9: Navigate with grace.

Here's a dirty little secret. People who do good work aren't always good to each other.

If, indeed, movements are born of pain and rage, and sustained by the powerful urge to protect and fight for what we love, you can bet that extreme emotions are involved. Stakes are high, resources often low, and those who have been marginalized and harmed might understandably grab and guard power viciously. As for lawyers, our reputations precede us: we are often high-achieving, competitive perfectionists, overworked and over-stressed. The pressures and personalities involved in movement work are a potent cocktail, and perhaps it should be expected that the best and worst traits of our peers, and ourselves, will be amplified.

As with losing, difficult personalities are an inevitability; developing a facility for navigating your own quirks, and those of others, is an invaluable skill. Infighting can poison a movement; dividing and conquering is also a traditional tool of the master. Our lawyerly urge for accountability does not mean there is always someone to blame (especially on our own team). The system is often stacked against us, and we rarely have the human or financial resources of those we oppose. Remembering who the opposition really is, and focusing on changing that broken system, must be our North Star, rather than being "right."

In Conclusion:

Rule #10: Winning the case isn't everything. Winning meaningful change is.

The master's tools will never dismantle the master's house. They may allow us temporarily to beat him at his own game, but they will never enable us to bring about genuine change.

Audre Lorde's words can be discouraging to someone who became a lawyer to use the tools to overthrow a master that values corporate rights over human rights, that sacrifices people, and that dooms the planet to a wasteland. But as I have been engaging with the people who contributed to this book and their ideas, and reading my own damned rules, I remind myself to consider Lorde's words in their context and totality. So I return to Rule #1, and the less-often quoted part of her statement: "Make common cause with those others identified as outside the structures." This is a far cry from the professional distance we're trained to maintain as we put our own views, opinions, and causes aside in order to effectively serve (but not ally with) our clients. Rather than rely on existing law and precedent to advance our clients' cases, Lorde urges us "to define and seek a world in which we can all flourish."

Here is how I read Lorde and apply her to my own life and work. Once we (1) use our master's tools to "define and seek" a new world (rather than tweak what we have, relying on existing precedent) and (2) envision this world to be one in which all (not only our clients) flourish, then we too can be vehicles for transformative change that brings down the master's house.

In my own work as a movement lawyer and in working with the contributors to this book, I have learned that we *can* use the law, very effectively, to beat the master at his own game—and we must. Once we understand and take our place in a movement in which our legal tools are just one part of a rich and diverse ecosystem of skills, knowledge, wisdom, beauty, rage, pain, and joy, we *can* bring about genuine change. That's the win that all of us must fight for.

FROM IRAC TO VISTA

IRAC is the methodology for legal analysis that every American law student is drilled in: **Issue, Rules, Application, Conclusion**:

- State the legal **Issue** at stake,
- Review the **Rules** that are relevant to the issue by looking at precedent and statute,
- **Apply** and analyze those rules to the issue at hand,
- Come to a **Conclusion** based on this process.

There are entire books and courses dedicated to this topic. But when you start with the narrow *legal* issue you want to sort, rather than a broader assessment of what you want to achieve and why, you are working from a technocratic baseline that may limit the impact of your advocacy. And so, rather than sticking with IRAC, the process of making this book has helped me to develop what we can call VISTA, which organizes the Rules for Radical Lawyers into the beginning of a "radical lawyers checklist" to fill in those blanks in your traditional legal education. Think of VISTA as your IRAC for strategic campaigning, applied here to the *Doe v. Unocal* case described in the first chapters of this book.

- **Vision**—Articulate the idealized change you and the movement(s) you're part of are seeking. Ask the questions: What will change in the world if we are successful? What systems and structures will be different if we achieve this vision?

  - For Doe v. Unocal, *our vision was a world where human rights were paramount to corporate rights, and where people in Burma could live with the dignity and justice of human rights protection. (Make sure sure you're aligned on this with your clients and the movements they are part of.)*

- **Impacts**—Articulate the specific impacts and outcomes that contribute to this vision.

  - *In* Doe v. Unocal *these were: punishment and accountability for the fossil fuel corporations; remedy for our clients to make them whole and let them move on; an opportunity for our clients to tell their stories and be heard; a change to the system (ending corporate impunity for human rights abuses committed abroad); and prevention of future*

human rights abuses in Burma. (Once more, make sure sure you're
aligned on this with your clients and the movements they are part of.)

- **Strategy**—Once you have clarity on your big vision, and the specific impacts you seek to contribute to it, and you are aligned on that vision and impacts with your clients, then decide which legal strategies are best deployed to deliver those outcomes.

  - *In* Doe v. Unocal *we chose to focus on litigation as our primary legal strategy, understanding how this would need to be connected to legislative and policy efforts we could contribute to when appropriate. Can your legal strategy actually deliver the vision your client wants and needs? We made legal history when we won jurisdiction, but when our clients asked if that meant they could go home, I was reminded of the limits of the law. That feeling was reinforced when disappointed movement activists expressed a feeling of betrayal that our clients chose to end the case with a settlement. We could not have avoided those legal limits, but we could have avoided the activist ire by having extensive conversations with clients and movement leaders in advance of litigation, aligning around a common vision, and then being transparent up front about which legal strategies could deliver what pieces of that vision, and for whom.*

- **Tactics**—Within your strategies are the even more specific tactics that you must use to support your strategy overall. If the Vision and Impacts are the "what," the Strategy and Tactics are the "how," with tactics being the various actions you take to achieve your overall strategic goals.

  - *In* Doe v. Unocal, *our tactics included federal court litigation under the Alien Tort Statute; state court litigation under California tort laws; legislative advocacy for federal sanctions; state legislative advocacy for selective purchasing laws; exposing and highlighting legal risks in shareholder advocacy; media and public relations tactics.*

- **Audience**, and **Adversaries**, and **Allies**. There are three A's, and you need to know them equally well.

  - Your audience is the decision maker you appear before, with the power to grant or deny your demands. Make sure your strategy speaks to and influences them through the different tactics (messages and messengers) you might deploy, depending on whether your audience is a judge, jury, mediator, or government official. Always remember, however, there are additional audiences with power to influence or deliver the change you seek: the media, the government, investors, the movements and the communities your clients come from. Legal strategies must not exist in a vacuum; they have the power to shift public opinion, spur government action, or inspire community mobilization.

- *In* Doe v. Unocal, *our primary audience was members of the judiciary—the federal judges who delivered game-changing decisions and set a new legal bar for global corporate complicity in human rights abuses, and the state judge who presided over our proceedings from discovery through trial and settlement.*

- Likewise, you must understand your adversaries, and choose the tactics that actually get them to make the changes that you are demanding.

  - *In* Doe v. Unocal, *we knew that our corporate adversaries were concerned most about their bottom line and their brand. We thus reinforced our legal strategies with shareholder advocacy to elevate the financial risks associated with their investment in Burma, and media strategies to tarnish their name and their brand.*

- Finally, tailor these tactics to mobilize powerful allies, whose power might come in numbers or because your adversaries or audience are accountable to them, or awed or influenced by by them.

  - *In* Doe v. Unocal, *our allies were in the Free Burma Movement, in the labor movement, the environmental movement, the human rights movement, and the anti-globalization movement. They represented millions of citizens from around the world, many in democratic countries that had the power to issue sanctions on the Burmese regime and thus prevent further investment in their military junta.*

About the Contributors

Phelister Abdalla is the national coordinator of the Kenya Sex Workers' Alliance (KESWA), committed to examining the strengths and weaknesses of international human rights and domestic legal frameworks as they apply to sex work. Phelister is an active sex worker herself, and is particularly focused on ensuring that sex workers are included as active participants in the planning, decision-making, and implementation of the KESWA programmes. She is part of a public interest litigation case in Kenya that aims to reform the anti–sex work laws there, and, by so doing, give sex workers a better chance of safe and dignified lives. This forms part of a broader strategy aimed at remedying the violations sex workers face.

Alejandra Ancheita is founder and executive director of ProDESC, an organization that has, since 2005, advanced the rights of Mexican workers and Indigenous and agrarian communities. At ProDESC she achieved unprecedented results in the application of accountability mechanisms to transnational corporations. For this, she received the Martin Ennals Award, dubbed the "Nobel Prize of Human Rights," in 2014, and was recognized in 2015 by the Mexican Senate. She has a law degree from the Universidad Autónoma Metropolitana in Mexico and an LLM from Fordham University. She was awarded an honorary doctorate by the Université Paris Nanterre in 2019. She is a member of the Global Reference Group of Bread for The World; of the Martin Ennals Foundation board; of the Bonavero Institute of Human Rights at the University of Oxford; and of the academic boards of the law faculties at the Universidad Iberoamericana and the Universidad Autónoma Metropolitana–Cuajimalpa.

Joe Athialy is executive director of the Centre for Financial Accountability (CFA) in India, and works on accountability and transparency issues relating to national and international financial institutions. He was previously the acting Asia director of the Bank Information Center, and the campaigns and communication coordinator of Amnesty International.

Joe has been a grassroots social activist and a commentator for many years, and was a part of the Narmada Bachao Andolan (Save Narmada Movement) to stop the building of the Narmada Dam. He has done pioneering work, engaging with the World Bank Group and other multilateral development banks at the policy level as well as project monitoring. His work through CFA helped broaden the work on transparency and accountability of national and international banks in India and demystify the world of finance to a wide range of people and organizations.

Baher Azmy is the legal director of the Center for Human Rights, a national legal and advocacy organization based in New York City. He supervises litigation challenging government and corporate repression and protecting the human rights of vulnerable populations. Baher has litigated landmark cases including challenges to discriminatory stop and frisk policing practices; protecting the rights of immigrants, activists, and prisoner;, and challenging US detentions in Guantanamo, government surveillance and accountability for victims of torture. He regularly teaches civil rights law and US constitutional law in US law schools and produces scholarship on questions relating to access to justice.

Pavel Chikov is a Russian lawyer, human rights activist, and public figure. He heads the Agora International Human Rights Group, and was a member of the Presidential Council for Civil Society and Human Rights from 2012 to 2019. He has a law degree from Kazan State University, a master's in public administration from University of North Dakota, and a doctorate in law from the Academy of Sciences of the Republic of Tatarstan. Before he founded Agora in 2005, Pavel founded the Kazan Human Rights Center in Tatarstan, and was legal director of the Public Verdict Foundation, dedicated to the legal protection of human rights. He was a columnist for many years at several Russian titles, including Forbes.ru, RBC, *Vedomosti*, *Republic*, *Novaya Gazeta*. In 2014, Pavel Chikov and Agora were awarded the Rafto Prize in recognition of their services to the fight for human rights.

Jane Fonda is an Emmy award–winning actress, a two-time Oscar winner, and a political and environmental activist. She launched Fire Drill Fridays in 2019 and the Jane Fonda Climate PAC in 2022 to stem the tide of climate change and address the outsize influence the fossil fuel industry has on political systems. She sits on the boards of V-Day: Until the

Violence Stops; the Women's Media Center (which she cofounded in 2004); the Georgia Campaign for Adolescent Power & Potential: and Homeboy Industries. She is the author of *What Can I Do?: My Path from Climate Despair to Action*.

Ghida Frangieh is a Lebanese lawyer and researcher based in Beirut. She is a member of the Legal Agenda, a law and society organization with offices in Beirut and Tunis, and currently heads its Strategic Litigation Unit. She is involved in various campaigns to advance human rights with a focus on criminal justice and migration. In 2015, she co-founded the Lawyers' Committee for the Defense of Protesters, a platform to coordinate the efforts of lawyers during large-scale social mobilizations. Before joining the Tripoli Bar Association, she was a legal advisor for refugees and stateless persons at Frontiers Ruwad Association.

Njeri Gateru is cofounder and executive director of the National Gay and Lesbian Human Rights Commission in Kenya, and head of its legal department. She oversees administration and provides legal aid, litigation, documentation, and advocacy services to persons violated on the basis of their sexual orientation or gender identity and expression. The organization's mission is to promote and protect the equality and inclusion of LGBTQ individuals and communities in Kenya, and advance their meaningful participation in society. She was part of the legal efforts to get the anti-LGBTQ laws in Kenya repealed, an effort that was thwarted by a conservative judgement and currently on appeal.

Mark Gevisser is one of South Africa's foremost authors and journalists. His books include *The Pink Line: Journeys Across the World's Queer Frontiers*; *Lost and Found in Johannesburg*; and the award-winning *A Legacy of Liberation: Thabo Mbeki and the Future of South Africa's Dream*. His journalism and criticism has been published widely, in the *New York Times*, *New York Review of Books*, the *Guardian*, *Granta*, and many other publications. He is an experienced teacher of narrative nonfiction, and has taught at the University of Pretoria and run workshops for Commonwealth Writers and other organizations. His documentary feature film, *The Man Who Drove with Mandela*, won a Teddy Award at the Berlin Film Festival in 1999, and he has also worked as an exhibition curator and television scriptwriter. He was born and raised in Johannesburg, educated at Yale University, and now lives outside Cape Town.

Robin Gorna is an AIDS activist and feminist who has led and co-founded global and local campaigns and organizations, including SheDecides (a global sexual and reproductive rights movement) and Women4GlobalFund, as well as the Australian Federation of AIDS Organizations and the International AIDS Society. Her AIDS work began in 1986 in the community sector and she has also worked as a donor and in UN agencies. In 2003, Robin set up the UK Department for International Development's Global AIDS Policy Team, and then led the UK's HIV and health work in Southern Africa. She is currently vice chair of the Technical Review Panel for the Global Fund to Fight AIDS, TB and Malaria; she also represents people with lived experience of Long COVID as Co-Chair of the Global COVID Communities Board. Robin is the author of *Vamps, Virgins and Victims: How Can Women Fight AIDS?*, publishes widely, and is currently working on a memoir exploring the two pandemics.

Justin Hansford is professor of law at Howard University and executive director of its Thurgood Marshall Civil Rights Center. Justin was previously a Democracy Project fellow at Harvard University, a visiting professor at Georgetown University Law Center, and an associate professor at St. Louis University. He has a BA from Howard and a JD from Georgetown University Law Center. He received a Fulbright Scholarship to study the legal career of Nelson Mandela, and served as a clerk for Judge Damon J. Keith on the United States Court of Appeals for the Sixth Circuit. He is a leading scholar and activist in the areas of critical race theory, human rights, and law and social movements. He is a coauthor of the seventh edition of *Race, Racism, and American Law*, a member of the UN Permanent Forum of People of African Descent. Justin has served as a policy advisor for proposed post-Ferguson police reforms at local, state, federal, and international levels.

Mark Heywood has over three decades of experience in civil society in South Africa. He has founded or cofounded some of the country's most respected civil society organizations, including the Treatment Action Campaign, Corruption Watch, SECTION27, and the AIDS and Rights Alliance for Southern Africa (ARASA). From 2007 to 2012 he was deputy chair of the SA National AIDS Council (SANAC), and chair of the UNAIDS Reference Group on HIV and Human Rights from 2006 and 2012. His books include the memoir *Get Up! Stand Up!* and poetry volume *I Write What I Fight*, and his publications include more than thirty peer-reviewed articles and hundreds of articles in popular media. He is currently editor of *Maverick Citizen*, where he publishes regularly. Mark has been a visiting scholar at Temple University, the O'Neill Institute at Georgetown University, and the Bonavero Institute of Human Rights, Oxford University.

Benjamin Hoffman is an attorney with EarthRights International. He first joined EarthRights in 2011, spending three years in the Amazon office in Lima, Peru, providing litigation support to communities from the Andean-Amazonian region resisting the harmful consequences of resource extraction and mega-development projects. Through this work, he contributed to EarthRights's goal of better integrating community collaboration and co-empowerment in human rights advocacy strategies and methodology; he is the coauthor of several law review articles on the topic. He then worked for five years co-teaching the Columbia Law School Human Rights Clinic, continuing his work to disrupt global corporate-community power imbalances in the business and human rights fields, including in the context of workers' rights advocacy. For his contributions to the law school, he received the 2016 Faculty Honors Award from the Columbia Society of International Law. He rejoined EarthRights in 2019.

David Hunter is professor of law at American University's Washington College of Law, where he teaches and researches international and comparative environmental law and the relationship of human rights and environmental law. He serves on the boards of Accountability Counsel, the Center for International Environmental Law (CIEL), the Environmental Law Alliance Worldwide US, Friends of Green Advocates, and the Project on Government Oversight. He has previously served on the boards of the Bank Information Center, Greenpeace US, and EarthRights International, as well as the steering committee of the World Commission on Environmental Law. While working at CIEL, he accompanied local communities around the world as they sought justice through international legal strategies, and became a leading advocate for and architect of nonjudicial grievance mechanisms in international development finance.

Ka Hsaw Wa is cofounder and executive director of EarthRights International. He is a member of the Karen ethnic nationality from Burma/Myanmar. His activism began in 1988 after he was arrested and tortured for his organizing role in the student uprising calling for human rights, democracy, and an end to military rule. He has lived in exile for twenty-five years, documenting evidence of human rights and environmental abuses throughout Southeast Asia, which has been instrumental in the creation of new legal strategies for corporate and government accountability. He leads EarthRights's global campaign and its legal and training programs including the innovative EarthRights School at the Mitharsuu Center for Leadership and Justice. Ka Hsaw Wa is the recipient of numerous awards including the Goldman Environmental Prize, the Reebok Human Rights Award, and the Magsaysay Award. He has an MA in service, leadership, and management from the School for International Training.

Julia Lalla-Maharajh, OBE, spent eighteen years working in the corporate transport and infrastructure sectors. After volunteering in Ethiopia in 2008, she came to understand more about female genital cutting. Volunteering in Senegal and the Gambia she witnessed the kind of sustainable, effective change that led her to found and lead the Orchid Project in 2011, with a vision of a world free from female genital cutting. She now focuses on social change and social justice, and is a successful public speaker. She is one of the *Evening Standard*'s "Power 1,000: London's Most Influential People" and was awarded an OBE for services to ending female genital cutting. At the 2019 UN General Assembly Julia was given the Ally Award by survivors of female genital cutting. She is a board member of VSO, the international volunteer charity, and chair of Under One Sky, a homelessness charity.

Kumi Naidoo is an international activist who began his journey at fifteen, participating in South Africa's liberation struggle. He obtained a BA in political science from the University of Durban-Westville in 1985 but was forced to flee the country in 1987. In exile he studied for a doctorate in political sociology from Oxford as a Rhodes scholar. He returned to South Africa in 1990 and has since been involved in a vast range of initiatives for social justice, including being executive director of the South African National NGO Coalition. Kumi was secretary general and chief executive officer of CIVICUS from 1998 to 2008; executive director of Greenpeace International from 2009 to 2016; and secretary general of Amnesty International from 2018 to 2020. He was the founding chair of the Global Call to Action Against Poverty and of the Global Call for Climate Action. He is a Professor of Practice at Thunderbird School of Global Management at Arizona State University.

Nana Ama Nketia-Quaidoo is director for community development at Advocates for Community Alternatives (ACA), a US-based organization that operates in West Africa. Prior to joining ACA, she contributed to community projects sponsored by USAID as a field officer and monitoring and evaluation specialist. She also worked as programs manager for Gender and Environmental Monitoring Advocates (GEMA), where she was directly involved in helping communities affected by mining to identify alternative sources of livelihood. As a broadcast journalist and news editor at Ahomka FM, a community radio station, she became an active member of Journalists for Human Rights in Ghana's central region. Nana Ama is a trained teacher who taught English and Ghanaian languages in a community senior high school for seven years. She holds a masters in human resource management from the University of Cape Coast Business School, and a bachelors in Ghanaian languages from the University of Education Winneba.

Katie Redford is a lawyer with expertise in human rights, climate change, and corporate accountability. She is executive director of the Equation Campaign, which confronts the climate crisis by "supporting movements on the ground to keep fossil fuels in the ground." She was a cofounder and director of EarthRights International, where she oversaw litigation, training, and campaigns programs to hold corporations and other perpetrators legally accountable for human rights and environmental abuses worldwide. Katie received an Echoing Green fellowship in 1995 to establish EarthRights, and has been an Ashoka Global Fellow, a Rockwood Leadership fellow, and a Bellagio resident fellow. She serves on various nonprofit and philanthropic boards and teaches at the University of Virginia School of Law and the Washington College of Law. Katie is a graduate of Colgate University and the University of Virginia School of Law, and a member of the Bar of the Supreme Court of the United States and the Massachusetts State Bar.

Jennifer Robinson is an Australian barrister at Doughty Street Chambers in London, specializing in human rights, media, public, and international law. She is best known for her work as counsel to Julian Assange and WikiLeaks, placing her at the center of one of the most important and controversial free speech cases of our time. She has acted in freedom of speech and freedom of information cases for journalists and media organizations, including the *New York Times*, BBC World Service, and the International Consortium of Investigative Journalists. She has appeared in human rights and climate justice cases before the British courts, the European Court of Human Rights, the Inter-American Court of Human Rights, and the International Court of Justice. She regularly engages with UN special mechanisms and has conducted human rights missions for the International Bar Association. Her book with Dr. Keina Yoshida, *How Many More Women?*, on how the law silences women, was published in 2022.

Ayisha Siddiqa is a Pakistani American researching the intersections of environmental and human rights law at New York University's Climate Litigation Accelerator. She is the cofounder and finance director of Polluters Out, and executive director of student affairs at Fossil Free University. She was one of the leaders of the 2019 Youth Climate Strike in New York City. Her climate work focuses specially on the rights of marginalized Black, Indigenous, and Brown communities and she believes that storytelling is a key component of achieving climate justice.

Eimear Sparks is a sexual and reproductive health and rights advocate and program advisor to the Movement Accelerator Program at the International Planned Parenthood Federation, European Network. She is a former 25x25 young leader in the SheDecides network, and has experience campaigning for abortion rights including during the Repeal the 8th campaign in Ireland and with Women on Waves during their Mexico campaign in 2017. She holds a bachelor's degree in European studies and a master's in inequalities and social sciences.

Klemenytna Suchanow is a Polish activist, writer, and researcher. She has a degree in Polish and Spanish studies from the University of Wrocław, and a doctorate in literary studies. An activist for women's rights, judicial independence, and freedom of assembly, she is one of the founders of the Polish Women's Strike, a grassroots feminist movement that has mobilized in opposition to the government's attack on abortion rights since 2016.

Krystal Two Bulls, an Oglala Lakota and Northern Cheyenne organizer from Lame Deer, Montana, has been actively involved in resisting the Dakota Access Pipeline. She is a coordinator for the Drop the MIC (military-industrial complex) campaign at About Face: Veterans Against the War, a group of post-9/11 service members and veterans organizing against war, militarism, and the military-industrial complex. She is a US Army veteran who served for eight years. She is also the founder and director of Voices of the Sacred, an organization dedicated to the empowerment and leadership development of Native youth and veterans.

Marissa Vahlsing joined EarthRights in 2011, when she helped launch EarthRights's new Amazon office in Lima, Peru and assisted in developing its Amazon legal program. Since then, she has focused on developing and implementing legal and advocacy strategies to defend the rights of frontline communities facing oil pollution, mining, land-grabbing, and paramilitary violence in cases against corporations, governments, and financial institutions. She has litigated several landmark human rights and environmental justice cases before US courts, including *Doe v. IFC*, *Doe v. Chiquita Brands*, and *Maxima Acuna-Atalaya et al. v. Newmont Mining*. Marissa has also developed and served as counsel on cases before the Inter-American Commission and Court and appeared as counsel in Colombia's Special Jurisdiction for Peace (JEP). Marissa is a graduate of Harvard Law School and holds a BA in political science from Swarthmore College. She was also a 2005 recipient of a Harry S. Truman scholarship.

David Wicker, seventeen years old at the time of this book's publication, is a climate justice activist from northern Italy fighting to raise awareness of the climate crisis and to put pressure on institutions in order to drive climate action. David contributed to the foundation of the Turin chapter of Fridays for Future and to the formation of the national Fridays for Future Italy, in 2019. Since then, he has organized strikes and protests that have brought tens of thousands of people onto the streets of Turin several times. He has also interacted with local and national institutions in Italy as well as international bodies such as the European Parliament and the United Nations. He is a student at the United World College of Armenia, looking to link his passion for computer science to the power of activism and to climate science and policy.

Farhana Yamin is an internationally recognized environmental lawyer and climate change and development policy expert. She has advised leaders and ministers on climate negotiations for thirty years, representing small islands and developing countries and attending nearly every major climate summit since 1991. In addition to founding Track 0, she is an associate fellow at Chatham House, a Director of Impatience, Senior Advisor to SYSTEMIQ, an FRSA and Visiting Professor at University of the Arts, London, and deputy chair of the Climate Vulnerable Forum expert advisory group. She is currently the Coordinator of the Climate Justice & Just Transition Donor Collaborative Project. She was second on the BBC's 2020 Power List, with the judges describing her a "powerhouse of climate justice." She is a columnist at Business Green and appears regularly in the media. She trained as an outdoor education leader and did a number of courses on nature connection, including how to support racialized minorities to access and enjoy green spaces. She works part time at the Doc Society coordinating the Climate Reframe Project, which seeks to amplify the voice of racialized minorities/people of colour in the UK environment movement.

JingJing Zhang is a prominent Chinese environmental lawyer, the founder of the Center for Transnational Environmental Accountability (CTEA), and a lecturer in law at the University of Maryland School of Law. As the inaugural litigation director at the Beijing-based Center for Legal Assistance to Pollution Victims between 1999 and 2008, JingJing won several milestone environmental litigation cases in the Chinese courts and was called "China's Erin Brockovich." She is now working on transnational environmental and climate lawsuits to ensure Chinese companies under China's Belt and Road Initiative comply with environmental laws and international human rights norms in Africa and Latin America. JingJing earned her MPA from Harvard University Kennedy School of Government and her law degrees from China.

More About the Power of Law, Power of People Project

See https://www.therevolutionwillnotbelitigated.com/.

This book is the result of a two-year project initiated by Katie Redford and Robin Gorna when they were residents at the Rockefeller Bellagio Center, in March 2018. With funding raised from the Bertha Foundation and others, Katie and Robin brought twenty lawyers and activists together, from ten different countries, to a subsequent meeting at Bellagio, in September 2019, facilitated by Rhea Suh. The task of the participants was to share their experiences of how legal strategy and movement building work best together toward meaningful social change.

Katie Redford is a movement lawyer who co-founded EarthRights International, and has worked intensively in the fields of corporate accountability and environmental and climate justice. Robin Gorna is a seasoned activist in the AIDS and gender rights movements. Inspired by the slogan of the Bertha Foundation's Justice Program—"It takes a lawyer, an activist, and a storyteller to make meaningful change"—they invited a fellow Bellagio resident, the journalist and author Mark Gevisser, to join the project. Mark ran a writer's workshop at the September 2019 meeting, founded on the principle that "the best theories of change come from a reflection on practice." The result is the collection of personal essays that comprise this book—although not all participants in the meeting were able to contribute to the book, and additional authors have joined the process too.

All these essays are published at www.therevolutionwillnotbelitigated.com. This website is specifically designed to provide students, activists, and professionals with tools for thinking about the role that legal advocacy plays in movements and movement building. The website and its content were designed by Kai Keane and Jesse McElwain.

At Bellagio, the participants had a lot to disagree upon and argue about. But these five common understandings emerged, and became the guiding principles for this project:

1. *The relationship between movement building and any legal strategy is symbiotic and interdependent, and legal advocacy needs to be understood as just one of many strategies to bring about change.*

    When movements and lawyers work together, the shift in power and transformational impact is greater than the sum of their parts. Lawyers are masters of legal procedure. They must also become expert in the procedures that unleash power outside the courtroom: education, access to information, community organizing, agency, and media exposure.

2. *There is no blueprint for how to shift power, but there is a common pattern of experience.*

    Movements are born of pain and anger. They navigate uncertainty and chaos using the imperfect tools of the law to seek justice and relief. Movements are sustained by creativity and community, and they channel their momentum, chaos, and power through strategy, empathy, and joy.

3. *Justice is about shifting power, not just winning a case.*

    The journey toward justice does not end with a courtroom victory. Movement lawyers must look beyond the confines of law to comprehend what a shift of power may mean to each client. You can lose the case but win the struggle, if your client has more power at the end of it.

4. *Power begins to shift when you tell your story.*

    Storytelling is a form of justice. The law can render people invisible; people need to be seen and heard—rather than just documented to be used as data and evidence. "Victims" become active citizens when—through legal process—they become informed and visible, the tellers of their own stories and the agents of their own destiny. Lawyers and activists have their own stories to tell too. Being there as a lawyer helps shift power by validating and giving voice to your client. Being there as a plaintiff or a witness compels those with power to take notice—and has the power to shift their perspective, and thus power itself.

5. *The law can shift power, but only to a point, and to understand its own power, we must understand its limitations and how we can both work within it and expand it*

"The master's tools will never dismantle the master's house," Audrey Lorde famously said. "They may allow us to temporarily beat him at his own game, but they will never enable us to bring about genuine change."

To the extent that the law is "the master's tool" we need to learn how to use it to play the game—but also to transform it, so it can bring about meaningful change.

CPSIA information can be obtained
at www.ICGtesting.com
Printed in the USA
JSHW082104210223
38077JS00001B/1